HowNet and the Computation of Meaning

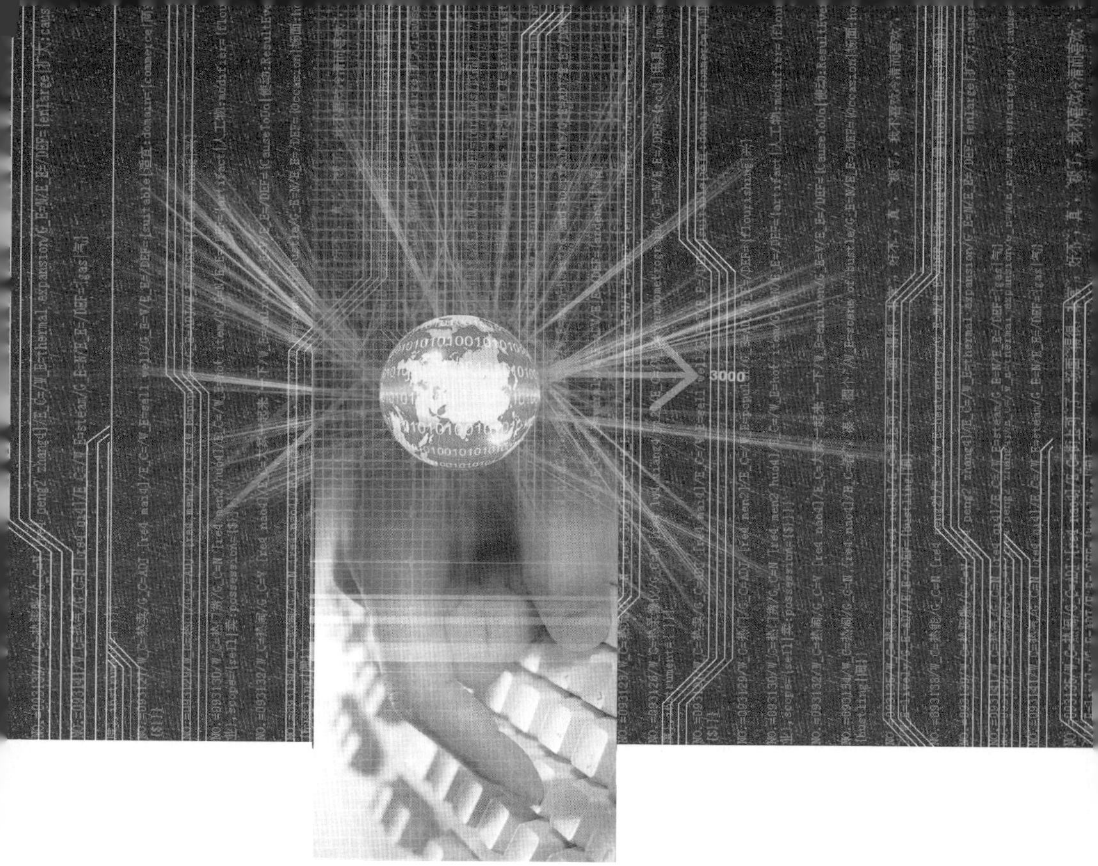

HowNet and the Computation of Meaning

Zhendong Dong

Qiang Dong

World Scientific

NEW JERSEY • LONDON • SINGAPORE • BEIJING • SHANGHAI • HONG KONG • TAIPEI • CHENNAI

Published by

World Scientific Publishing Co. Pte. Ltd.
5 Toh Tuck Link, Singapore 596224
USA office: 27 Warren Street, Suite 401-402, Hackensack, NJ 07601
UK office: 57 Shelton Street, Covent Garden, London WC2H 9HE

British Library Cataloguing-in-Publication Data
A catalogue record for this book is available from the British Library.

HOWNET AND THE COMPUTATION OF MEANING
(With CD-Rom)

ISBN 981-256-491-8

Printed in Singapore by World Scientific Printers (S) Pte Ltd

Foreword

Dictionaries are no doubt indispensable tools for everyone, particularly for those who write or otherwise use language in their work. In this age of the information society, as computers are used to write text, as well as to search, summarize, generate, and even translate languages, dictionaries for computer-based language processing have become increasingly important as well.

Over the past 50 years, many electronic dictionaries have been created for computer use, but almost none of them have offered a high degree of both reliability and ease of use for natural language processing. WordNet in English and the EDR dictionary in English and Japanese are perhaps the only two dictionaries that are accessible for use by computer. Now, the completion and broad dissemination of the HowNet dictionary for Chinese and English, created by Zhendong Dong, is truly a piece of good news for researchers in the field of natural language processing around the world.

I used the term "dictionary" in the above to describe all of these systems, but the goals, contents and features of WordNet, EDR dictionary, and HowNet are quite different and quite unique, so that readers are to be careful about the word "dictionary" used here. They must, first of all, read Chaps. 1 and 2 of this book carefully to understand the goals and contents of HowNet.

The creation of a dictionary is a long process of trial and error, and it is a process that is never truly complete. Particularly in the case of HowNet, where the definitions are given by a set of basic sememes and relations, the settings for these sememes and relations must have required a huge amount of time and labor. Zhendong Dong's efforts in overcoming these difficulties and creating a truly rich and detailed dictionary based on clear definitions are worthy of great respect. I have no doubt that HowNet will be used for generations to come as a most extensive and reliable Chinese and English dictionary for computer applications, such as the "Koki" character dictionary has been used centuries as a standard dictionary of Chinese. The contents of HowNet are many times more detailed and rich than those found in the Koki dictionary.

Now that 18 years of long and patient efforts have finally borne fruit, and HowNet has reached the stage of circulation and use, Zhendong Dong has written this book to provide details of HowNet's content and unique features, as well as its description system and software with which the system is used. His explanation of the system's applications in natural language processing will also be of great value to natural language processing researchers throughout the world.

I have been a close friend of Mr. Dong for many years, and each time we meet I gain an even deeper respect for his sincere character, his gift for language, and his great determination and indefatigable efforts to create HowNet, which no doubt will continue in perpetuity.

I hope that this book will be read widely — and that HowNet will come to be used — not only by researchers in the field of natural language processing, but by many people throughout the world who are involved in the study of languages.

長尾真

Makoto Nagao
President, National Institute of Information and
Communications Technology (NICT)
Former President, Kyoto University
July 2005

Preface

The striking advance of computers and especially the emergence of Internet ushered in the information society. Information has become wealth of the society as well as a resource of the globe. Today when one wants to acquire any information, say, where to buy an antique camera, which is the most suitable hotel in Birmingham, or some knowledge about Chinese characters and radicals, he can surf the Internet or the World Wide Web to retrieve it. If he gets it, but if it is not in his native language, then he may use a language translation tool which is attached to the search engine. Unfortunately, in many cases he may get into some embarrassing position. For example, the search engine may drown him in hundreds of thousands — if not millions — of results to his retrieval, in which there are so many duplications, and the translation tool may give him a translation so awkward that he may take it as another foreign language. All this shows that it may not be hard to retrieve some information with a keyword on the Internet, but it is not so easy to get precisely what one actually needs; it may not be difficult for a computer to look up a translation of a word in a bilingual dictionary, but it would by no means be easy to translate a real text. When the first computers appeared in 40s of the last century, the scientists' first attempt of its application was to deal with natural languages. However, 60-year experience has proved that natural language processing (NLP) is really a very hard nut to crack.

In order to improve the technology of NLP, the scientists in the field have tried so many ways, one of which is to create large-scale knowledge resources, including machine-tractable dictionaries. HowNet is one of the cases in which great effort has been devoted to the building of knowledge resources.

HowNet is unique with its definition in a set of basic sememes (the smallest units of meaning) and semantic relations. HowNet has been now widely applied in a lot of subject areas of NLP, such as word similarity measurement, information extraction, text categorization, question answering, word sense disambiguation, etc.

HowNet demonstrates its prominent power in the computing of meanings. If anyone wants to know what the coverage and depth of the meaning computation that HowNet can achieve, he can try the Mini-HowNet and its affiliated tools which are attached to this book. For example, if he wants to know the semantic distance between "doctor" and "dentist", and between "doctor" and "nurse", the tool, called Concept Similarity Measure, will tell that the first pair is much closer than that of the second pair. If anyone wants to know how meanings are computed by HowNet, how it can achieve such an extent and depth, or the theory of meaning and its computation, he should read this book. To play with the Mini-HowNet and its affiliated tools while reading this book will be of great fun!

This book is not the termination of the development of HowNet, but the beginning of its new stage. At this moment to look back into the past and recall some of the great events and figures that exercised influence on the development of HowNet will be of significance. In the late 80s, in Makoto Nagao's frequent academic visits to China, I interpreted for him and learned a great deal from his rich experience in building semantic dictionary, especially the principles for semantic classification of nouns and verbs. From 1987 to 1992 when I was the chief technical leader of Chinese team participating in the machine translation project among Japan and other four Asian countries, I learned quite a lot from various kinds of MT dictionaries of Japanese IT companies and labs, especially from Japan's EDR concept dictionary. In 1988 I was invited by Antonio Zampolli to attend the Summer School on computational linguistics. During the 1-month course, for the first time I learned ontology from Sergei Nirenburg's lecture, and visited the knowledge base built in the lab of Pisa University. In 1993 when I worked in Tokyo, I visited Hozumi Tanaka of Tokyo Institute of Technology, during the whole morning of discussion, he gave me lots of valuable advice and gave me many papers which described taxonomy or discussed semantic categorization. My 3-year work in Institute of Information Systems in Singapore was a substantial preparatory stage for the research of HowNet. I would like to thank all my friends who have rendered their help in the creation of HowNet. At this moment my deep memorial goes to Chen Liwei, late President of Chinese Information Processing Society, who was the respected guide to my research career.

Finally, thanks to my wife who is always a strong supporter of my life and work.

Zhendong Dong

Contents

Introduction

Language is an essential carrier of human beings' thoughts and the most important vehicle of human communications. When the first computer appeared in the 40s of the last century, one of its first applications people tried to accomplish was to process natural languages, for instance, to develop automatic translation systems. Natural language processing (NLP), a subfield of artificial intelligence, has become a prominent research and development area. It aims at two closely-related goals: to enable computers to interact with humans using natural language capabilities, and to serve as applications for providing services such as automatic text understanding, extraction of knowledge from digital libraries, information retrieval, question answering systems, machine translation, automatic text summarization, speech recognition and speech synthesis. In addition, a new subject of research, computational linguistics has come into being. In more than half a century, it struggled a long way from one approach to another, philosophically, from empiricist (before 1960) to rationalist (1960–1985) first, and then from rationalist back to empiricist (since 1985). The rationalist approach is characteristic of its intelligent system using a set of rules to simulate the human linguistic competence. The empiricist approach is mainly based on statistics, large-scale corpora and machine learning. The new paradigm has shifted the research focus from selected sample to real-world texts and from "toy systems" to practical engineering solutions. Thus a new term of the research area has come into being, i.e. human language technology (HLT). Whenever a new paradigm shift appeared, a new breakthrough was anticipated and heralded naively.

Unfortunately, any breakthrough became in vain at last after a long expectation.

Nowadays more and more researchers have become aware of the inherent pitfalls and limitation of both approaches. They have begun to seek some so-called hybrid-integrated approaches and new knowledge resources. It is not wise to stick to only one approach to the end. Application demands are the mother of invention. Different types of food need different cuisines, kitchen utensils and cooking materials.

It is widely acknowledged by the HLT community that ambiguity in the language is the key problem in HLT or computational linguistics. The ambiguity haunts a language at all levels and nearly in all aspects. All kinds of the ambiguity in a language, either in word sense, syntactic structure, or discourse relations, can be summed up as a problem of meaning, for example:

(1) Word sense:
bank — river bank or financial bank?

(2) Morphological form:
lay — This hen doesn't lay. / She lay in bed all day.

(3) Syntactic structure:
 (a) He joined Beijing Institute of Computing which is well-known for HLT — What is well-known? The institute or computing?
 (b) He tried to translate with a MT system the book in which there is a lot of description of natural scenery — What governs "the book"?
 (c) The old man and woman refused to leave — Is the woman old or not?

(4) Ellipsis:
When A is added into B and C into D... — What is omitted?

(5) Anaphora:
Julia and I went to see Paula, because she wanted me to help her with her studies — What does "she" refer? Paula or Julia?

Let's look at a real example of the application of some HLT products — English part-of-speech taggers.

We had the following English sentence and input it in four English part-of-speech taggers that are found at the Internet can be tested freely.

"Numerous studies have shown that furry companions — just by their presence — can help lower blood pressure and cholesterol levels, raise chances of survival after a heart attack, reduce loneliness and depression and spread all-round good cheer."

Before the test by part-of-speech tagging, many words in the sentence are ambiguous in part-of-speech shown as follows:

"Numerous [a] studies [v/n] have [aux/v] shown [v] that [det/pron/conj] furry [a] companions [n/v] — just [adv/a] by [adv/prep] their [pron] presence [n] — can [aux/n/v] help [n/v] lower [n/v/a] blood [n] pressure [n] and [conj] cholesterol [n] levels [n/v], raise [n/v] chances [n/v] of [prep] survival [n] after [prep/conj] a [det] heart [n] attack [n/v], reduce [v] loneliness [n] and [conj] depression [n] and [conj] spread [n/v/a] all-round [a] good [a/n] cheer [n/v]."

Result of Tagger 1:

"Numerous [a] studies [n] have [aux] shown [v] that [conj] furry [a] companions [n] — just [adv] by [prep] their [pron] presence [n] — can [aux] help [v] **lower [v/a]** blood [n] pressure [n] and [conj] cholesterol [n] **levels [n/v], raise [n/v]** chances [n] of [prep] survival [n] **after [prep/conj]** a [det] heart [n] attack [n], reduce [v] loneliness [n] and [conj] depression [n] and [conj] **spread [n/v]** all-round [a] good [a] cheer [n]."

Result of Tagger 2:

"Numerous [a] studies [n] have [aux] shown [v] that [conj] furry [a] companions [n] — just [adv] by [prep] their [pron] presence [n] — can [aux] help [v] **lower [a]** blood [n] pressure [n] and [conj] cholesterol [n] **levels [n/v], raise [n]** chances [n] of [prep] survival [n] after [prep] a [det] heart [n] attack [n], reduce [v] loneliness [n] and [conj] depression [n] and [conj] spread [v] all-round [a] good [a] cheer [n]."

Result of Tagger 3:

"Numerous [a] studies [n] **have [v]** shown [v] **that [det]** furry [a] companions [n] — **just [a]** by [prep] their [pron] presence [n] — **can [v]** help [v] **lower [adv]** blood [n] pressure [n] and [conj] cholesterol [n] **levels [n/v], raise [n]** chances [n] of [prep] survival [n] after [prep] a [det] heart [n] attack [n], **reduce [?]** loneliness [n] **and [?]** depression [n] **and [?]** spread [v] all-round [a] **good [?] cheer [v]**."

Result of Tagger 4:

"Numerous [a] studies [n] have [aux] shown [v] that [conj] **furry [n]** companions [n] — just [adv] by [prep] their [pron] presence [n] — can [aux] help [v] **lower [a]** blood [n] pressure [n] and [conj] cholesterol [n] levels [n], raise [v] chances [n] of [prep] survival [n] after [prep] a [det] heart [n] attack [n], reduce [v] loneliness [n] and [conj] depression [n] and [conj] spread [v] **all-round [conj]** good [a] cheer [n]."

The above taggings in bold are incorrect. The only correct tagging should be as follows:

"Numerous [a] studies [n] have [aux] shown [v] that [conj] furry [a] companions [n] — just [adv] by [prep] their [pron] presence [n] — can [aux] help [v] lower [v] blood [n] pressure [n] and [conj] cholesterol [n] levels [n], raise [v] chances [n] of [prep] survival [n] after [prep] a [det] heart [n] attack [n], reduce [v] loneliness [n] and [conj] depression [n] and [conj] spread [v] all-round [a] good [a] cheer [n]."

Unfortunately, none of the above taggers could achieve 100% correct tagging. It should be pointed that part-of-speech tagging may be just one of the very early phases for English parsing. The early stage errors would lead to rippling erroneous results in the later stages and would no doubt cause the final failure in the parsing.

After careful observation, we can conclude that in appearance part-of-speech tagging belong to the syntactic category, but in essence it is an issue of meaning. In the final analysis, the ultimate goal of HLT is none other than to seek solutions to ambiguity of the computer-processed language. Can a computer really handle and solve the meanings of the language? Our answer is positive. If a computer can give the correct answer to your question: "What is the height of Mount Everest?" Is it able to handle the meaning of the sentence? If a computer can give a correct Chinese translation of your input sentence: "Can we get credit from your bank?" Is it able to handle the meaning of the sentence? We suppose the answer should be positive too. In a strict sense, the solution to HLT is to remove ambiguities at all levels in the processed language. The disambiguation should rely on the computation of meanings. In order to obtain satisfactory results in the computation of meaning, knowledge resources are indispensable. The computation of meaning at different levels needs various kinds of knowledge resources.

The long experience in working on HLT shows that in HLT we need three types of knowledge: intralinguistic knowledge, interlinguistic knowledge, and extralinguistic knowledge. Intralinguistic knowledge incorporates a wide range of conventional linguistic areas such as phonetics, morphology, syntax, semantics and pragmatics. By interlinguistic knowledge, we mean cross-language knowledge, such as comparative linguistics, or the knowledge that we especially apply in language translation or recently in cross-language information retrieval. Extralinguistic knowledge in fact is common sense knowledge or world knowledge. Different tasks need different kinds of knowledge. We should be very clear about how to use knowledge, how to use the right knowledge in the right place.

What HLT needs is computer-oriented knowledge resources rather than human-oriented resources. Human-oriented knowledge and computer-oriented knowledge resources are quite different in nature and in the way of acquisition and representation. These two types of knowledge resources may benefit each other but can never substitute each other. In these past ten years, we have noticed two unhealthy tendencies in HLT, that is, a self-claimed "computational linguistics" without computation or with no care about the possibility of materialization by the computer and a computational linguistics with computing only and without linguistic considerations or without any care about linguistic peculiarities. Besides, we have also noticed some misunderstandings about the building of linguistic knowledge resources. Some people thought that the computer-oriented knowledge resources should be built in an automatic way or at least not by human-coding.

They believe in machine-acquired knowledge resources only. It is really naive to go from one extreme to another. Different kinds of knowledge resources serve different application demands.

This book is intended to discuss computation of meaning for HLT and the construction of linguistic knowledge systems. The book is not a users' manual of HowNet, but is a writing which theoretically manifests the process as well as the basis of the computation of meaning. The book reveals how the computation of meaning is actually based on sememes rather than concepts and demonstrates how accurate and how deep the computation of meaning can be made when a knowledge system like HowNet is used. In addition, through the detailed presentation of HowNet, the book elaborates the acquisition of sememes, the representation of taxonomy and axioms, the materialization of meaning computing, and the evaluation of linguistic knowledge systems.

We would like to express our special thanks to Hao Changling, who is an active member of HowNet team and has offered her valuable effort in assembling and editing the book.

Chapter 1

MEANING AND ITS REPRESENTATION

What is meaning? Or what is the meaning of meaning? "Meaning" is really a very difficult issue. Traditionally, meaning is discussed in the subject fields of philosophy and linguistics. This book is intended to discuss meaning in terms of HLT in general, and the construction of computer-oriented knowledge resources and the computation of meaning in particular. Linguistically, meaning exists in various levels such as word sense, the meaning of a phrasal structure, sentential meaning, and textual meaning. In this book, we would like to focus on the meaning of concepts, or linguistically, on senses of words and expressions. The computer-oriented understanding of meaning differs greatly from the human-oriented one.

First of all, let's take a look at some definitions of word in human-oriented lexicons. Suppose we want to know the meaning of the English word "possess", we may look it up in an English dictionary, say, Longman Dictionary of Contemporary English (LDOCE) and then find that the first sense of the word "possess" is defined as follows:

1 to own; have: *He possesses 2 cars*

If we do not know the meaning of "own" yet, we have to go on to look it up again, and find the definition is as follows:

1 to possess (something), esp. by lawful right, *who owns this house/this dog*?

So here we find a loop: starting from "possess", and then to "own" and going back to "possess". It is not unique, but has its counterpart. In

Chinese dictionaries the cases of recursive definitions can also be found here and there. Needless to say, to humans all the above definitions may be perfect. If a computer could really understand and process them, then all the tasks of HLT might have been fulfilled! That is the reason why we need computer-oriented representation.

How can we testify that someone really understand the meaning of "possess"? Let's make a simple experiment by asking him the following questions:

"If you possess a car, do you have the car?"
"If you possess a car, does the car belong to you?"
"If you buy a car, do you possess it?"
"If you borrow a car, do you possess it?"
"If you possess a car, can you give it to anybody?"

If anyone can give correct answers to the questions, we take it for granted that he may have understood the meaning of "possess".

Secondly, let's compare the definitions of the word "paper" in three different dictionaries: WordNet, LDOCE and Contemporary Chinese Dictionary (bilingual version) and try to see its meaning in them.

(1) Definition in WordNet:
"a material made of cellulose pulp derived mainly from wood or rags or certain grasses"

(2) Definition in LDOCE:
"material made in the form of sheets from very thin threads of wood or cloth, used for writing or printing on, covering parcels or walls, etc."

(3) Definition in Contemporary Chinese Dictionary
"substance made from cellulose fibers derived from rags, wood, etc. often with other additives, and formed into flat thin sheets suitable for writing, painting or printing on, or for decorating walls, wrapping, etc."

If we make analysis of these definitions, we may extract the following understandings:

(a) Paper is a kind of material or substance;
(b) it is made from cellulose pulp derived from wood, rags, etc.;
(c) paper is in the form of sheet;
(d) it can be used for writing, painting, wrapping, etc.

We may be enlightened by the aforesaid experiment and comparison that meaning can be understood through the relations. We can understand the concept of “possess” through its relations with some other concepts, like the concepts of “buy”, “belong”, “own”, “lose”, “give”, etc. Similarly, the concept of “paper” can be understood through its relations with the concepts of “material”, “write”, “print” and “wrap”, etc., and the relations based on the attributes such as form, use, softness, contrast, and so on. The relations which represent meanings can be divided into two categories: Concept Relation (CR) and Attribute Relation (AR).

When we say we understand the meaning of a concept, it means that we know its concept relations and its attribute relations to some extent. For example, when we say we understand the meaning of “chair”, we may know that it is a piece of furniture on which one person can sit, which typically has a back. Our understanding of the meaning of “chair” may be represented by the relations among the concepts “chair” and “furniture”, “sit”, etc., and by the relations among the attributes “form”, “weight”, “size”, “color”, etc., which a chair may have.

It should be pointed that any concept relation will fall into a net, which is called Concept Relation Net (CRN) and any attribute relation will fall into a net too, which is called Attribute Relation Net (ARN).

1.1. Concept Relation Net (CRN)

As discussed above, it is believed that every concept has a relation net, called Concept Relation Net (CRN), by which the actual meaning of the concept is represented, and by which computers, or even human, can understand and manipulate its meaning. CRN consists of 3 components: concept nodes, connection arcs, and relations. See Fig. 1.1.

Concept nodes: "doctor", "disease", "hospital", "patient"...
Relation arcs: →, ←, ←→
Relations: [hypernym], [hyponym], [antonym], [meronym], [agent], [patient], [instrument], [location]...

CRN is elastic or extendable as it varies with individual persons. In other words, different individual has different CRN, even of the same concept. This reflects different levels of knowledge among people. The more knowledge one masters, the more concepts he will master, and what is more, the larger or more complicated CRN of the concepts he will know. It can be imagined that a 6-year child may know "doctor" but his CRN of "doctor" would be far from that as shown in Fig. 1.1, which is believed to be mastered by an ordinary adult. The same case goes with mankind as a whole. Mankind increases his knowledge with each passing year when he enlarges his volume of concepts and at the same time, the CRN of the concepts.

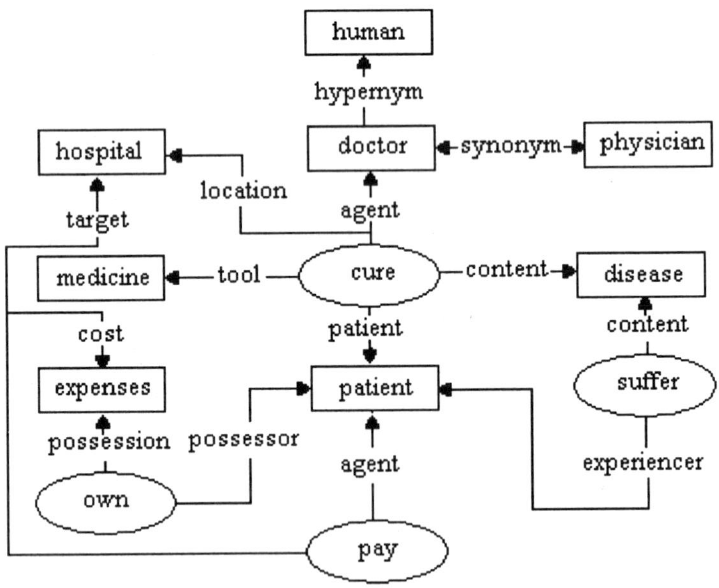

Fig. 1.1. Concept Relation Net (CRN) of "doctor".

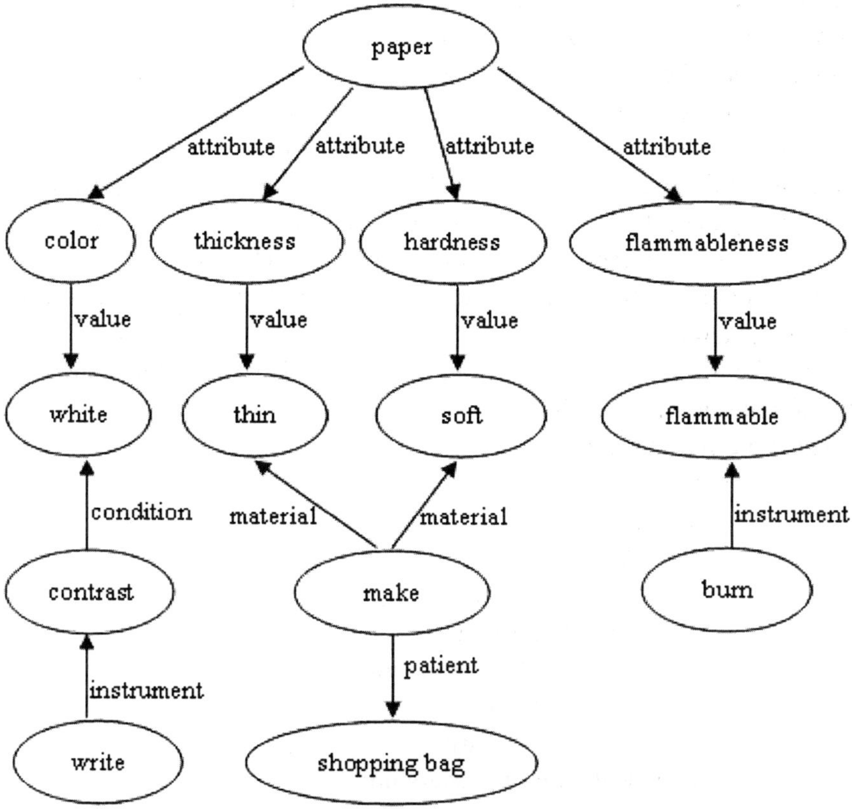

Fig. 1.2. Attribute Relation Net (ARN) of "paper".

1.2. Attribute Relation Net (ARN)

Careful observations find that the meanings of concepts are displayed not only by their CRN but also by the relations among attributes of the concepts, as called Attribute Relation Net. That is to say, in many cases it is the attributes of a concept that act in the role of meaning representation. Figure 1.2 reveals that it is not "paper" as a whole that is related to "write", but only one of its attributes, say "color", is related to "write" with "contrast" as the condition. Therefore in a strict sense, "paper" is not necessarily related to "write". We can sometimes even write on the sand with a twig or on the table with our wet finger. On the contrary, we cannot write on a piece of white paper with a chalk or on the blackboard in black ink. Therefore, for writing, what affects may not be the whole lot of the concept like “paper”, but some attributes of the concept. Besides, we can use “paper” to wrap up something because of its attributes of the material which are almost the same as cloth or plastic.

Meanings at all levels, say, of a word, of a sentence, or of a text, can be represented and understood through relations. The meaning of a word and the meaning of a sentence differs in that the former is static and the latter is dynamic.

To take the word “buy” as an example. “Buy” is represented by several relation nets as follows:

(a) Hypernymous net:

event
==> act
==> ActSpecific
==> AlterSpecific
==> AlterRelation
==> AlterPossession
==> take
==> buy

(a-1) Relation of possession:

event
==> static
==> relation
==> possession
==> own
==> possess

Here (a) and (a-1) indicate that when the action of “buy” happens, it will change the relation of possession. If you buy anything, you will possess it.

(b) Hyponymous net:

The hyponymous net of the word “buy” is exemplified by the following words and expressions:

act as a purchasing agent, book, book a ticket, booking, buy and get everything ready, buy at a high price, buy at negotiated price, buy at reduced prices, buy goods wholesale, buy grain, buy liquor and imbibe it, buy on credit, buy more of the same securities, buy property, buy the whole lot, buy to resell, buying and selling, deal in, deal in small business, fraudulently purchase, illegally buy up, go shopping, insure, mail order, order, place an order, purchase by mail, purchase from abroad, purchase in advance, renew one's subscription, rush to purchase, shopping, subscribe

Hyponymous net makes “buy” connect all its hyponyms.

(c) Role of agent — Who buys

The role of agent of the word “buy” represented by the following words and expressions:

bargainer, buyer, buying party, client, customer, emptor, frequenter, home buyer, itinerant trader, orderer, patron, pedlar, policy-holder, purchaser, purchasing agent, purchasing station, regular customer, shopper, stockbroker, stockjobber, subscriber, vendee

(d) Role of location — Where one buys

The role of location of the word “buy” represented by the following words and expressions:

24-hours shop, bazar, black market, book store, car market, chain store, chemist's shop, cigarette stall, cloth store, confectionery, convenience store, fair, fish market, flagship store, flea market, florist, food market, shopping mall

Roles usually play a significant part in relation net in representing static meanings, and even more important part in representing dynamic meanings. If we want to test whether a person comprehend a sentence or a paragraph, a common method we usually adopt is to raise a few questions about the sentence or the paragraph. For example, if we have a testing sentence as follows:

“Mary’s brother bought her the book their father wrote in 1980”.

The questions we can put to test a person's comprehension of the sentence. It is believed that all the questions are relation-oriented, for instance:

(1) Who bought the book? — Agent

(2) For whom did Mary's brother buy the book? — Beneficiary

(3) What did Mary's brother buy? — Possession

(4) Whose father wrote the book bought by Mary's brother? — Agent

(5) When did Mary's father write the book? — Time

It would not matter whether a person knows the names of relations, such as "agent", "possession", and "time". If a person comprehends the sentence and can answer the questions correctly, he would be clear about the relations.

Chapter 2

OVERVIEW OF HOWNET

This chapter is intended to give a panoramic picture of HowNet — its brief history of research and development, its nature and architecture, its main characteristics.

2.1. The History of HowNet

The research and development of HowNet can be dated back to the end of 1980s. Even in the very beginning, the aim of construction of HowNet was very clear, that is, to construct a common-sense knowledge system or an extralinguistic knowledge system. In 1988 Zhendong Dong wrote:

"Knowledge is assumed to be a system, which contains a relation-base and an inference device. There are two types of relations in the relation-base: one is the relations between concept features, the other is the relations between events. A concept is composed of two parts, i.e. concept core and relevant features of the concept. The inference device works on the basis of the relation-base. And also, there are two types of inferences. One is based on concept feature relations of which the typical is shown by the substitution. For example, one may dry his hands by rubbing them against his shirt after washing when he does not have a handkerchief at his disposal. The other is based on event relations of which the typical can be seen in a who-done-it story.

How to Build the Knowledge System?

Since it is utterly impossible to build a practical knowledge system overnight, we have to set limitation to it and to build it step by step. Then shall we make it limited by a specific domain or scenario? We suggest that, instead, we should have it limited by the numbers of concepts deliberately selected and by the numbers of the features attached to the selected concept. And we should proceed step by step from the static to the dynamic, from the concept feature relations to the event relations, from the low layer, i.e. more concrete and simple to the high layer, i.e. more abstract and complex, and from the relation-base to the inference device. Currently much effort has been given to build the taxonomy. It is desirable to select from the taxonomy some essential concepts (e.g. bread, eat, boy, etc.) and determine a certain concept feature circle (e.g. flour for bread, mouth for eat, etc.) in order to build a first-layer prototype of the concept feature relation-base. Next, in the same circle we can try to build a second-layer prototype which is base on more abstract concepts and their features, e.g. food for bread, grain for flour, digest for eat, etc. after that we can try to build the relation network between the selected concept features. The higher and more abstract layer the relation network is based on, the more successful our work will be. It must be emphasized that our aim is not to build an overall knowledge base of mankind, but to build a universal relation system by which ordinary people, normally experts of all the fields, can build their own knowledge base."

Dong's writing in 1988 depicted the general conception of the construction of HowNet.

The research and development of HowNet underwent 5 stages:

(1) Conceptual design (1988–1993): working out the overall scheme, extracting primitives or sememes, discovering the types of relations among concepts and among attributes of concepts; in addition, creating biaxial theory of the categorization of event concepts;

(2) Experiments (1993–1997): experimental coding of data in knowledge dictionary, comparison with WordNet;

(3) Engineering implementation (1997–1999): large-scale coding, programming the browser and management tools, release of the first version of HowNet;

(4) Revision (1999–2003): overall revision of Knowledge Database Mark-up Language (KDML); re-coding the data in knowledge dictionary, and release of HowNet 2000 version;

(5) Development of second resources as evaluation tools (2003–2005): developing Concept Relevance Calculator (CRC) and Concept Similarity Measure (CSM), checking, evaluating and modifying data coded, and release of the latest version of HowNet.

HowNet is ever growing with its constant improvement and updating in general, and its development of new second resources or application tools in particular.

2.2. The Nature of HowNet

One of the frequent questions raised to us is: "Is HowNet an ontology, or a thesaurus, or a WordNet-like lexical database?" Our answer is: HowNet is none of these. HowNet is an on-line extralinguistic knowledge system for the computation of meaning in HLT. HowNet unveils inter-concept relations and inter-attribute relations of the concepts as connoting in lexicons of the Chinese and their English equivalents. HowNet is unique with the following salient characteristics:

HowNet is an extralinguistic knowledge system. Compared with some existing linguistic knowledge resources, such as Roget's thesaurus, WordNet and EDR dictionaries, HowNet is unique in the following aspects:

(1) The definitions of concepts are based on sememes and described in a structured mark-up language which is easy to compute by a computer;

(2) It reveals not only the concept relations within the same part-of-speech (POS) categories, but also those cross-POS categories, especially the semantic-role relations between nouns and verbs;

(3) The representation is based on concepts denoted by words and expressions in both Chinese and English;

(4) It can be self-tested, self-evaluated by using HowNet-based tools, including Concept Relevance Calculator and Concept Similarity Measure.

The comparison of a HowNet entry record with the word definitions in LODCE and WordNet may give us a rough picture of the uniqueness of HowNet. Let's take "doctor" and "prison" (only one sense of each) for example:

(1) LDOCE:

doctor n **2** a person whose profession is to attend to sick people (or animals;) *an animal doctor*

prison n a large (government) building where criminals are kept locked up as a punishment for as long as the law has decided: *The thief was sent to prison for a year.*

(2) WordNet:

doctor, doc, physician, MD, Dr., medico — (a licensed medical practitioner; "I felt so bad I went to see my doctor")

prison, prison house — (a correctional institution where persons are confined while on trial or for punishment)

(3) HowNet:

NO.=127941
W_C=医生
G_C=N [yi1 sheng1]
E_C=
W_E=doctor
G_E=N
E_E=
DEF={human|人:HostOf={Occupation|职位},
    domain={medical|医},{doctor|医治:agent={~}}}

NO.=054998
W_C=监狱
G_C=N [jian1 yv4]
E_C=
W_E=prison
G_E=N
E_E=
DEF={InstitutePlace|场所:domain={police|警},
{detain|扣住:location={~},
patient={human|人:modifier={guilty|有罪}}},
{punish|处罚:location={~},
patient={human|人:modifier={guilty|有罪}}}}

The concept definition (DEF) in HowNet is not written in natural language but in a mark-up language, whose basic units are sememes such as "human|人", "InstitutePlace|场所","Occupation|职位", "medical|医", "doctor|医治", "detain|扣住" and semantic roles and features such as "HostOf", "agent", "modifier" and "domain".

The definition of "doctor" can be literally paraphrased as follows:

"A doctor is a human being, who has the attribute of occupation; he doctors (gives medical treatment to); he belongs to the domain of medicine".

The definition of "prison" can be literally paraphrased as follows:

"A prison is an institutional place, which is the location where guilty people are detained and punished. The place belongs to the domain of police and law".

Obviously the definition in HowNet is formal or structured and machine-tractable. We deliberately name HowNet a *system* because it is not merely a static database, but a dynamic and computer-tractable implement and because it does not only include a lexical database, but also includes a set of taxonomies and documents of axioms which are all capable to be manipulated and used for various kinds of the computation of meaning.

2.3. The Architecture of HowNet

HowNet knowledge system consists mainly of the following components.

(1) Knowledge dictionary

Knowledge dictionary is the essential database of HowNet system. It is bilingual of Chinese and English. Currently it contains over 160,000 records like the examples of "doctor" and "prison" shown above, including over 84,000 unique forms of Chinese words and expressions and over 80,000 unique forms of English words and expressions.

(2) Taxonomy bank

HowNet taxonomy bank includes the following sub-banks: entity taxonomy bank, event taxonomy bank, attribute taxonomy bank, attribute-value taxonomy bank, the bank of secondary features list, the bank of antonymous sememes list, the bank of converse sememes list and the bank of event role and feature.

(3) Maintenance tools

The maintenance tools include all kinds of programs for data management.

(4) The devices of computation of meaning

HowNet the device of computation of meanings are developed to make self-testing of knowledge data and to push HowNet nearer to practical applications. The devices currently mainly include: HowNet browser, Concept Relevance Calculator (CRC), Concept Similarity Measure (CSM), and Query Expansion Tool (QET).

The detailed presentation of each of the components will be given in the next chapters. The architecture of HowNet knowledge system is shown in Fig. 2.1.

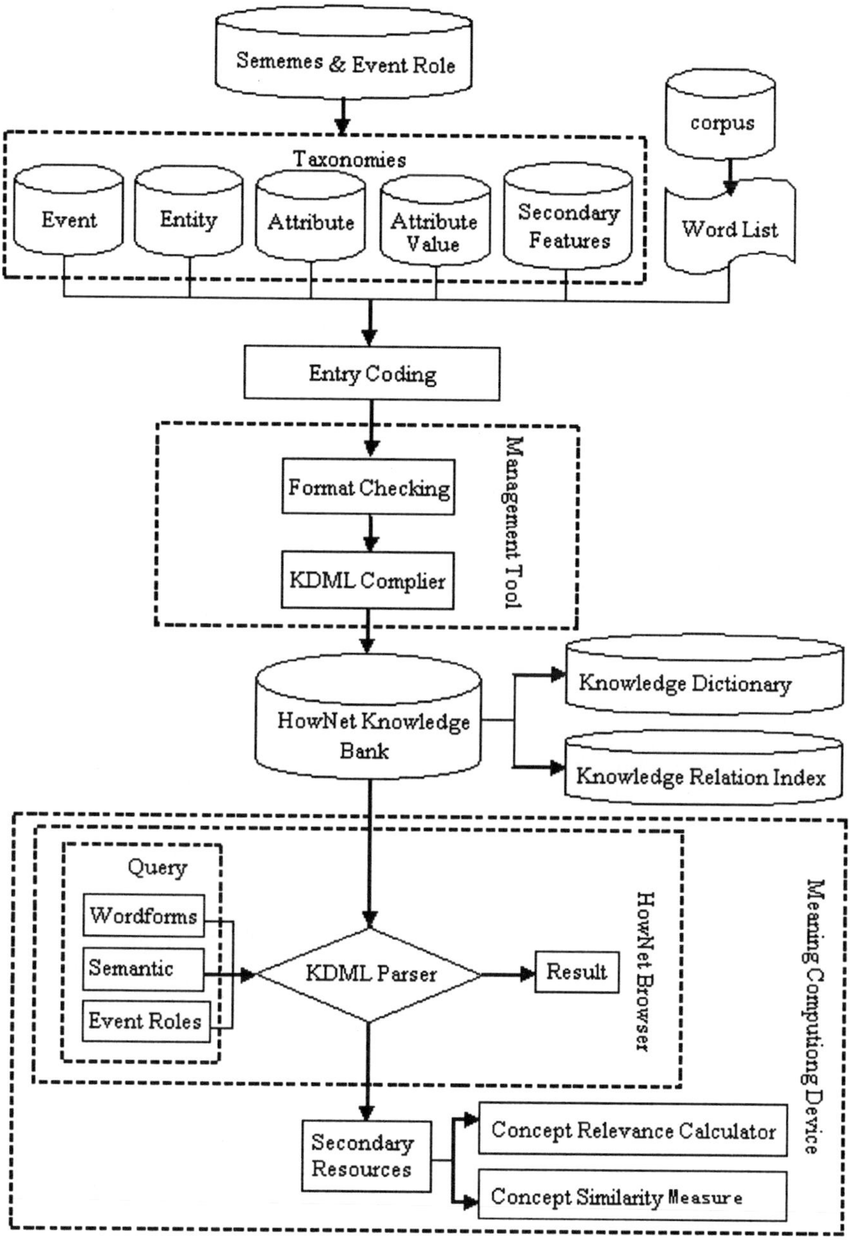

Fig. 2.1. Architecture of HowNet Knowledge System.

Chapter 3

SEMEMES

3.1. What is a Sememe

When any computation is to be carried out, a basic computation unit should be first decided. Numeric figures are taken as the basic units for computation in mathematics. As aforementioned, in computing a natural language, we too should determine its basic or smallest units.

Syntactically the smallest units are conventionally regarded as words. The higher-level syntactic computation such as phrasal structures or sentential structures are all based on words. However, when we intend to compute meanings implied in the words and language structures, we should then determine a set of the smallest units of meanings. Some take concepts as the basic units, some select a small set of words called primitive vocabulary. They consider that these smallest units cannot be discomposed any more. For example, the meaning of "hijack" can be discomposed into "take", and "by force", and the meaning of "pedestrian" can be discomposed into "human", and "travel by foot", but the meaning of "take", "human" "travel" and "by force" seem to be unable to be discomposed further or at least, is not easy to discompose any further. LDOCE selects 2000 basic words as its core glossary that has been used for all the explanations and examples in the dictionary. Can they be used as the sememes for building our knowledge system? Unfortunately the answer is negative. The units in the primitive vocabulary or core glossary used in LDOCE are not the sememes that we intend to use to build an extralinguistic knowledge resource and to compute meanings, because they keep part of natural language characteristics and so remain ambiguous. Are there any basic or non-discomposed meaning units in reality then? If so, where can we get them? How can we acquire them? How can we know if the selected set has adequate coverage or is powerful enough for the computation of meaning?

3.2. Acquisition of a Sememe Set

We consider that we should know where we can discover this full set. Can we select thousands of words and try to discompose their meanings to discover the sememe set? How big a vocabulary should we select? How can we know that no serious omissions of the sememes would be made? After a few years of exploration we at last found that the Chinese language displays a considerable amount of semantic information even at the character level. The composition of Chinese characters and the Chinese way of formation of concepts suggest that they might involve a sophisticated and pragmatic system of sememes.

3.3. Inspiration from Chinese

It is reported by Chinese linguists that although there are over 50,000 characters in the Chinese script, a highly educated Chinese knows roughly about 6,000 characters and an ordinary Chinese people know even much lesser in their daily life. Besides, this rather limited knowledge is adequate to sustain the long-time updating of vocabulary, since the way to enlarge the Chinese vocabulary is to create or even loan new words and expressions by forming new combinations of characters instead of coining new characters. Chinese words and expressions are generally formed by characters and Chinese characters are basically composed of radicals. The number of the commonly-used Chinese characters is limited and the number of radicals is even limited. According to Xu Shen's etymological dictionary, over 99% of the included Chinese characters display some semantic information relevant to the real-world concepts that they denote. Most characters are composed of two parts: meaning component and phonetic component.

The meaning component reveals sense or give some hint of relevant sense while the phonetic component indicates possible pronunciation of the character, for example, the character "洋" (ocean) is made of two parts. Its first part "氵"(Chinese call it "three drops of water") is the meaning part which denotes "水" (water), and its second part "羊" indicates the pronunciation of the character. It is interesting to find that all the following Chinese characters have the same meaning part "氵": "江(river)", "湖(lake)", "溪(stream)", "海(sea)", "流(flow)", "泥(mud)", "漕(transport by water)", since their meanings are all related to "water".

More examples about meaning part and phonetic part are listed below:

"妈(mother)" =	meaning 女(woman)	+	phonetic 马
"房(house)" =	meaning 户(household)	+	phonetic 方
"吐(vomit)" =	meaning 口(mouth)	+	phonetic 土
"柏(cypress)" =	meaning 木(tree)	+	phonetic 白
"睛(eyeball)" =	meaning 目(eye)	+	phonetic 青

There are 214 radicals in Chinese, which we can roughly find in the following categories as shown in Table 3.1.

Table 3.1. Classes of Chinese radicals.

Class	Radical
nature	sun(日), moon(月), water(氵), gold(金), earth(土), rain(雨), mountain(山), sound(音), steam(气)
human	man(亻), father(父), son(子), woman(女)
animal	horse(马), bird(鸟), fish(鱼), insect(虫), dog(犬, 犭)
plant	grass(艹), tree(木), wheat(麦), millet(黍)
artifact	dish(皿), cart(车), boat(舟), knife(刂), arrow(矢)
material	rice(米), grain(禾), silk(糸), leather(革), tile(瓦)
part	mouth(口), hand(扌), foot(足), heart(心, 忄), eye(目), blood(血), tooth(齿), skin(皮)
attribute	color(色)
time	evening(夕), morning(辰)
location	city (邑, 阝), village(里), field(田)
fact	sickness(疒), death(歹), life(生)
action	see(见), eat(饣), fly(飞), walk(辶)
value	big(大), small(小), long(长), old(老), red(赤), black(黑), white(白), blue(青), sweet(甘), fragrant(香)

All Chinese characters are composed of radicals or a radial itself is a character. Meanwhile, nearly all Chinese words and expressions are formed by combination of characters or a character itself can be regarded as a word. Table 3.2 displays the composition of Chinese characters by radicals, where we can clearly see how it carries meanings.

Table 3.2. Composition of Chinese characters with Radicals.

radical	meaning	character
氵	water	河(river) 海(sea) 溪(stream) 流(flow)
钅	gold	银(silver) 铁(iron) 钳(tongs) 锈(rust)
火	fire	火* 烟(smoke) 烤(roast) 烧(burn) 烫(scold)
灬	fire	热(hot) 煮(boil) 煎(fry) 照(shine)
米	rice	米* 粮(grain) 粥(gruel) 粟(millet)
女	woman	女* 妻(wife) 她(she) 婚(marry) 娇(tender)
足	foot	足* 蹄(hoof) 趾(toe) 跑(run) 踢(kick)
饣	eat	饼(cake) 饿(hungry) 饱(full) 蚀(erode)

Some Chinese characters can be used as single-character words, such as “走(walk)”, “医(give medical treatment)”, but some can not, they can only appear as a component in multi-character words and expressions. In reality there are much more multi-character words and expressions than single-character words. In other words most Chinese words and expressions are multi-character combination. Again the combination of Chinese words and expressions are even more semantically dependent. Therefore we can find a lexical, and even further phrasal, system of the Chinese language which is very distinct from Indo-European languages. The system follows a line as shown in Fig. 3.1.

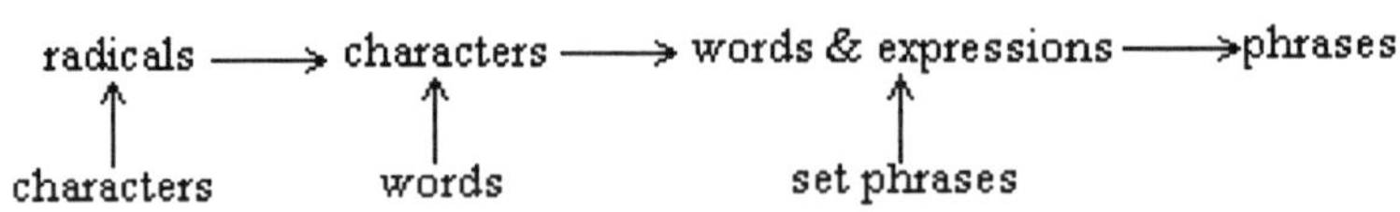

Fig. 3.1. Chinese lexical formation line.

In fact there is no clear-cut demarcation line between so-called words and phrase in Chinese. This may be the reason why some Chinese grammarians argue that there are no words at all but only characters and coined a term as "character-phrase" to replace conventionally-called words. We consider the debate on "word or character" has a common ground that they are both eager to give a hard specification of the Chinese language. Unfortunately Chinese is not so clear-cut and hard, but it is soft. We have to recognize and adopt its "softness". Let's look at the following two groups and study the Chinese way of formation of concepts, needless to care about if they are words or phrases, though in conventional dictionaries they are all taken as words.

Word	**Character1**		**Character2**
医务(medical matters) =	医(treat)	+	务(affairs)
医师(doctor) =	医(treat)	+	师(skilled person)
医院(hospital) =	医(treat)	+	院(institution)
医术(medical skill) =	医(treat)	+	术(skill)
医学(medicine) =	医(treat)	+	学(knowledge)
医药(drug) =	医(treat)	+	药(drug)
医科(medical course) =	医(treat)	+	科(knowledge)
医德(doctor's ethics) =	医(doctor)	+	德(ethics)

Word	**Character1**		**Character2**
学院(college) =	学(study)	+	院(institution)
研究院(institute) =	研究(research)	+	院(institution)
产院(maternity hospital) =	产(childbirth)	+	院(institution)
保育院(nursery) =	保育(childcare)	+	院(institution)
法院(court) =	法(law)	+	院(institution)
画院(art academy) =	画(painting)	+	院(institution)
疗养院(sanatorium) =	疗养(recuperate)	+	院(institution)
剧院(theatre) =	剧(drama)	+	院(institution)

In the first group (related to medicine) we find all the Chinese expressions share a character "医" meaning "to give medical treatment" while in the second group (related to organization) we find all the expressions share a character "院" meaning "institution". This is the typical Chinese way of formation of words and expressions. Here we use the term "words and expressions" instead of the term of sole "words", as we can see that it is really very difficult to define "Chinese word". We believe that it is more important for us to represent the real meaning of the words and expressions than trying to give any evidence to justify the existence or non-existence of Chinese words. Anyway if we leave alone for the time being the argument about "word or no word" in the Chinese language, we may at least assume that all the words and expressions above-listed are phrase-like. It is clear that they are combined by two meaningful components. We believed that the sememes we tried to acquire must be there among them.

Hence, inspired by the aforesaid facts, we began an experiment in 1989. We selected about 4000 frequently-used Chinese characters, extracted and listed all their senses. Note that we used a 3-part combination of an English word plus a Chinese word or expression with a "|" in between to represent the senses, and sememes in HowNet later on. Here in order to save space we omit the Chinese part. In other words, the symbol like "abandon|" in the following table is no longer an English word but a representation of senses or a sememe. Then we made a sense table out of the 4000 characters as exemplified in Table 3.3.

Table 3.3. Sense list.

character	sense
放	abandon| add| lend| put| shoot|
丢	abandon| lose| throw|
置	buy| put|
借	borrow| lend| use|
用	eat| expense| need| use|
吃	eat| destroy| exhaust| suffer|
食	eat| edible|
费	exhaust| expenditure| extravagant|
快	fast| sharp| soon|
疾	disease| fast|
餐	eat| food|

By deleting all the duplications, we extracted our initial testing sememe list including around 1500 different senses, and we noticed that although they covered the 4000 characters, there was some subtle difference between similar senses. It needed some slight modification or adjustment. It took us three years to do trial tagging over 50,000 Chinese words and expressions and their English equivalents using our initial sense list of 1500 sememes. This process itself was a large-scale linguistic engineering and experiment, which, though labor-intensive and time-consuming, proved to be very valuable for the subsequent research and development of HowNet.

Next we would take some of the sememes in Table 3.3 and see how they govern the concepts when they are used to tag both English and Chinese words and expressions.

Let's take "eat|" and "use|" as the examples of sememes.

(1) "eat|" is extracted as a sememe meaning "to take solid food", it can be used to tag:

English: eat, take, take in, etc.

Chinese: 吃, 餐, 用, 食, 进, etc.

(2) "use|" is extracted as a sememe meaning "to make work", it can be used to tag:

English: use, utilize, utilise, apply, employ, etc.

Chinese: 用, 动, 使, 采用, 利用, 应用, 运用, etc.

Chapter 4

CONCEPT CLASSIFICATION AND PROPERTY DESCRIPTION

In building a semantic knowledge resource like a thesaurus or ontology, we may confront a choice of approaches to the scheme of concept organization, either the concept classification or the property description using sememes or primitives. Up till now most current semantic knowledge resources such as Roget's Thesaurus and Japan's EDR concept dictionary adopt the former approach. Before the development of HowNet, we had worked on a large-scale English-Chinese dictionary for a MT system, in which we adopted concept classification approach for its semantic part. However, when we constructed HowNet, we gave up the old approach of pure concept classification and turned to a hybrid approach, that is, a combination of the two approaches with the priority to the property description. It would be proper and fit for us to share our experience in both the approaches with our readers.

This chapter will be devoted to the discussion on the pros and cons of the two approaches.

4.1. Concept Classification

In concept classification, a set of classes and subclasses should be worked out. In some classification scheme, the classes and subclasses are organized into a class hierarchy; some schemes just have their classes in a discrete way. A pure concept classification, with or without a hierarchical organization, may be a good approach to building a human-oriented thesaurus, or a word finder, because the purpose of classification is to make it easier for readers to find relevant or synonymous words and expressions.

4.2. Arbitrariness and Purpose of Classification

It is not an easy task to assure faithfulness and accuracy in modeling the complicated relations that exist among real-world concepts. The developers' subjective arbitrariness would no doubt impede the consistency and coherency, and even further hinder the effectiveness in its applications.

In reality, arbitrariness is inevitable in classification. Is it really possible to achieve any classification which can be free from its developers' views on the real world or a specific domain of the world? It is known that different libraries have their own library classification systems, such as Library of Congress Classification, Chinese Library Classification, or specific-domain classification systems like National Library of Medicine Classification, and so on. It is hard to say which has better accuracy or which has avoided arbitrariness and subjectiveness. In addition, when careful comparison is made between a classification system in common-sense lexical database and in botany or zoology, it is found that there is a big difference in their organization. Any classification system would inevitably reflect its developers' realm of knowledge.

In discussion of classification issues, more emphasis should be placed on the purpose to attain rather than the arbitrariness and subjectiveness. The aim for classification varies with what it serves, for example, for the library the purpose is to make a good arrangement of books, whereas for a lexical database such as a thesaurus or a word finder, the purpose is to help a reader choose the right word he wants. In these two cases we rarely pay much attention to the logic relations among the books or the words themselves. Classification is really a very common practice in developing world knowledge resources. However, the purpose of this kind of classification should be completely different. The purpose of the classification for knowledge resources is to discover the relations among real-world concepts in general, and to achieve a hierarchy of hypernym/hyponym relations among them in particular. It must be bore in mind that the relation of hypernym/hyponym is just one of numerous kinds of relations among real-world concepts.

4.3. Classification by Top-down or Bottom-up

There are two ways to classify concepts, i.e. top-down and bottom-up. We find that top-down is most frequently adopted, especially by traditional linguists and that it seems easy to use top-down way when concepts of things such as animals, plants, instruments, etc. are classified. However, HowNet adopts the bottom-up way instead. The reason to do so is that classification of concepts is not the focus for HowNet. The aim of HowNet is to find the primitives to represent the concepts as precisely as possible and to form the relation nets among concepts and attributes. In other words, we tried to exhaust the most primitive senses. After we believe we have found all the sememes, or most of primitive senses, we rearranged in a hierarchy and extracted the classes. Let's take event concepts as an example. We first extracted all the event senses from 4000 Chinese frequently-used single-character words, then we reshuffled them and removed all the duplications, finally we obtained about 800 event senses. We used these 800 event senses as sememes to code verbs (including phrasal expressions) both in Chinese and English and meanwhile to do some necessary adjustments. By doing so we finally produced a hierarchical classification of event concepts. The detailed illustration of sememes extraction was given in Chap. 3.

4.4. General Guidelines for Concept Classification in HowNet

In classification in HowNet we strictly observe the following general guidelines:

(1) Only concepts are taken into consideration. It is concepts that are classified but not words, for example, it is the concept "plant" that is the

hypernym of the concept "tree", because a word may be ambiguous, but a concept is not. When we say "plant" is the hypernym of "tree", the "plant" should be the concept of "a living organism" and the "tree" should be the concept of "a tall perennial plant".

(2) A hyponym concept must inherit all the essential attributes of its hypernym concept, meanwhile it must have at least one attribute that its hypernym concept does not possess.

(3) No class as miscellany or grab-bag is allowed to exist in classification scheme. Whenever an entity is found to fall out of any one of classes, the whole classification scheme is to blame and re-design of the classification scheme has to be made.

(4) Any class can be taken as a sememe in defining real-world concepts. In other words, the determination of the sememes adopted in HowNet and the classification of concepts are simultaneously conducted.

(5) Different types of concepts such as things, parts, events, attributes, should have their own unique classification schemes.

(6) No overlapping is allowed, in other words, any one concept is allowed for only one class, or one immediate hypernymous concept. In HowNet the primitives can compensate such a case when it is really inevitable.

Last but not the least important, if we intend to build a semantic or world knowledge classification scheme, the interference of syntax should be avoided because syntax is language-dependent. Moreover, divergence of criterion in classification scheme is always harmful especially for computer-oriented knowledge resources, not only for the classification of event concepts, such as take, buy, have, put, walk, etc. but also for all kinds of classification, the best classification scheme should have a unified and consistent classification criterion. The criterion should embody the essence of what are to be classified. All the factors that many dictionaries have adopted are by no means the essence of event concepts, for instance, the domains that the events usually appear in, the body parts that the events happen with, the feelings that the events express, etc. Besides, if these are all adopted as the criteria in classification, the scheme would be spoiled.

In contrast to the classification of entities or things, or linguistically, of nouns, the classification of events, or linguistically, of verbs diversifies greatly with different grammars or schools. For entities or things, more or less similar schemes of classification could be found although they came from various grammars or schools. Most of them were arranged in a hierarchy with classes of "inanimate" and "animate", and then "animal", "plant", "human", "artifact", "instrument", and so on. However, for the classification of events very few similar schemes could be found. What's the reason? It is because there are too many different aspects from which events can be observed. We consider that two facets are harmful and should not be encouraged. One is the interference of syntax; the other is multi-criterion. HowNet adopts a biaxial theory for event classification, which is generally acknowledged to be one of the most significant originality of HowNet. The theory will be discussed in detailed in Chap. 6.

4.5. Root-nodes in HowNet

When discussing the top-level of classes, we will answer the question: what are the entities that are exclusively most essential in the world. It is believed that nothing in the world can fall out of the top-level classes and no overlapping should happen across the top-level classes. We maintain a philosophy on the world that all *things* (physical and metaphysical, including their *parts*) are in constant *motion* and are ever changing in a given *time* and *space*. Things evolve from one state to another as recorded in the change in their *attributes* with the display of their corresponding *values*. Hence we assert that there are seven top-level classes. They are *thing*, *part*, *attribute*, *time*, *space*, *event* and *attribute-value*. The relations of the root-nodes are shown in Fig. 4.1.

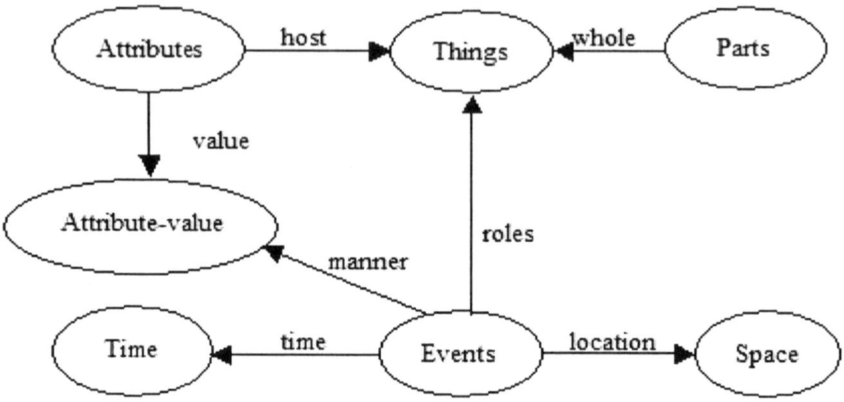

Fig. 4.1. Relations of root-nodes.

Chapter 5

SEMANTIC ROLES

5.1. What is a Semantic Role

A semantic role is defined by HowNet as the inherent relation that a participant has with the event in a real or imagined context, which is also known as thematic role, theta role or deep case.

When discussing semantic roles or deep cases, some people very often tend to ask a seemingly theoretical question: "If we adopt a scheme of deep cases, how many cases should we have in a language?" We believe that HowNet can give a satisfactory answer, because we have observed and coded over 95,000 meanings of Chinese and English words and expressions with inherent semantic roles.

Before the penetrating discussion of the semantic roles in HowNet, two points should be emphasized:

(1) Semantic roles should be defined without any consideration of syntactic structure;

(2) They are strictly specified and matched to every event class, thus to every event in both Chinese and English.

5.2. Semantic Roles in HowNet

HowNet uses 91 semantic roles. They are categorized into two groups: main semantic roles and peripheral semantic roles, which are further sub-classified as follows:

(1) Main semantic roles

(a) principal semantic roles: 6

agent, coagent, existent, experiencer, possessor, relevant

(b) affected semantic roles: 11

isa, ContentProduct, PartOfTouch, PatientPart, PatientProduct, content, contrast, partner, patient, possession, target

(2) peripheral semantic roles

(a) time: 12

DurationAfterEvent, DurationBeforeEvent, EventProcess, SincePeriod, SincePoint, TimeAfter, TimeBefore, TimeFin, TimeIni, TimeRange, duration, time

(b) space: 10

LocationFin, LocationIni, LocationThru, SourceWhole, StateIni, StateFin, direction, distance, location, source

(c) resultant: 8

ResultContent, ResultEvent, ResultIsa, ResultWhole, Purpose, result, sequence, succeeding

(d) manner: 11

accompaniment, aspect, cost, degree, frequency, instrument, manner, material, means, method, times

(e) modifier: 16

HostOf, MaterialOf, OfPart, PatientAttribute, PatientValue, RelateTo, Belong, concerning, descriptive, host, modifier, quantity, range, restrictive, scope, whole

(f) basis: 6

AccordingTo, CoEvent, beneficiary, cause, concession, condition

(g) comparison: 2

ContentCompare, QuantityCompare

(h) coordination: 6

and, besides, but, except, or, transition

(i) commentary: 2

comment, emphasis

Each of the illustrations of them below includes three parts: (1) definition and discussion; (2) contextual example (in italic); (3) sense example (in quotation marks) of words and expressions in HowNet.

1. AccordingTo — the entity that an event is based on, e.g.
In accordance with the regulations, the medicine should be destroyed

"size"

DEF={classify|分类:
AccordingTo={Size|尺寸:host={physical|物质}}}

"customization"

DEF={produce|制造:AccordingTo={aspiration|意愿}}

2. CoEvent — specially designed by HowNet to denote the event which has the role frame that its "cognate" entity shares, e.g.

My belief in his sincerity
Cf. I believe in his sincerity

"belief" shares the same role frame as "believe": experiencer and target.

"wish"

DEF={aspiration|意愿:CoEvent={expect|期望}}

"environmental protection"

DEF={fact|事情:CoEvent={protect|保护:
patient={Environment|情况:host={entity|实体}}}}

3. ContentCompare — the content in comparison, which is rarely shown explicitly in a sentence and usually denotes a certain attribute, e.g.

This factory makes *shoes* twice as much as our factory (*quantity*)
This brand of milk powder is the best (*quality*)
He is *taller* than his brother (*tallness*)

4. ContentProduct — something that is produced by the events such as "compile", "write", "draw" types, etc., e.g.

They compiled *a new dictionary*
The publication of *the book*
The boy is drawing *a horse*

"publishing house"
DEF={InstitutePlace|场所:{publish|出版:
ContentProduct={publications|书刊},agent={~}}}

5. DurationAfterEvent — a period of time ever since an event ends, e.g.
It is *3 weeks* since I arrived

"long parting"
DEF={farewell|离别:DurationAfterEvent={time|时间:
modifier={TimeLong|长时间}}}

6. DurationBeforeEvent — a period of time before an event happens, e.g.
After *three years* of hard work, the experiment succeeded at last.

7. EventProcess — the process of an event, e.g.
In the operation, the program may be affected by this virus

"course of treatment"
DEF={process|过程:{doctor|医治:EventProcess={~}}}

8. HostOf — the attribute that a concept is its host, e.g.
"teacher"
DEF={human|人:HostOf={Occupation|职位},
domain={education|教育},{teach|教:agent={~}}}

9. LocationFin — the location where an entity locates after an event of "AlterLocation" type happens, e.g.
They left *for Tokyo*
Please put them *in the box*

"go home"
DEF={GoBack|返回:LocationFin={family|家庭}}

10. LocationIni — the location where an entity locates before an event of "AlterLocation" type happens, e.g.

He fled *from the house* in fire

She will leave *UK* next week

"leave home"

DEF={leave|离开:LocationIni={family|家庭}}

11. LocationThru — the location where an entity goes through when an event of "AlterLocation" type happens, e.g.

He came to Moscow *via London*

"intersection"

DEF={part|部件:whole={route|道路},
{cross|越过:LocationThru={route|道路},location={~}}}

12. MaterialOf — the entity that is the product which an entity is its material, e.g.

"flour"

DEF={material|材料:MaterialOf={edible|食物},
material={crop|庄稼}}

13. OfPart — the part of an entity in the events of "include" type and "exclude" type, e.g.

The device includes *two components*

"illustration"

DEF={image|图像:{contain|包含:OfPart={~},
whole={publications|书刊}}}

"humpbacked"

DEF={disable|残疾:OfPart={part|部件:
PartPosition={body|身},modifier={hind|后},
whole={AnimalHuman|动物}}}

14. PartOfTouch — the part which is touched in the event of "AlterForm" type while its whole is the patient of the event, e.g.

He slapped the boy *in the face*
His leg was broken in the accident
She cut her *finger*

"clap one's hand"
DEF={beat|打:PartOfTouch={part|部件:whole={part|部件:
PartPosition={hand|手},whole={human|人}}}}

15. PatientAttribute — the attribute or sometimes the attribute value, which is changed in the events of "AlterAttribute" type, e.g.

"air-conditioning"
DEF={adjust|调整:PatientAttribute={Temperature|温度}}

16. PatientPart — the part which is moved in the events of "CausePartMove" type, e.g.

He nodded *his head*
She blinked *her eyes*
She shed *tears* when she heard the news

"bow"
DEF={CausePartMove|部件他移:
PatientPart={part|部件:PartPosition={body|身},
whole={human|人}}}

17. PatientProduct — the entity which is produced in the events of "CauseToExist" type, e.g.

The boy is making *a wood gun* for himself
railway construction
The institute was set up last year

"brewery"
DEF={InstitutePlace|场所:domain={industrial|工},
{produce|制造:
PatientProduct={drinks|饮品},location={~}}}

18. PatientValue — the value which is changed in the events of "AlterAttribute" type, e.g.

Wash hands *clean* first

Don't paint the wall *red*

"heighten"

DEF={AlterForm|变形状:PatientValue={high|高}}

19. QuantityCompare — the quantity in comparison, e.g.

This street is *two miles* longer than that

This factory make shoes *twice* as much as our factory

20. RelateTo — a concept to which another concept has an indistinct relation, e.g.

"hurricane"

DEF={wind|风:RelateTo={WeatherBad|坏天},
modifier={strong|强}}

"bloom"

DEF={pregnant|怀孕:RelateTo={plant|植物}}

"put"

DEF={provide|供:RelateTo={fund|资金},
domain={finance|金融}}

21. ResultContent — the result in the events of "punish" type, e.g.

He was sentenced *to death*

"fine"

DEF={expenditure|费用:{punish|处罚:ResultContent={~}}}

22. ResultEvent — the event which is caused by "MakeAct" and is done by the patient, e.g.

He asked her *to come early*

She was asked to *come early*

"hurt"
DEF={beat|打:ResultEvent={wounded|受伤}}

23. ResultIsa — the entity which is referred to in the events of "CauseToBe" and "CauseNotToBe" types, e.g.
We called him *Little Snake*
He was appointed as *our new coach*

"discharge"
DEF={dismiss|罢免:ResultIsa={Occupation|职位}}

24. ResultWhole — the whole in the events of "include" and "classify" types, e.g.
When did he join the *army*
This kind of words may be classified into *verb category*

"call up"
DEF={include|纳入:ResultWhole={army|军队},
domain={military|军}}

25. SincePeriod — a period of time since when an event occurs and lasts till now, e.g.
Over the past *three years*, she is looking for him

26. SincePoint — a point of time since when an event occurs and lasts till now, e.g.
She likes singing *since childhood*

27. SourceWhole — the whole as the source in the events of "AlterInclusion" type, e.g.
We should expel the officials like him *from the public service*

"demobilize"
DEF={discharge|开除:SourceWhole={army|军队},
domain={military|军}}

28. StateFin — the new state into which something changes after an event happens, e.g.

The book has been translated into *many languages*

"upstart"

DEF={human|人:{prosper|发达:StateFin={rich|富},agent={~},
manner={sudden|骤然}}}

29. StateIni — the initial state from which something changes before an event happens, e.g.

Is it translated *from Chinese*?

"come around"

DEF={BeRecovered|复原:StateIni={dizzy|昏迷}}

30. TimeAfter — the event happens before another, e.g.

After graduating, he went to Shanghai

"tea break"

DEF={time|时间:{rest|休息:
TimeAfter={discuss|商讨},duration={~}}}

31. TimeBefore — the event happens after another, e.g.

They finished the experiment *before the school was over*

"dress rehearsal"

DEF={drill|练习:TimeBefore={perform|表演},
domain={entertainment|艺}}

32. TimeFin — the point of time up to which an event lasts, e.g.

We've been working from morning *to night*

We won't start *until Bob comes*

33. TimeIni — the point of time from which an event begins, e.g.

She has lived here *ever since*

We've been working *from morning* to night

34. TimeRange — the period of time which covers from the present till an event occurs in the future, e.g.

How soon will he come

I'll come *in a minute*

35. accompaniment — two or more events happen in accompaniment, e.g.

He slept *with the window opened*

Don't talk too much *while eating*

"risk investment"

DEF={provide|供:accompaniment={dangerous|危},
domain={economy|经济},possession={fund|资金}}

"take a walk with pet birds"

DEF={walk|走:accompaniment={bird|禽},manner={idle|闲}}

36. agent — the doer or actor of any event of "act" type in HowNet; it is not necessarily animate nor with volition, e.g.

He bought a watch yesterday

Most birds and some insects fly

He was killed by *a young girl*

Can *the system* really translate the text

His treatment of the data

The stone hit her head

The tree was broken *by strong wind*

The ship sailed in the sea

"buyer"

DEF={human|人:domain={commerce|商业},
{buy|买:agent={~}}}

37. and — the concepts coordinates, e.g.

He likes singing *and dancing*

38. aspect — Chinese aspect only. See Sec. 3, Chap. 14 for details.

39. belong — a member which belongs to a whole, e.g.
He is the headmaster *of the high school.*

"New York"
DEF={place|地方:PlaceSect={city|市},
belong="US|美国",modifier={ProperName|专}}

40. beneficiary — the entity which an event benefits, e.g.
He bought *me* a book for 5 dollars
For whom the bell tolls?

"serve the people"
DEF={do|做:beneficiary={human|人:quantity={mass|众}}}

41. besides — another event that occurs, e.g.
He not only *can read it*, but *can write it*
In addition, I wrote a report

42. but — implies in spite of a certain situation, e.g.
I'd like to join you, but I am afraid I can.

43. cause — the cause of an event, e.g.
Why didn't he come yesterday
He died of *illness*
I am sorry *he didn't come*
Thanks for *your prompt reply*

"tsunami"
DEF={mishap|劫难:cause={mishap|劫难:cause={shiver|颤动:
agent={land|陆地}}},location={waters|水域}}

"food poisoning"

DEF={disease|疾病:cause={eat|吃:
patient={physical|物质:modifier={poisonous|有毒}}}}

44. coagent — the entity that should acts equally together with another, in the events such as "talk", e.g.

This morning, I played chess *with Mary*

"Iran-Iraq War"
DEF={fact|事情:CoEvent={fight|争斗:
coagent="Iran|伊朗""Iraq|伊拉克"},
domain={military|军},modifier={ProperName|专}}

45. comment — the speaker's view which normally related to the whole event rather than the individual element, e.g.

Hopefully, the computer can manipulate them
In the final analysis, knowledge is strength
As a matter of fact, nobody likes it
Of course I will be responsible for that

46. concerning — the entity which concerns, e.g.

He knows a lot about *religious rules*

"zoology"
DEF={knowledge|知识:concerning={animal|兽}}

47. concession — the state showing willingness to admit a point that goes against the event, e.g.

Although he lost the game, he was the best

"have a false appearance"
DEF={useless|无用:concession={GoodLooking|好看}}

48. condition — the state on which the event depends, e.g.

I will take it *if it is less expensive*
We will go *unless it rains*
He will join us *on condition that he is invited*

Take it *in case it rains*

"buy one, get one free"
DEF={obtain|得到:condition={buy|买},
manner={FreeOfCharge|免费}}

49. content — the entity or event which is affected by the event types of "ActGeneral", "StateMental", "AlterMental", etc. And it differs from "patient" in that it is not changed in the same way as "patient", e.g.

I have been engaged *in NLP* for over 20 years
It started *raining*
Telephone numbers are difficult to remember
He said *he would come*
English is taught in that school

"homesickness"
DEF={thought|念头:CoEvent={ThinkOf|思念:
content={family|家庭}}}

"unbelievable"
DEF={impossible|不会:scope={believe|相信:content={$}}}

50. contrast — the concept which is correspondent to the main body in the events of "comparison", "AlterComparison", "suit relation" or "win" and "surpass" types, etc., e.g.

He is as tall *as his brother*
He is taller than *his brother*
It is different *from them*
My opinions are similar *to his*

"outdoors"
DEF={location|位置:contrast={room|房间},
modifier={external|外}}

"asphyxia"
DEF={phenomena|现象:CoEvent={BeSimilar|相像:
contrast={die|死}}}

51. cost — the entity one pays in purchase or for service, e.g.
How much did you pay for it
He bought me a book from them *for 5 dollars*
I sold him my car *for $100*
I paid *100 dollars* for my room a day

"postage"
DEF={expenditure|费用:{post|邮寄:cost={~}}}

52. degree — the position on a scale of intensity or quality, e.g.
How big is it
The place is *extremely* large
We all love the boy *very much*
I took it when it was *less* expensive

"largish"
DEF={big|大:degree={ish|稍}}

"light green"
DEF={green|绿:degree={light|淡}}

"at full speed"
DEF={fast|快:degree={extreme|极}}

53. descriptive — the attribute value which modifies an entity in a "isa" type event, e.g.
The house is *very big*
Is it *really difficult* to write a novel?

"flush"
DEF={become|成为:descriptive={red|红}}

54. direction — the direction which an entity faces in the event of "TimeOrSpace" and "AlterLocation" types, e.g.

The house faces *the south*
Suddenly a car came *up to me*

"move south"
DEF={AlterLocation|变空间位置:direction={south|南}}

55. distance — the extent of space between two objects or places, e.g.
He walks *ten miles* to come here

"neighbour"
DEF={human|人:{reside|住下:agent={~},
distance={near|近}}}

"go far to"
DEF={LeaveFor|前往:distance={far|远}}

56. duration — the period of time for which the event lasts, e.g.
How long have you been in the city
We have stayed here *for 3 days*

"shelf life"
DEF={time|时间:{store|保存:duration={~}}}

57. emphasis — special forcefulness of expression that gives importance to something singled out, e.g.
Only she can do it

58. except — excepting or being excepted, e.g.
All should come to report except *those who have submitted their papers*

59. existent — the main entity in the events of "TimeOrSpace" and "ExistAppear" types, e.g.
Where is *my book?*
Your book is on his desk

The room is facing the south
There are *two books* on the table
The man disappeared in the dark
Six traffic accidents happened this morning
There comes *the bus*

"fall ill"
DEF={happen|发生:existent={disease|疾病}}

"case rate"
DEF={Rate|比率:host={place|地方},
scope={happen|发生:existent={fact|事情:
modifier={guilty|有罪}}}}

60. experiencer — the topic in the events of "state" type except "ExistAppear", e.g.
Their plan to improve the quality of products failed
He was ill
He likes swimming
The man was disappointed
I forget his phone number
The competition will start soon
It threatens to rain

"doghouse"
DEF={house|房屋:{alive|活着:
experiencer={livestock|牲畜},location={~}}}

"busybody"
DEF={human|人:{FondOf|喜欢:experiencer={~},
target={MakeTrouble|捣乱}}}

61. frequency — the frequency an event repeats, e.g.
How often do you go there in a year?
He *rarely* comes to see us these days
Sometimes I do, *sometimes* I don't

"rebuild"

DEF={build|建造:frequency={again|再}}

62. host — the concept which is the host of an attribute, e.g.

"color"

DEF={Color|颜色:host={physical|物质}}

"temperament"

DEF={Behavior|举止:host={AnimalHuman|动物}}

63. instrument — the entity which is used as a tool in an event, e.g.

We can do that *with a computer*

He came *by train*

"banquet"

DEF={fact|事情:CoEvent={entertain|招待:
instrument={edible|食物}}}

"propose a toast"

DEF={congratulate|祝贺:instrument={drinks|饮品}}

64. isa — the entity which is referred to in the events of "isa" relation type, e.g.

Horses are *animals*

Necessity is *the mother of invention*

She became *one of my best friends*

"epaulet"

DEF={fittings|配件:whole={clothing|衣物},
{mean|指代:instrument={~},isa={Rank|等级}}}

65. location — the location where an event happens, e.g.

Where is my book?

He is *in the office*

There is a book *on the table*

He lives *in London*
He wrote the book *in a small village*

"reception center"
DEF={InstitutePlace|场所:{entertain|招待:location={~}}}

66. manner — the way in which the event happens, e.g.
How did they treat their parents?
It should be done *very effectively*
Don't do it *in a hurry*

"cheer"
DEF={cry|喊:manner={joyful|喜悦}}

67. material — the entity out of which something is made, e.g.
Wine is made *out of grapes*

"seafood"
DEF={food|食品:material={fish|鱼}}

68. means — the event or the fact by which an event is completed, e.g.
How can you make it?
She made her wishes known *by means of* signs
Dough is made by *mixing flour and water*

"exchange and get"
DEF={obtain|得到:means={exchange|交换}}

69. method — the entity by which an event is completed, e.g.
He finished the work *by traditional craft*

"trick"
DEF={plans|规划:{deceive|欺骗:method={~}}}

70. modifier — the attribute-value which modifies an entity, e.g.

new car
blue sky
high-risk group

"white clouds"
DEF={CloudMist|云雾:modifier={white|白}}

71. or — the concept which is an alternate, e.g.
you *or me* go there

72. partner — the entity which is correspondent to the main body in the events of "connective", "AlterConnection", "TimeOrSpace" or "HaveContest" types, etc., e.g.
She doesn't relate well *to her mother*
The marriage of a queen concerns *the people*
I'll come *with my brother*
The Chinese team had the competition *with the Korean team*
Can we mingle this medicine *with that drug?*

"bullfight"
DEF={compete|比赛:partner={livestock|牲畜}}

73. patient — the entity which is affected, and typically changed in the events of "act" types, e.g.
They smuggled *a lot of drugs*
Oil exporting is the main economic resource of the country
The computer was repaired by him
His treatment *of the data*
He will be punished severely
The mother dressed *her baby patient*
She dried her *skirt* in the sun
The manager encouraged *us* to develop *new technology*

"fish"
DEF={catch|捉住:patient={fish|鱼}}

74. possession — the entity is owned in possession relation, e.g.
John has *three cars*
How much I owe you?
the teacher's *book*
Honor belongs to the people
Whose *pen* is this?
He bought a *watch* yesterday
Unfortunately I didn't get the *post*

"forfeit"
DEF={abandon|放弃:possession={rights|权利}}

75. possessor — the owner in possession relation, e.g.
John has three cars
How much *I* owe you
Teacher's book
Honor belongs *to the people*
Whose pen is this?

"beneficiary"
DEF={human|人:{obtain|得到:possession={Advantage|利},
possessor={~}}}

76. purpose — the intention for which an action is done, e.g.
He came *for the purpose of seeing his family*
He came *to see his family*
He came *for talking to her*
In order to catch up with them, we have to work harder

"ring"
DEF={tool|用具:{PutOn|穿戴:instrument={~},
purpose={decorate|装饰}}}

"oblation"
DEF={tool|用具:{submit|交:possession={~},
purpose={salute|致敬}}}

77. quantity — the quantity of something, including, approximate of number itself, e.g.

ten people
two directions
about five years
a little sugar

"every family"
DEF={family|家庭:quantity={many|多}}

78. range — the range an event covers, e.g.
They *all* came

"generality"
DEF={Role|功用:host={entity|实体},range={extensive|泛}}

"read extensively"
DEF={read|读:range={extensive|泛}}

79. relevant — the topic in the events of "relation" types except possession relation, e.g.

What's *this?*
Horses are animals
It is difficult *to write a novel*
His carelessness led to the failure of the task

"synonym"
DEF={expression|词语:{BeSame|相同:relevant={~},
scope={information|信息}}}

80. restrictive — the entity used to restrict something, but not in attribute nor in possession, e.g.

a dictionary *of modern Chinese*
the dog *running after the boy* was caught
the teacher corrected the mistake *he made in his homework*

"waste gas or steam"

DEF={gas|气:restrictive={waste|废物}}

81. result — the result caused by an event, e.g.

His carelessness led *to the failure of the task*

He was almost beaten *to death*

She was so frightened *to say a word*

"pack full"

DEF={fill|填入:result={full|满}}

82. sequence — the order in which some events occur, e.g.

This is his *first time* to come to New York

"display for the first time"

DEF={CauseToAppear|显现:sequence={first|首次}}

83. scope — the area within the limits an event affects, e.g.

They are the same *in color* but different *in size*

This article is easy *to read*

Of course I will be responsible *for that*

"devaluate"

DEF={BecomeLess|减少:scope={Worth|价值}}

84. source — the source which a possession (physical or mental) is obtained, e.g.

I bought it *from a second-hand bookstore*

They robbed *him* of his watch

We learned much *from him*

"purchase from abroad"

DEF={buy|买:source={place|地方:modifier={foreign|外国}}}

"well"

DEF={facilities|设施:
{take|取:possession={water|水},source={~}}}

85. state — the state in which something happens, e.g.
Most of the miners lead *a very miserable life*

86. succeeding — the event which follows another, e.g.
They discussed and *made the decision*

"encircle and suppress"

DEF={surround|包围:domain={military|军},
succeeding={destroy|消灭}}

87. target — the entity which is affected but not changed, e.g.
Give *me* the book
We all respect *him* greatly
Who taught *you* chemistry?
He spoke *to her*

"model"

DEF={human|人:{imitate|模仿:target={~}}}

"favourite"

DEF={entity|实体:{like|爱惜:target={~}}}

88. time — the time when an event happens, e.g.
When did you get it?
He lived in England *3 years ago*
He arrived *on Monday morning*
She entered *while I was reading the letter*

"runner-up"

DEF={human|人:{win|获胜:experiencer={~},
time={compete|比赛}}}

"morning dew"
DEF={RainSnow|雨雪:time={time|时间:
TimeSect={morning|晨}}}

89. times — the specific times which the event repeats, e.g.
I played cricket *5 times* last week

90. transition — the passage from one subject to another in discourse, e.g.
Some people like fat meat, *whereas others hate it*

91. whole — the entity which is the whole of its parts, e.g.
These organizations will be subordinate *to the State Department*

"bud"
DEF={part|部件:PartPosition={embryo|胚},
whole={plant|植物}}

"watch strap"
DEF={fittings|配件:whole={tool|用具:{tell|告诉:
content={time|时间},instrument={~}}}}

"digestive organ"
DEF={part|部件:PartPosition={viscera|脏},
whole={AnimalHuman|动物},
{digest|消化:instrument={~}}}

"stomach"
{part|部件:PartPosition={viscera|脏},
whole={part|部件:PartPosition={viscera|脏},
whole={AnimalHuman|动物},{digest|消化:instrument={~}}}}

The last two examples show the relation of the "part" of a "part" ("digestive organ" is the part of "animals" while "stomach" is the part of "digestive organ", so it is the part of a part).

Chapter 6

TAXONOMY

By taxonomy we mean the classification of sememes in a hierarchical structure. Taxonomy mainly provides the hypernym-hyponym relations of concepts. In correspondence to the root nodes of sememes discussed in Chap. 4, HowNet organizes its sememes into the following 4 taxonomies: (1) taxonomy of events; (2) taxonomy of entity, including things, parts, time and space; (3) taxonomy of attributes; and (4) taxonomy of attribute-values. In this chapter, apart from the 4 taxonomies, we will discuss the secondary features list and the antonymous and converse sememes lists.

6.1. Event Taxonomy

Event is something that happens in a given time and space, and linguistically in most situations are denoted by verbs. In HowNet there are 812 classes of events.

Event concepts can be observed and analyzed in their multiple semantic facets, which can be classified into two types: intrinsic and extrinsic. The former includes (1) development of things (including the development of physical things and the development of metaphysical substance); (2) correspondence between static events and dynamic events; (3) entailment of events; and (4) cognate RoleFrame between incidents (denoted usually by verbs) and facts (denoted usually by nouns). The latter includes: (1) involvement of things in events; (2) relations between events and attributes and attribute-values; (3) shifting of semantic roles of events; and (4) features of subject domains.

The event concepts can be sub-classified into the following two higher-level groups as shown in Fig. 6.1.

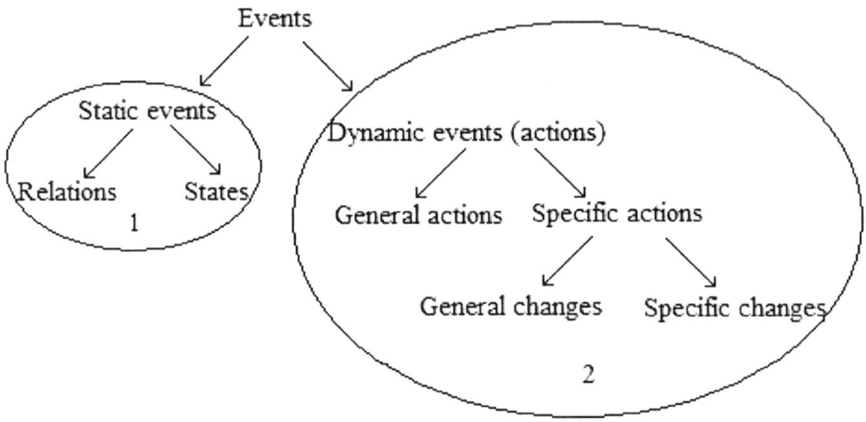

Fig. 6.1. Higher levels of event hierarchy.

The first group denotes no actual actions while the second denotes actual actions. The first group is sub-classified into two sub-groups: the event of relation and the event of state. The second group, the event of action, is also sub-classified into two sub-groups: general actions such as "do", "make", and specific actions such as "eat", "buy", "walk".

6.1.1. *Biaxial theory*

It is generally acknowledged that the most significant originality or uniqueness of HowNet is its biaxial theory of events. The theory is based on 812 classes of events with which presently over 20,000 Chinese and English verbs respectively have been tagged. The theory unveils an intrinsic biaxial scheme of events. The two axes are intersected each other. One of the axis is the development of things, the other is the correspondence between static events and dynamic events. Biaxial theory is proved to be one of the most important discoveries made by HowNet researchers.

6.1.1.1. *Development of things*

The basic functions of events reflect what happens to things i.e. the states that things lie in and the change that things undergo.

Although things differ greatly in form and nature, they are in common in terms of their basic process of development. Physical things, either animate or inanimate, or social units, undergo the same basic process of development, that is, a process of development of coming into being, then growing up and maturing, gradually becoming old and weak, finally passing from physical life. In other words, they undergo a process from living to death or from appearance to disappearance. As for any happenings, for example, a meeting or a birthday party, or a company or even a government undergoes nearly the same basic process of development, it begins or emerges , may get into a climax or flourishing afterwards, and finally comes to an end or perishes. Psychological features are roughly sub-classified into feelings and cognition. They too may undergo a process from appearance to disappearance like the other types of things, but there is one outstanding feature attracts our attention, i.e. apart from the similar process of development from rising to fading, they may be expressed or shown.

6.1.1.2. *Correspondence between static events and dynamic events*

We have discovered a perfect correspondence between the concepts of static events and the concepts of dynamic events. Any relation or state is caused or changed by its corresponding action, for example, events denoting the relation of possession such as "have", "own" or "lose" correspond to the events denoting the change of the possession relation such as "take" and "borrow" or "give" and "lend". We discuss more details on the correspondence between relation events and relation-change events, between state events of and state-change events respectively in the following two sections.

(1) Correspondence between relation events and relation-change events: There are 9 sub-classes of relation events we discover and represent in HowNet.

(a) Relation of is-a, e.g.

He *is* head of the department
She *became* a school teacher

(b) Relation of possession, e.g.
My brother *has* a car
She *lost* the money

(c) Relation of comparison, e.g.
She *resembles* her mother very much
They *differ* in color

(d) Relation of fitting, e.g.
This *suits* his needs
The two proposals *conflict*

(e) Relation of inclusion, e.g.
The list *includes* the names of many famous writers
The cost for the trip *excludes* food

(f) Relation of relatedness, e.g.
The case *relates to* his family
It *has nothing to do with* her

(g) Relation of cause-result, e.g.
The heavy fog *resulted* in the accident
The problem *roots* in her depression

(h) Relation of location/time, e.g.
Where *is* my handbag
The house *faces* south

(i) Relation of arithmetic, e.g.
Five *minus* three equals two
The bill *amounted to* $1000

As shown above obviously, all the 9 classes of events denote neither actions nor states. They only express some special kinds of relations, for example, in "He is a teacher", the event "is" expresses an is-a relation, and in "My brother owns a car", the event "owns" expresses a possession relation, that is, a relation between "my brother" and "the car". Similarly, in "My father is in London", the event "is" expresses a location-relation, that is, a relation between "my father" and "London". The events do not indicate any state of "my brother" and "the car" or "my father" and "London", nor do they express any actions on them. All the above 9 classes of relations are caused by their corresponding relation-change events. The correspondence is illustrated in Table 6.1.

Table 6.1. Correspondence between relation event and relation-change event.

	Relation events	**Relation-change events**
(a)	be, become, be not …	appoint, demote, call …
(b)	have, own, have not …	take, buy, give, borrow, sell …
(c)	resemble, differ …	compare, equalize …
(d)	suit, conflict, disagree …	observe, conform, breach …
(e)	contain, exclude, belong …	join, admit, expel, dismiss …
(f)	connect, have to do …	link, disconnect, divorce …
(g)	incur, result in, root …	infect, affect …
(h)	lie, be situated, face …	move, swim, send, stop …
(i)	plus, minus, amount to …	add, multiply, reduce, divide …

To put it in a nutshell, any relation between entities is caused by an action which is corresponding to the relation, for example, the relation of *possession* such as "possess", "own" or "do not have" is caused by the actions denoting the *change of possession* like "take", "buy", "borrow", and "give", "sell", "lend", etc.

(2) Correspondence between state events and state-change events

The state events denote the states that an entity is situated in. The main sub-classes of state events are formed into a hierarchy as follows:

```
{State}
├ {State Physical}
│ ├ {Appear}
│ ├ {Begin}
│ ├ {State Normal}
│ ├ {State Good}
│ ├ {Recovered}
│ ├ {Change}
│ │ ├ {Change-in-Appearance}
│ │ ├ {Change-in-Quantity}
│ │ ├ {State Bad}
│ │ ├ {End}
│ │ └ {Weather-Change}
```

```
│ ├ {Change-Not}
│ └ {Disappear}
└ {State Mental}
  ├ {Feeling}
  ├ {Attitude}
  ├ {Volition}
  └ {Cognition}
    ├ {Have-Knowledge}
    ├ {No-Knowledge}
    ├ {Misunderstand}
    └ {Unable}
```

The correspondence between the concepts of state events and the concepts of state-change events is illustrated in Table 6.2.

Table 6.2. Correspondence between state event and state-change event.

	State events	**State-change events**
(a)	appear, expose ...	disclose, veil, unveil ...
(b)	be born, come into being ...	produce, bring forth ...
(c)	be alive, live, survive ...	raise, bring up, support ...
(d)	boom, progress ...	develop, improve ...
(e)	suffer, ill, break down ...	affect, damage ...
(f)	recover, get well ...	treat, cure, repair, mend ...
(g)	die, pass away, perish ...	kill, murder, suicide ...
(h)	disappear, vanish, get lost ...	hide, conceal, destroy, ruin ...
(i)	joy, rejoice ...	please, delight, satisfy ...
(j)	be annoyed ...	annoy, displease, provoke ...
(k)	anger, see red ...	anger, make angry ...
(l)	perceive, feel, sense ...	look, listen, smell, taste ...
(m)	know, cognize, learn ...	read, study, tell, teach ...
(n)	Misunderstand ...	deceive, fool, mislead ...

HowNet discovers any state is caused by a kind of corresponding state-change event. For example, in "a baby *was born*", this state was caused by a state-change event, "its mother *gave birth*". "*Giving medical treatment*" is a state-change event which may cause the state of "*recovery*".

In HowNet only relation-change events and state-change events are actions.

6.1.2. *Event frames*

In the event taxonomy of HowNet, each of 812 classes of events is attached to an event frame based on semantic roles as shown in Fig. 6.2.

```
├ {own|有} {possession|领属关系:possession={*},possessor={*}}
│  ├ {obtain|得到} {own|有:possession={*},possessor={*},source={*}}

├ {AlterPossession|变领属} {AlterRelation|变关系:agent={*},possession={*}}
│  ├ {take|取} {AlterPossession|变领属:agent={*},possession={*},source={*}}
│  │  ├ {steal|偷} {take|取:agent={*},manner={covert|隐秘},possession={*},
│  │  │           source={*}}
│  │  ├ {buy|买} {take|取:agent={*},beneficiary={*},cost={*},
                 domain={commerce|商业},possession={*},source={*}}
```

Fig. 6.2. HowNet Event frame.

Each frame includes three parts:

(a) hypernym:

as *take*|*取* for steal|偷 and buy|买; *AlterPossession*|*变领属* for take|取; *AlterRelation*|*变关系* for AlterPossession|变领属; *own*|*有* for obtain|得到;and *possession*|*领属关系* for own|有

(b) indispensable roles:

as agent={*}, possession={*}, source={*}, manner={covert|隐秘}

(c) feature(s):

as domain={commerce|商业}

The event frames ensure two types of event relations: vertical relations and crosswise relations. The vertical relations of the events are based on the hypernyms; the crosswise relations are ensured by the roles. It is noted that only absolutely necessary semantic roles are included in the event frames, in other words, whenever an event happens the indispensable semantic roles will inevitably participate in. If any one of the listed roles was absent, the event would not stand. It should be noted that not all the indispensable roles have to appear in a real context at the same time. For example, when the event "buy" happens, "buyer" (agent), "something to be bought" (possession), "some place from which someone buys" (source), "money to be paid for purchase" (cost), "for whom someone buys" (beneficiary) must participate in logically, but not necessarily appear in one sentence in a real text. Sometimes they may come in different sentences. For example,

"My brother bought her the book in a second-hand book store"

my brother	→ agent
her	→ beneficiary
the book	→ possession
second-hand book store	→ source

Though the sentence does not mention the money paid for the book, it is certain that the agent has paid for it. If not, the action would not be "buying" any more!

As for "time" and "space" or "location", they are deliberately omitted in the event frames because any event happens in a certain time and place with no exceptions even though they do not appear in the context.

In the event frames some roles may be specified with definite sememes as their values, such as manner={covert|隐秘} in the frame of "steal|偷", but for most cases there are no definite values yet, so wildcards are used. The next section — "Typical actors or selectional restriction" will be devoted to the detailed discussion.

6.1.3. *Typical actors or selectional restrictions*

HowNet uses an innovative term "typical actor" instead of "selectional restriction". We consider that "selectional restriction" is too tough, not as flexible enough as "typical actor". As we have specified the indispensable roles in the event frames, we will further specify who or what will usually plays the roles, that is, who will be the actors for the role, for example,

{eat|吃}
{metabolize|代谢:agent={animate|生物→},patient={food|食品}}

{drink|喝}
{metabolize|代谢:agent={animate|生物→},patient={drinks|饮品}}

Cf. the event frames, without the typical actors

{eat|吃}
{metabolize|代谢:agent={},patient={*}}*

{drink|喝}
{metabolize|代谢:agent={},patient={*}}*

The typical actors for the events "eat" and "drink" are: "animate and its hyponyms (indicated by "→")" for the agents, and "food" and "drinks" for the two patients respectively. By typical actor, we mean that in most cases they may be the correct *selections*, but they are by no means *restrictions*, or they should be used exclusively. In other words, we do not want to make any tough rules on the selections of the concept for a specific role. Our past experience in NLP tells us that the performance of NLP systems was often harmed by over-restrictive semantic selections, especially when the systems handle large-scale real texts.

6.2. Entity Taxonomy

HowNet entity taxonomy contains the sememes of things, parts, time and space as its top-level nodes. In HowNet there are 151 classes which cover "things", "time", "space", and "parts". The main scheme of the hierarchy is shown in Fig. 6.3.

In contrast to the classification of physical things, traditionally the classification of so-called abstract things varies greatly with different language resources. In most of them it seems a subclass of abstract things or nouns is adopted, which naturally includes those concepts (or nouns) of attribute. However, we consider that in terms of semantics the nature of concreteness or abstractness is not an essential one. HowNet has adopted a unique scheme.

```
- {entity|实体}
  ├ {thing|万物}
  │  ├ {physical|物质}
  │  │  ├ {animate|生物}
  │  │  │  ├ {AnimalHuman|动物}
  │  │  │  │  ├ {human|人}
  │  │  │  │  │  └ {humanized|拟人}
  │  │  │  │  └ {animal|兽}
  │  │  │  ├ {plant|植物}
  │  │  │  └ {bacteria|微生物}
  │  │  ├ {inanimate|无生物}
  │  │  │  ├ {NaturalThing|天然物}
  │  │  │  ├ {artifact|人工物}
  │  │  │  └ {waste|废物}
  │  │  └ {shape|物形}
  │  ├ {mental|精神}
  │  ├ {fact|事情}
  │  └ {group|群体}
  ├ {time|时间}
  ├ {space|空间}
  └ {component|部分}
```

Fig. 6.3. Skeleton of entity taxonomy.

6.2.1. *Things*

Things are the main entity that instigate or cause the happening of events. Things include physical things, metaphysical things and social units. Physical things are objects with material form while metaphysical things are those without material form. Physical things include animate beings and inanimate substance. Metaphysical things include psychological features and happening. Things can be sub-classified as shown in Fig. 6.4.

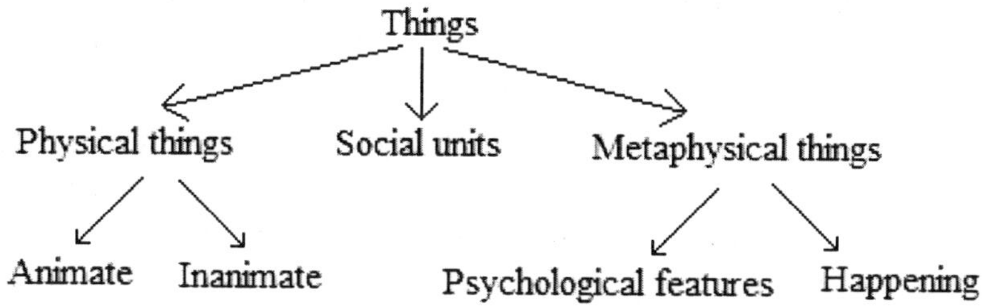

Fig. 6.4. Top levels of thing hierarchy.

Similar to the taxonomy of events in HowNet, the taxonomy of entity is not merely a hierarchy of the hypernym-hyponym relations of entities, but also a representation of sememe definitions. In a sense, it prepares for the axioms and rules of inference. Let's take part of it and give detailed explanation. See Fig. 6.5.

```
{entity|实体}
├ {thing|万物} {entity|实体:{ExistAppear|存现:existent={~}}}
│ ├ {physical|物质} {thing|万物:HostOf={Appearance|外观},{perception|感知:content={~}}}
│ │ ├ {animate|生物} {physical|物质:HostOf={Age|年龄},{alive|活着:experiencer={~}},
│ │ │ │                {die|死:experiencer={~}},{metabolize|代谢:experiencer={~}},
│ │ │ │                {reproduce|生殖:agent={~},PatientProduct={~}}}
│ │ │ ├ {AnimalHuman|动物}  {animate|生物:HostOf={Sex|性别},
│ │ │ │ │                    {AlterLocation|变空间位置:agent={~}},
│ │ │ │ │                    {StateMental|精神状态:experiencer={~}}}
│ │ │ │ ├ {human|人}     {AnimalHuman|动物:HostOf={Name|姓名}{Wisdom|智慧}
│ │ │ │ │ │              {Ability|能力},{think|思考:agent={~}},{speak|说:agent={~}}}
│ │ │ │ │ └ {humanized|拟人} {human|人:modifier={fake|伪},{forge|伪造:PatientProduct={~}}}
```

Fig. 6.5. Part of entity taxonomy.

This part of taxonomy of entity should be interpreted as follows:

(1) One of the hyponyms of entity is "thing"; one of the hyponyms of "thing" is "physical thing"; one of the hyponyms of "physical thing" is "living thing"; one of the hyponyms of "living thing" is "animal"; one of the hyponyms of "animal" is "human"; and finally, "personified thing" is the hyponym of "human". This is part of the hierarchy of hypernym-hyponym relations as shown more clearly as in Fig. 6.5.

(2) The sememe definitions convey the following detailed information about the concepts:

(a) "thing" is an "entity" which "exists (in the world)";

(b) "physical thing" is a "thing" which has the attribute of "appearance" and can be "perceived";

(c) "living thing" is a "physical thing" which has the attribute of "age", and may "live", "die", and "has metabolic process", and can "reproduce offspring" as well as "is reproduced";

(d) "animal including human" is a "living thing" which has the attribute of "sex", and can "move", and may "experience mental states (such as feelings)";

(e) "human" is an "animal" which has the attributes such as "name", "ability" and "wisdom", and can "think" and "speak";

(f) "personified thing" (such as ghost, fairy) is a "human" which is "fake".

(3) Inheritance of properties of the hypernyms

As aforesaid, HowNet specifies that any concept inherits all the fundamental properties of its hypernym and must have at least one property that its hypernym does not own. Hence in the part of entity taxonomy shown in Fig. 6.5, "human" inherits all the listed properties of its hypernyms. "Human" has not only the attributes of "name", "ability" and "wisdom", but also has the attributes of "sex" (from "animal"), "age" (from "living thing") and "appearance" (from "physical thing"). In addition, "Human" not only can "think" and "speak", but also can "move" and "experience mental states" (from "animal"), and may "live", "die", "metabolize", "reproduce offspring" and "be reproduced" (from "living thing").

(4) Coverage and pass-on of hyponyms

(a) According to the taxonomy of entity:

{thing|万物} *{entity|实体:{ExistAppear|存现:existent={~}}}*

"thing" may "ExistAppear|存现";

meanwhile according to the taxonomy of event as shown in Fig. 6.6:

```
├ {ExistAppear|存现}
│ ├ {exist|存在}
│ │ └ {ComeToWorld|问世}
│ ├ {ExistNot|不存在}
│ ├ {appear|出现}
│ │ │ └ {exposure|露出}
│ └ {happen|发生}
```

Fig. 6.6. Part of event taxonomy.

"thing" then may "ExistAppear|存现", "exist|存在", "ComeToWorld|问世", "ExistNot|不存在", "appear|出现", "exposure|露出", or "happen|发生".

Again according to the taxonomy of entity:

{animate|生物} *{physical|物质:HostOf={Age|年龄},*
{alive|活着:experiencer={~}},{die|死:experiencer={~}},
{metabolize|代谢:experiencer={~}},
{reproduce|生殖:agent={~},PatientProduct={~}}}

"living thing" may "metabolize|代谢"(processes necessary for life); meanwhile according to the taxonomy of event as shown in Fig. 6.7:

```
├ {metabolize|代谢}
│ ├ {digest|消化}
│ ├ {absorb|吸收}
│ ├ {eat|吃}
│ ├ {drink|喝}
│ ├ {feed|喂}
│ ├ {excrete|排泄}
│ └ {respire|呼吸}
```

Fig. 6.7. Part of event taxonomy.

"living thing" then may "digest|消化", "absorb|吸收", "eat|吃", "drink|喝" "feed|喂", "excrete|排泄", or "respire|呼吸". This is what we mean by "coverage of hyponyms".

(b) According to the taxonomy of entity as the follows:

```
├ {thing|万物}
│ ├ {physical|物质}
│ │ ├ {animate|生物}
│ │ │ ├ {AnimalHuman|动物}
│ │ │ │ ├ {human|人},
```

"human" may "absorb|吸收", "eat|吃", "drink|喝" or "respire|呼吸". This is what we mean by "pass-on of hyponyms".

6.2.2. *Components*

In HowNet we use the sememe "component|部分" to refer to the root-node of "part". "Component|部分" includes two subclasses of sememes: "part|部件" and "fittings|配件" as shown in Fig. 6.8:

```
- {entity|实体}
  ├ {thing|万物}
  └ {component|部分} {entity|实体:whole={entity|实体:
     │                    {contain|包含:OfPart={~}}},modifier={other|另}}
     ├{part|部件} {component|部分:whole={entity|实体:
     │                {contain|包含:OfPart={~}}},modifier={other|另}{necessary|必要}}
     └{fittings|配件}{component|部分:whole={entity|实体:
              {contain|包含:OfPart={~}}},modifier={other|另}{unnecessary|不必要}}
```

Fig. 6.8. Component in entity taxonomy.

This part of taxonomy of entity is interpreted as follows:

(1) "thing" and "component" are sister-nodes whose hypernym is "entity". And "component" has two hyponyms: "part" and "fitting";

(2) The sememe definitions give the further information about the concepts:

(a) "component" is an "entity" which takes another "entity" as its whole;

(b) "part" is a "component" which takes another "entity" as its whole and is a necessary part of it; "fitting" is a "component" which takes another "entity" as its whole but is not absolutely necessary, for example, the sole of shoes is "part"; the shoelace of shoes is "fitting" as HowNet defines.

The philosophy on which we understand a "component" states firstly that all objects are probably part of something else and at the same time, all objects can also be taken as the *whole* of something else. Doors and windows are components of buildings and limbs are components of animals. However, at the same time, buildings form the components of a block or street. A human is part of a family or society that he/she belongs to. All things can be divided into their respective components. *Space* can be segmented into "upper part", "lower part", "left side", "right side" while *time* can be seen from "the past", "the present" and "the future". Nothing can only function as a component but not the whole, and the reverse is true.

Secondly, as we pointed out previously, a hyponym concept inherits the principal properties of its hypernym. Hence it is inappropriate to regard a component as the hyponym of its whole. Component is as independent as its whole. Component does not inherit the main attributes of its whole. A "bomber" or a "fighter" inherits the main attributes from its hypernym "airplane", but a "wing" never carries the main attributes of an "airplane". A human being as his/her main properties, can think and speak, but his/her hand or leg cannot.

Thirdly, component is taken as a constituent in a larger whole, thus in HowNet all the concepts which are defined as "part", its "whole" class must be specified without exception, for example,

"roof"
DEF={part|部件:PartPosition={head|头},*whole={house|房屋}*}

"twig"
DEF={part|部件:PartPosition={limb|肢},*whole={plant|植物}*}

"memory"
DEF={part|部件:*whole={computer|电脑}*,
{store|保存:instrument={~}}}

Moreover, the role and function of the component resemble the human body, for instance, "hilltop", "hillside", "mountain foot", "table leg", "back of chair", "estuary". "Doors" and "windows" of a building are analogous to the relevant components of the human body such as the eyes, mouth etc. It is interesting to note that the same analogy applies to various languages. This shows how similar the mankind shares their views on the relations between a component and its whole.

6.2.3. *Space*

In fact many things imply the concept of space, such as land, waters, sky and places, or institutions such as schools, hospitals, shops, or buildings, houses, or even many artifacts such as vehicles, furniture, containers. By "space" as one of seven root-node classes, we mean those that are highly abstract and sub-classified into two classes:

(1) directions, such as east, west, wind direction;
(2) locations such as address, point, entrance, inside.

In the entity taxonomy, the hierarchy and sememe definitions of space are found in Fig. 6.9.

```
{entity|实体}
 ├{space|空间} {entity|实体:{event|事件:location={~}},modifier={abstract|抽象}}
 │ ├{direction|方向} {space|空间:{event|事件:direction={~}},modifier={abstract|抽象}}
 │ └{location|位置} {space|空间:{event|事件:location={~}},modifier={abstract|抽象}}
```

Fig. 6.9. Space in entity taxonomy.

6.2.4. *Time*

Similar to space or place, time has its own, as we called, sections, rather than subclasses or parts, because they are neither subclasses nor parts. In HowNet they are placed in the taxonomy of secondary features.

A question is frequently raised: why you do not classify time into "point of time" and "period of time"? The suggested two subclasses sound reasonable and sometimes may be useful, but it is very difficult to manipulate them in practice. Whether it is a point of time or a period of time may in many cases depend on the view from the relevant event. For example, is "afternoon" a period of time or a point of time? It seems to us in many cases it depends on the event related to it. Let's compare the following sentences:

He spent a quiet afternoon in the park
He will arrive this afternoon

Time has its own special sections and features as specified in secondary features list of HowNet as follows:

```
├ {TimeSect|时间段}
│  ├ {dynasty|朝代}
│  ├ {lifespan|终生}
│  └ {year|年}
│     └ {season|季}
│        ├ {spring|春}
│        ├ {summer|夏}
│        ├ {autumn|秋}
│        ├ {winter|冬}
│        └ {month|月}
│           ├ {TenDays|旬}
│           └ {week|周}
│              └ {day|日}
│                 ├ {daytime|白昼}
│                 │  ├ {morning|晨}
│                 │  └ {afternoon|午}
│                 ├ {night|夜}
│                 └ {hour|时}
│                    └ {minute|分钟}
│                       └ {second|秒}
├ {TimeFeature|时间特性}
│  ├ {beginning|始}
│  ├ {ending|末}
│  ├ {middle|间}
│  └ {festival|节}
```

6.3. Attribute Taxonomy

The way we understand *attribute* is that any object necessarily owns a set of attributes. Similarities and differences between the objects are determined by the attributes that they carry. There will be no objects without attributes. Human beings are attached with natural attributes such as race, color, gender, age, ability to think, ability to use language as well as social attributes such as nationality, family origin, job, wealth, etc. Under specific conditions, it is true to say that the attached attributes are even more important than the host itself, a fact most evident in the "next-best alternative" exercises associated with our daily life. For instance, if we want to clamp a nail on the wall but does not have a hammer, what would be the best alternative tool? Obviously, it would be something that carries attributes close to a hammer, where in this case, weight and hardness would be the key attributes. The relation between the attributes (e.g. weight and hardness, etc.) and their host (a hammer) is unbending. The attributes simply come with the host and vice versa. The attribute-host relation differs from the part-whole relation. HowNet reflects the difference by way of coding specifications such that attributes are necessarily defined in terms of the possible classes of host, for example,

"depth"

DEF={Depth|深度:*host={physical|物质}*}

"depth"

DEF={Abstruseness|深浅:*host={Content|内容}*}

In fact, the definitions of attributes in natural language also indicate their host as usual. Let's take the definitions of "depth" in WordNet:

"depth" — extent downward or backward or inward;

"depth" — degree of psychological or intellectual depth

The attribute taxonomy of HowNet contains 247 classes of sememes, and they are classified into 7 subcategories as shown in Fig. 6.10.

```
{Attribute|属性}
├ {Appearance|外观}
├ {Measurement|量度}
├ {Property|特性}
├ {Relationship|关系}
├ {Situation|状况}
├ {QuantityProperty|数量特性}
└ {Quantity|数量}
```

Fig. 6.10. Skeleton of attribute taxonomy.

6.4. Attribute-value Taxonomy

Each attribute inherently points to its host on the one hand, and points to its corresponding values on the other. In other words, there exists an inherently inter-referential relation between attributes and attribute values. We consider all the attributes have their corresponding values meanwhile all attribute-values have their own corresponding attributes. The attribute-value taxonomy of HowNet contains 889 classes of sememes. As we mentioned above that in HowNet the attributes are classified into 7 subcategories, the attribute-values can inherently be classified into 7 subcategories which corresponds to the attribute subcategories shown in Fig. 6.11.

```
{Attribute|属性}                      {AttributeValue|属性值}
├{Appearance|外观}                    ├{AppearanceValue|外观值}
├{Measurement|量度}                   ├{MeasurementValue|量度值}
├{Property|特性}                      ├ {PropertyValue|特性值}
├{Relationship|关系}                  ├ {RelationshipValue|关系值}
├{Situation|状况}                     ├ {SituationValue|状况值}
├{QuantityProperty|数量特性}          ├ {QuantityPropertyValue|数量特性值}
└{Quantity|数量}                      └ {QuantityValue|数量值}
```

Fig. 6.11. Correspondence between attributes and attribute-values.

In HowNet Browser a detailed list of the attributes and their corresponding attribute-values is provided for computing their relations, for example:

```
{AppearanceValue|外观值}
├{ColorValue|颜色值}                → {ValueOf={color|颜色}}
│    ├ {colored|彩}
│    ├ {plain|素}
│    ├ {red|红}
│    ├ {yellow|黄}
│    ├ {blue|蓝}
│    ├ {green|绿}
│    ├ {purple|紫}
│    ├ {brown|褐}
│    ├ {white|白}
│    ├ {black|黑}
│    ├ {grey|灰}
│    ├ {RedBrown|赭}
│    ├ {BlueGreen|青}
│    └ {colorless|无色}

{MeasurementValue|量度值}
├{LengthValue|长度值}               →{Length|长度}
│    ├ {LengthLong|长}
│    └ {LengthShort|短}
├{StatureValue|高矮值}              → {Stature|高矮}
│    ├ {StatureTall|身高}
│    └ {StatureShort|身矮}

{PropertyValue|特性值}
├{SoundQualityValue|音质值}            → {SoundQuality|音质}
│    ├ {euphonious|好听}
│    └ {cacophonic|难听}

{RelationshipValue|关系值}
├{IntimacyValue|亲疏值}             → {IntimacyValue|亲疏值}
│    ├ {intimate|亲密}
```

```
│    ├ {distant|疏远}
│    ├ {friend|友}
│    ├ {enemy|敌}
│    └ {antagonistic|不容}

{SituationValue|状况值}
├{FateValue|命运值}              → {Fate|命运}
│    ├ {fortunate|好运}
│    ├ {misfortunate|倒霉}
│    ├ {auspicious|吉祥}
│    └ {inauspicuous|不祥}

{QuantityValue|数量值}
├{AmountValue|多少值}              → {Amount|多少}
│    ├ {many|多}
│    ├ {few|少}
│    ├ {single|单}
│    ├ {double|复}
│    ├ {mass|众}
│    ├ {fragment|部}
│    ├ {some|些}
│    ├ {sufficient|足}
│    ├ {insufficient|不足}
│    └ {half|半}
```

6.5. Secondary Features List

Secondary features list includes 113 semantic features. They are all the units of the computation of meaning too like the 4 classes of sememes discussed above. They are categorized into 7 subclasses (domain, position of parts, time section, time feature, place section, grammatical person, some adjunct features) and arranged in a hierarchical structure as follows:

```
- Secondary Feature
   ├ {domain|领域}
```

```
│  ├ {economy|经济}
│  │  └ {industrial|工}
│  ├ {sport|体育}
│  │  ├ {TableTennis|乒乓球}
│  │  └ {badminton|羽毛球}
│  └ {physics|物理}
├ {PartPosition|部件位置}
│  ├ {head|头}
│  ├ {body|身}
│  └ {BodyFluid|体液}
├ {TimeSect|时间段}
│  └ {year|年}
│     └ {season|季}
│        └ {month|月}
│           └ {day|日}
│              └ {hour|时}
├ {TimeFeature|时间特性}
├ {PlaceSect|地域}
│  ├ {country|国家}
│  ├ {county|县}
│  ├ {district|区}
│  ├ {ResidentialArea|居民区}
│  └ {village|乡}
├ {PersonPro|人称}
├ {adjunct|修饰语}
│  ├ {question|疑问}
│  ├ {neg|否}
│  └ {MaChinese|语助}
└ {aspect|体}
   ├ {Vdirection|动趋}
   ├ {Vprocess|动程}
   └ {Vresult|动果}
      ├ {Vachieve|达成}
      ├ {Vfail|未达成}
      └ {Vtry|试试}
```

According to the regulations, all the features in the secondary features list are not allowed to be used as the categorial sememe, that is, the first unit in the definitions of any concepts in defining a concept. For example, in the definition of the word "morning", its first unit is {time|时间},which is correct in HowNet definition.

"morning"

{time|时间:TimeSect={morning|晨}}

6.6. Antonymous and Converse Sememes Lists

In HowNet, two attribute-values imply opposite sememes are antonyms while two events imply opposite sememes are converse. The opposite sememes of attribute-values and events are specified in the antonymous sememes list and the converse sememes list respectively. In HowNet, the antonymous relations and the converse relations of concepts are not manually coded, but are computed based on these two lists. The antonymous relation has 242 pairs of sememes of attribute-value concepts, part of which is shown in Fig. 6.12 while converse relation has 112 pairs of sememes of event concepts. Some of the examples are shown in Fig. 6.13.

{HighQuality|优质}	{inferior|劣质}
{HighRank|高等}	{LowRank|低等}
{LowVoice|低声}	{loud|高声}
{aged|老年}	{child|少儿}
{alike|似}	{different|异}
{always|总是}	{never|从不}
{beautiful|美}	{ugly|丑}
{beneath|下}	{upper|上}
{benevolent|仁}	{wicked|歹}
{biased|不公正}	{fair|公正}
{big|大}	{small|小}
{fast|快}	{slow|慢}
{fat|胖}	{bony|瘦}
{many|多}	{few|少}

Fig. 6.12. Part of antonymous sememe pairs.

{BecomeMore|增多}	{BecomeLess|减少}
{ComeToWorld|问世}	{perish|灭亡}
{ExistNot|不存在}	{exist|存在}
{ExpressAgainst|谴责}	{praise|夸奖}
{MarryTo|嫁}	{MarryFrom|娶}
{MoveItDown|下移}	{lift|提升}
{OwnNot|无}	{own|有}
{satisfied|满意}	{unsatisfied|不满}
{PayAttention|注意}	{despise|轻视}
{PickOut|拔出}	{insert|插入}
{PlayDown|贬低}	{PlayUp|鼓吹}
{PutOn|穿戴}	{StripOff|剥去}
{sleep|睡}	{awake|醒}
{teach|教}	{study|学习}

Fig. 6.13. Part of converse sememe pairs.

Chapter 7

KNOWLEDGE DICTIONARY OF HOWNET

The knowledge dictionary is the essential database of HowNet. It serves as the foundation on which all the computation of meaning in HowNet is based. The nature and quality of HowNet depends mostly on its volume and quality. The general status of the dictionary is usually displayed by HowNet browser and the statistic data shows its ever-growing and updating. In terms of knowledge data, the knowledge dictionary of HowNet is composed of two databases: taxonomy database and lexical database.

The taxonomy database contains all the taxonomies (event, entity, attribute, attribute-value) and the special lists (secondary features list, antonymous sememes list, and converse sememes list) that we presented and discussed in Chap. 6. The browser can display the size and hierarchy of each taxonomy and list. The lexical database contains Chinese and English lexical entries in the form of records. Each record is composed of 8 items:

NO.=	Serial number
W_C=	Chinese word or expression
G_C=	Chinese part-of-speech, phonetic transcription
E_C=	Examples for Chinese word or expression
W_E=	English word or phrase
G_E=	English part-of-speech
E_E=	Examples for English word or phrase
DEF=	Concept definition

A couple of concrete examples are shown below:

NO.=022935
W_C=大夫
G_C=N [da4 fu1]
E_C=妇科~，请~看病，全国有名的~，老~，~哪有不会看病的
W_E=doctor
G_E=N
E_E=My doctor said I had high blood pressure
DEF={human|人:
    HostOf={Occupation|职位},domain={medical|医},
    {doctor|医治:agent={~}}}

NO.=009326
W_C=博士
G_C=N [bo2 shi4]
E_C=
W_E=doctor
G_E=N
E_E=She is a doctor of philosophy in physics
DEF={human|人: {own|有:possession={Status|身分:
    domain={education|教育},modifier={HighRank|高等
    degree={most|最}}},possessor={~}}}

The first item "serial number" is not meaningful but only for casual statistics in data management and updating. The rest of items needs further explanation and discussion.

The data structure looks very human-oriented. We consider that the record should be well-readable and easy for developers to maintain and update the data when necessary.

7.1. Lexical Entry

The latest version of HowNet database statistics currently totals 84,000 Chinese words and expressions and 80,000 English words and expressions. The figures represent the absolutely unique word forms (Chinese) or strings (English) irrelevant to the syntactic category or the difference in pronunciation. For example, the English word "lay" is taken as a unique word in HowNet knowledge database, no matter how many parts-of-speech it may falls into. The Chinese word "行" is taken as a unique word although common Chinese dictionaries usually take it as different entries according to their different meanings, different pronunciation and different parts-of-speech.

7.1.1. *Chinese words and expressions*

All the Chinese words and expressions in HowNet are mainly selected by means of comparison among the following resources: two word lists based on two large-scale corpora in modern Chinese each of which contains over 400 million Chinese characters, and on a few medium-size popular modern Chinese dictionaries. Similar to the compilation of any other general Chinese dictionary, either computer-oriented or human-oriented, the first difficult problem that HowNet confronts is the determination and selection of words and expressions. We would like to leave detailed and somewhat theoretical discussion to Chap. 14, which is specially devoted to Chinese peculiarities.

In selecting words and expressions, HowNet observes the following principles:

(1) to admit the reality that in the Chinese language there is no clear-cut demarcation between multi-character words and multi-character phrases; never try to find any golden rule for distinguishing them in HowNet;

(2) to avoid using the term of "word", but to use the term of "word and expression" instead;

(3) to select the entries based mainly on their frequency in the corpora;

(4) to design a sophisticated mark-up language which is highly competent to define all kinds of entries no matter how big their linguistic units are and how complicated their internal structures are formed.

(5) to include as many frequently-used Chinese function words and expressions as possible, because Chinese has very few pure function words and expressions which have no content senses. Moreover, it is

widely acknowledged by Chinese grammarians that Chinese syntax is mainly based on two mechanisms: one is the word order and the other is the employment of function words and expressions. If we mimicked WordNet and ignored Chinese function words and expressions, the lexicon would be terribly incomplete and would be very awkward to the users.

7.1.2. *English words and expressions*

All the English words and expressions in HowNet under W_E are mainly natural English words or phrases and at the same time are the equivalents to the Chinese words and expressions under W_C. Only part of them are the literal explanations of its Chinese source as HowNet is bilingual, mainly Chinese-to-English. If chance leaves choice between literal explanations and natural English equivalents, the latter always takes priority, because we consider that HowNet is computer-oriented and is concept-based. For example:

NO.=015921
W_C=沉鱼落雁
G_C=ADJ [chen2 yv2 luo4 yan4]
E_C=
W_E=exceedingly beautiful
G_E=ADJ
E_E=
DEF={beautiful|美:degree={extreme|极}}

The W_E in this example is a phrase in natural and plain English, but the literal translation of its source "沉鱼落雁" should be as follows: "(of feminine beauty) make fish sink and birds alight".

One and the same Chinese word or expression with the same concept definition is allowed to have two or more than two of its English equivalents, that is, in a one-to-many mapping. This is the same case with English to Chinese, so in fact in HowNet a many-to-many mapping is formed between the words and expressions in the two languages. For example, Chinese word “词典” has 2 English equivalents: “dictionary” and “lexicon”; English word “dictionary” has 4 Chinese equivalents: “辞典”, “辞书”, “词典”, and “字典”.

7.2. Part-of-Speech (POS)

Part-of-speech in both Chinese and English, as the basic and necessary syntactic information, is given to each entry of words and expressions in HowNet.

7.2.1. *Part-of-speech of Chinese*

In this item two kinds of data are provided: (1) Chinese part-of-speech and (2) Chinese phonetic transcription in Pinyin.

The asymmetry in POS between Chinese and English should be considered normal and should be reflected in bilingual dictionaries. We code Chinese part-of-speech and English part-of-speech independently. One Chinese part-of-speech may correspond to two or more than two English parts-of-speech. In HowNet the major cases of asymmetry in POS can be found as shown below.

Chinese part-of-speech	**English part-of-speech**
Verb	Verb / Noun
ADJ	ADJ / ADV / Noun
Verb	Verb / ADJ

Look at the following examples of correspondence cases between Chinese POS and English POS.

Chinese part-of-speech	**English part-of-speech**
① 讲解 (Verb)	explain (Verb) explanation (Noun)
② 缓慢 (ADJ)	slow (ADJ) slowly (ADV)

	slowness (Noun)
③ 生成 (Verb)	generate (Verb) generative (ADJ)

With the above general survey, we may realize that the problem of Chinese part-of-speech is really a challenge not only to the compilation of human-oriented Chinese dictionaries but to the construction of any computer-oriented extralinguistic knowledge systems relating to Chinese. Because of the uniqueness of Chinese, HowNet observes special guidelines in dealing with the issues of part-of-speech.

Firstly, in determination of the part-of-speech of a Chinese word or expression, we take the following factors into consideration:

(1) semantics or meaning as the first priority, because Chinese is heavily-based on semantics rather than syntax;

(2) formation rules of message structure; Chinese words have no inflexions, nor prefixes and suffixes denoting parts-of-speech in a strict sense as English like "ex-", "pre-", "-tion", "-ness", "-ful", "-ly", but it has some rules of internal structure of words and expressions, which are mainly based again on semantics and convey certain information (this is the reason why we create the term — message structure). Some of the rules of message structure formation are given below with corresponding examples:

Rules	**POS**	**Examples**
① event/fact + human	NOUN	行人，走私犯，毒品走私犯
② thing + event	NOUN	客运，水污染，文物走私
③ event/fact + attribute	NOUN	坐姿，睡相，转速，货运量
④ value + attribute	ADJ	长效，高品质，高中奖额
⑤ time + event/fact	VERB	春耕，假日游，暑期补习

Note: The part-of-speech of the phrases of Type ② is coded as noun in HowNet. However it should be pointed out that it refers only to the phrase as a whole, in other words, the whole phrase is a noun, but the word "走私" in it remains as a verb. Owing to this treatment, the phrase is then coded in HowNet as follows:

W_C=毒品走私
G_C=N [du2 pin3 zou3 si1]
E_C=
W_E=smuggling of drugs
G_E=N
E_E=
DEF={fact|事情:CoEvent={transport|运送:manner={guilty|有罪},
patient={addictive|嗜好物:modifier={guilty|有罪}}}}

(3) roles in the distribution in context; In HowNet we deliberately avoid using the term of "grammatical functions", but use roles in the distribution in context instead.

Secondly, The correspondence between Chinese parts-of-speech and the concept classes in HowNet is shown below:

Concept class	**Chinese part-of-speech**
Entity	Noun
Thing	Noun / Pronoun
Component	Noun
Space	Noun
Time	Noun
Attribute	Noun / Classifier
Attribute-value	Adj / Adverb / Numeral
Event	Verb
Function Word	Preposition / Conjunction / Adverb

7.2.2. *Part-of-speech of English*

HowNet follows established English grammar in treating English part-of-speech. It may seem unfamiliar to English users that there is a contradiction between English part-of-speech and concept classification. The correspondence between English parts-of-speech and the concept classes in HowNet is shown below:

Concept class	English part-of-speech
Entity	Noun
Thing	Noun / Pronoun / Adj
Component	Noun
Space	Noun
Time	Noun
Attribute	Noun / Unit
Attribute-value	Adj / Adverb / Noun / Numeral
Event	Verb / Noun / Adj
Function Word	Preposition / Conjunction / Adverb

A few examples are given below to show an English noun corresponding to attribute-value and an English adjective corresponding to event:

NO.=015954
W_C=沉寂
G_C=ADJ [chen2 ji4]
E_C=
W_E=quietness
G_E=N
E_E=
DEF={quiet|静}

Cf. WordNet:

tranquility, tranquillity, quietness, quietude — (a state of peace and quiet)

NO.=032427
W_C=发展
G_C=V [fa1 zhan3]
E_C=
W_E=developmental
G_E=ADJ
E_E=
DEF={CauseToGrow|使成长}

Cf. WordNet:

developmental — (of or relating to or constituting development; "developmental psychology")

7.3. Example

As a rule each sense of a polysemous word and expression should have some examples. These examples are collected and given according to the following two guidelines:

(1) They are used mainly to help to distinguish the senses in word sense disambiguation (WSD) by the computer, but not merely to explain the meanings;

(2) They should be given as many as possible and they should be as easy as possible.

Temporarily in HowNet only Chinese words and expressions have examples. Look at Chinese examples in the following records:

NO.=012582
W_C=参加
G_C=V [can1 jia1]
E_C=49 年以前~工作的，~战斗，~北伐，~维新，~会议，~政治运动，~反右斗争，~运动会，~比赛，~舞会，~游行示威，~他的生日派对，~悼念胡耀邦，老同学聚会你~吗，~静坐示威，
W_E=attend
G_E=V
E_E=
DEF={engage|从事}

NO.=012585
W_C=参加
G_C=V [can1 jia1]
E_C=早年~共产主义青年团，~国民党，~共产党，~民主党派，~北伐军，~维新派，~什么教会，~少年体操队，~反动会道门，~帮派组织，~到打假的行列里来，~少先队，我什么党派也不~

W_E=join
G_E=V
E_E=
DEF={include|纳入}

As shown above, the Chinese word "参加" has two senses: "be engaged in" and "join". We can see that for the sense "be engaged in or attend", the objects of "参加 (represented by "~")" are the words or expressions denoting various kinds of activity, such as "work", "fight", "meeting", "sports meet", "birthday party", "demonstration", etc. while for the meaning "join", the objects of "参加 (represented by "~")" are the words or expressions denoting various kinds of organizations, such as "political party", "army", "gym team", etc. To take one more example:

NO.=056434
W_C=江
G_C=N [jiang1]
E_C=~河，~堤，~岸，~面，~底，~水，大~，~深，~宽，沿~，~对岸，~对面，过~，在~里游泳，~很深，沉入~底，~都干了，在~上，~桥，~中的小船
W_E=river
G_E=N
E_E=
DEF={waters|水域:modifier={linear|线}}

NO.=056433
W_C=江
G_C=N [jiang1]
E_C=姓~，~姓，~先生，~太太，~小姐，~女士，老~，小~，~大哥，~叔，~公，~爷爷，~伯伯，~伯母，~老爷，~家老二，~氏家族，~经理，~主任，~校长，~院长，~处长，~总理，~书记，~教授，~老师，~大夫，~护士长，~队，~总，~工
W_E=Jiang
G_E=N
E_E=
DEF={surname|姓}

The Chinese word "江" has two senses: "river" and "used as a Chinese surname". The examples given to these two senses may seem insignificant or even a bit silly. However they are believed to be very useful to WSD by the computer. These examples are formed into a specific annotated mini-corpus, which will be able to contribute much to WSD by analogy.

7.4. Concept Definition

This is the most important of all the items of a record. In this item the concept definition of a word or expression is given. The computation of meaning in HowNet mainly depends on the concept definitions. As mentioned previously, the concepts are defined on the basis of sememes.

Moreover, it should be reminded that the definitions in HowNet are not merely coded in a single semantic category, but are written in a special mark-up language, called Knowledge Database Mark-up Language (KDML), which is powerful enough to differentiate even very subtle ambiguities in word meanings. This feature will guarantee effective computation of meaning. To take the following words for example and compare them with Longman Dictionary and see what accuracy HowNet definitions can achieve.

"nurse"

DEF={human|人:HostOf={Occupation|职位},
domain={medical|医},{TakeCare|照料:agent={~}}

Cf. Longman Dictionary

1. nurse – (a person, typically a woman, who is trained to take care of sick, hurt, or old people, esp. as directed by a doctor in a hospital)

"nurse"

DEF={human|人:HostOf={Occupation|职位},
{TakeCare|照料:agent={~},
patient={human|人:modifier={child|少儿}}}}

Cf. Longman Dictionary

2. nurse – (a woman employed to take care of a young child)

Thus we can find that the definitions of HowNet are so similar in actual meaning to those that are written in natural language, for instance, the HowNet definitions of "nurse" above-listed can be interpreted roughly as follows:

① nurse is a human who is a professional person and works (as the agent) to care for sick persons.

② nurse is a human who is a professional person and works (as the agent) to care for a child.

Chapter 8

KNOWLEDGE DATABASE MARK-UP LANGUAGE AND CONCEPT DEFINING

As previously discussed, different from ordinary dictionaries and WordNet, HowNet does not use natural language to define its words and expressions, but uses a formal language based on sememes and semantic roles. In order to help readers or users have a thorough understanding of the depth of the representation of the inter-concept relations and the inter-attribute relations in HowNet, a detailed presentation of the way that HowNet defines its concepts will be given in this chapter. Theoretically, with the detailed presentation, the readers may be aware of the necessity and possibility of defining large-scale knowledge data with sememes and the depth of its revelation of the concepts. Practically, the detailed presentation may help the users learn what and how to apply the knowledge of HowNet to their own research and development.

Description of concepts in HowNet is an attempt to present the relations between concepts and between attributes. As the description is so complex that a clear set of rules should be established, otherwise it would be very difficult to maintain consistency and robustness.

The method of description and the relevant rules ensure that the inter-concept relations and inter-attribute relations are expressed clearly and thoroughly. In this connection, the building of HowNet is also the design and building of such mark-up language. To date, the Knowledge Database Mark-up Language (KDML) includes 2099 sememes, 121 secondary features and 91 semantic roles as its vocabulary and adopts an extended BNF as its syntax.

8.1. Extended BNF of KDML

BNF is an acronym for Backus–Naur Form. The extended BNF of KDML is the syntax of the Knowledge Database Mark-up Language of HowNet. Most of the relations among concepts and attributes revealed in HowNet are not manually coded but computed by the HowNet's devices of computation of meaning. The realization of the computation of meaning is ensured by the extended BNF of KDML in which the concepts are defined.

The meta-symbols of the extended BNF of KDML are shown in Table 8.1.

Table 8.1. Meta-symbols of the extended BNF of KDML.

symbol	meaning
::=	defined as
|	or
< >	category names enclosed
[]	optional items enclosed
{}	repetitive items (zero or more times) enclosed

The extended BNF for KDML is as follows:

<Concept>::=
<concept expression>{<semicolon><concept expression>}
<semicolon> ::= ;
<concept expression> ::=
<left-brace><sememe>[<colon><concept modifier>
{<comma><concept modifier>}]<right-brace>
<left-brace> ::= {
<right-brace> ::= }
<colon> ::= :
<comma> ::= ,
<sememe> ::=<Event>|<Entity>|<Attribute>|<AttributeValue>
<Event> ::=<event sememe table>
<Entity> ::=<entity sememe table>
<Attribute> ::=<attribute sememe table>
<AttributeValue> ::=<attribute value sememe table>

<concept modifier> ::=
[<Role><equal>]<RoleValue>{<RoleValue>}
<equal> ::= =
<Role> ::= <semantic role table>
<RoleValue> ::= <concept expression>
|<left-brace><secondary feature><right-brace>
|<double-quote><ProperNoun><double-quote>
|<left-brace><swung-dash><right-brace>
|<left-brace><dollor-sign><right-brace>
|<left-brace><question-mark><right-brace>
<secondary feature> ::= <secondary feature table>
<ProperNoun> ::=<ProperNoun table>
<double-quote> ::= "
<swung-dash> ::= ~
<dollor-sign> ::= $
<question-mark> ::= ?

8.2. Identifiers of KDML and Referent Signs

8.2.1. *Identifiers of KDML*

As mentioned above, Table 8.2 shows the identifiers used in HowNet KDML and their functions.

Table 8.2. Identifiers of KDML.

identifier	function
{}	to quote sememe or feature
:	to introduce an extensive description
,	to separate description nodes of the same level
=	to introduce a value of a semantic role or a feature
;	to express coordination in compound concepts
""	to quote a specific value, such as proper names

(1) Curly braces — { }

Every sememe or secondary feature should be put in a set of curly braces. For example:

"policewoman"

DEF={human|人:HostOf={Occupation|职位},
domain={police|警},modifier={female|女}}

Note: "human|人", "Occupation|职位", "female|女" are sememes and "police|警" (one of the domain values) is a secondary feature.

(2) Colon — :

A colon should be used to introduce an extensive description of a sememe. For example:

"washing machine"

DEF={tool|用具:{wash|洗涤:instrument={~},
patient={clothing|衣物}}}

Note: The first ":" introduces an extensive description of the sememe "tool|用具", describing what kind of tool it is; the second ":" introduces a lower-level extensive description of the sememe "wash|洗涤", indicating what is washed and what is its relation with the tool, agent, method, time or instrument, etc.

(3) Coma — ,

Two same-level sections of the description of relations should be separated by a coma. For example:

"ring"

DEF={tool|用具:
{PutOn|穿戴:instrument={~}, purpose={decorate|装饰}}}

Note: The coma is used to separate two sections: "instrument={~}" and "purpose={decorate|装饰}", which are of the same level as they both express the relations with the event "wear" (PutOn|穿戴).

"emergency patient"

DEF={human|人:domain={medical|医},
{SufferFrom|罹患:experiencer={~}},

{doctor|医治:patient={~}},
modifier={urgent|急}}

Note: This example includes four same-level sections, which are all attached to the first sememe of the definition: "human|人".

(4) Equal sign — =

An equal sign is used to express the value of DEF, and a semantic role or secondary feature. For example:

"seller"

DEF={human|人:domain={commerce|商业},
{sell|卖:agent={~}}}

Note: The example shows the three kinds of values: "DEF=", "domain="(secondary feature) and "agent=" (semantic role).

(5) Semicolon — ;

A semicolon is used only to separate coordinating sections for a compound concept definition or a compound complex definition. For example:

"day and night"

DEF={time|时间:TimeSect={daytime|白昼}};
{time|时间:TimeSect={night|夜}}

(6) Quotation marks — ""

Some special values should be put in quotation marks instead of curly braces, such as proper names. For Example:

"California"

DEF={place|地方:PlaceSect={provincial|省},
belong="US|美国",modifier={ProperName|专}}

"Buddhism"

DEF={community|团体:
belong="Buddhism|佛教",domain={religion|宗教}}

8.2.2. *Referent signs*

There are three referent signs in HowNet KDML. They are "~", "?", and "$".

Table 8.3. Referents of KDML.

referent	function
~	to refer to the value of an explicit semantic role
?	to refer to the value of an implicit semantic role
$	to refer to the value of an implicit, passive semantic role

(1) Swung-dash — ~

The swung-dash is the value of a semantic role which attributes the concept the swung-dash refers to. For example:

"excavator"

DEF={tool|用具:{dig|挖掘:instrument={~}},
{pick|拾起:instrument={~}}}

Note: These two swung-dashes are the values of the semantic roles "instrument" of the two events "dig|挖掘" and "pick|拾起". They both refer to the entity "tool|用具". They imply that "excavator" serves as an instrument of two events "digging" and "picking".

"forbidden area"

DEF={place|地方:{GoInto|进入:LocationFin={~},
{prohibit|禁止:ResultEvent={~}}}}

Note: In this definition the first swung-dash refers to "place|地方" and indicates that it is a place which is the final location people get into. The second swung-dash as the value of "ResultEvent" refers to "GoInto|进入" and indicates that it is the event which is prohibited.

(2) Question mark — ?

The question mark is the value of an implicit semantic role. The value indicates that although the real relevant entity does not appear in the current word or expression, it will actually appear in the real context. For example:

W_C=属于
G_C=V [shu3 yv2]
E_C=
W_E=belong to
G_E=V
E_E=
DEF={BeMember|隶属:whole={?}}

Note: When both Chinese word "属于" and English phrase "belong to" are used in a real text, the entities as their whole shall appear unavoidably, though there is no definite entities in both of the word and phrase themselves.

NO.=008617
W_C=濒于
G_C=V [bin1 yv2]
E_C=
W_E=be on the brink of
G_E=V
E_E=
DEF={BeNear|靠近:partner={?}}

Cf.
NO.=008614
W_C=濒死
G_C=V [bin1 si3]
E_C=
W_E=be on the brink of extinction
G_E=V
E_E=
DEF={BeNear|靠近:partner={perish|灭亡}}

Note: When both Chinese and English expressions "濒于" and "be on the brink of" in Record NO.=008617 are used in a real text, the entities as their partners shall appear unavoidably, though there are no definite entities in both the expressions themselves. Different from Record NO.=008617, in Record NO.=008614, the definite entities denoted by the sememe {perish|灭亡} as their partners of "濒" and "be on the brink of " appear in both the expressions. So {?} can no longer be used in there.

(3) Dollar sign — $

The dollar sign is the value of an implicit and passive semantic role. The value indicates that there is a passive relation between the event and the entity which the value refers to. For example:

NO.=064755
W_C=可防守
G_C=ADJ [ke3 fang2 shou3]
E_C=
W_E=defensible
G_E=ADJ
E_E=a defensible stronghold
DEF={able|能:scope={defend|防守:patient={**$**}}}

Note: The meaning of both the Chinese expression and English word is "that can be defended", for instance, "a defensible position". If something is defensible, then it is defended; if something is defensive, then it defends. Compare the two examples in Record NO.=064755 above and Record NO.=034055 below. "A defensible stronghold" is a stronghold which is capable of being defended; "defensive weapons" are weapons that are used to defend.

NO.=034055
W_C=防御性
G_C=ADJ [fang2 yv4 xing4]
E_C=
W_E=defensive
G_E=ADJ
E_E=defensive weapons

DEF={able|能:scope={defend|防守}}

Let's compare more examples:

"convincing" (a convincing argument)

DEF={able|能:scope={persuade|劝说}}

"convincible" (a convicible person)

DEF={able|能:scope={persuade|劝说:patient={$}}}

"laudatory"

DEF={able|能:scope={praise|夸奖}}

"laudable"

DEF={able|能:scope={praise|夸奖:target={$}}}

Note: The sign "$" can help us to distinguish the above two pairs of words and expressions with their subtle difference.

Let's look at some more examples:

"instant noodles"

DEF={food|食品:modifier={able|能:manner={prompt|旋即},
scope={eat|吃:patient={$}}}}

"instant coffee"

DEF={material|材料:MaterialOf={drinks|饮品},
modifier={able|能:scope={StateChange|态变:
StateFin={liquid|液},manner={prompt|旋即}}}}

Note: The first example indicates that "instant noodles" is a kind of food which can be cooked and eaten instantly. However, in the DEF of the second example the dollar sign cannot be used because its related event does not belong to "action" category but to "state" category and thus "coffee" is not the patient of "drink|喝" but the experiencer of "StateChange|态变".

8.3. Defining Regulations

As aforesaid, the concepts are defined in a Knowledge Database Mark-up Language with the sememes as its key components. The defining of concepts observes some hard regulations.

8.3.1. *General regulations*

First of all, the defining of concepts observes the following general regulations:

(1) No DEFs should be left blank;

(2) The definition of each concept begins with DEF=;

(3) All the sememes, secondary features, identifier, and symbols must be those that are specified by HowNet database and KDML;

(4) Each sememe should be put in braces;

(5) The first unit, or the unit that is immediately after DEF=, termed as *categorial sememe*, must be a sememe of either entity, event, attribute or attribute-value; this first unit indicates the basic class that the defined concept belongs to;

(6) A sememe is allowed to be defined in an embedded way, for instance:

"call"

DEF={communicate|交流:instrument=
{tool|用具:{communicate|交流:instrument={~}}}}

In the definition, the first pair of braces contains the sememe represented by "call". The second pair of braces contains the sememe denoting a tool which is an instrument for communication (i.e. telephone). The third pair of braces contains the sememe denoting "communicate", and the fourth pair contains "~" which refers to the "tool" (indicated by "tool|用具"). The whole definition carries the meaning: "call" means "to communicate using an instrument that is a tool which can be used to communicate as an instrument". In other words, {tool|用具:{communicate|交流:instrument={~}}} is a definition for "telephone", which is embedded in the definition for "call".

(7) There are four types of concepts in terms of defining:

(a) Simple concept: with only one simple sememe as its categorical sememe, e.g.

"house" (Noun)
DEF={house|房屋}

"elaborate" (Verb)
DEF={explain|说明}

"pretty" (Adj.)
DEF={beautiful|美}

"pretty" (Adv.)
DEF={ish|稍}

(b) Compound concept: with two or more than two simple categorial sememes in coordination separated by semicolon(s), e.g.

"lanky"
DEF={StatureTall|身高};{bony|瘦}

"sooner or later"
DEF={early|早};{late|迟}

(c) Complex concept: the categorial sememe is attached to an extended elaboration, e.g.

"man"
DEF={human|人:modifier={male|男}}

"pedestrian"
DEF={human|人:{walk|走:agent={~}}}

"CPU"
DEF={part|部件:
PartPosition={heart|心},whole={computer|电脑}}

"inspiring"

DEF={able|能:scope={urge|促使:
ResultEvent={excited|激动}}}

(d) Compound-complex concept: with two or more than two sememes in coordination, at least one of them is a complex sememe, e.g.

"Sino-American"

DEF={RelatingToCountry|与特定国家相关:
RelateTo="China|中国"};
{RelatingToCountry|与特定国家相关:
RelateTo="US|美国"}

"chew carefully and swallow slowly"

DEF={masticate|咀嚼:manner={careful|细心}};
{swallow|咽下:manner={slow|慢}}

8.3.2. *Specific regulations*

The presentation of specific regulations will be done on the basis of the content of the concepts, for example, how to describe a thing with its function, a thing with a definite value, an attribute with a definite scope, or any utterance that expresses a definite content in a certain context, and so on and so forth.

To define specific concepts, there are two types of regulations: one for simple concepts and the other for complex concepts. In the following sections of the discussion about how to define various categories of concepts, the emphasis will be put on the complex concepts.

A comparison between HowNet definitions and natural language definitions will be made in some of the following examples given below. By doing so we can show what accuracy the definitions with sememes can be attained.

8.3.2.1. *Regulations for defining things*

(1) Simple concepts of things

A simple concept of things is defined with only one categorial sememe which belongs to the entity taxonomy except the following classes: component, time, space and their subordinate subclasses, e.g.

"sky"

DEF= {sky|空域}

(2) Concepts value-restrictive

A complex concept of things is defined with certain value(s). The values may be an attribute value or some other kinds such as relatedness, material, etc., e.g.

"lad"

DEF={human|人:modifier={child|少儿}{male|男}}

Cf. natural language definition:

a male child (a familiar term of address to a boy)

"lullaby"

DEF={music|音乐:modifier={able|能:
scope={urge|促使:ResultEvent={sleep|睡}}}}

Cf. natural language definition:

a quiet song intended to lull a child to sleep

"dough"

DEF={material|材料:MaterialOf={edible|食物}}

Cf. natural language definition:

a flour mixture stiff enough to kneed or roll

(3) Concepts function-restrictive

A concept is defined with its specific functions. The functions may be represented by various semantic roles, among which agent, instrument, location are most popular, e.g.

"ugly duckling"

DEF={human|人:{grow|成长:
StateFin={promising|前景佳},

StateIni={dismal|前景差},experiencer={~}}}

Cf. natural language definition:

an ugly or unpromising child who grows into a beautiful or worthy person

"pilot"

DEF={human|人:HostOf={Occupation|职位},
{drive|驾驭:agent={~},patient={aircraft|飞行器}}}

Cf. natural language definition:

someone who is licensed to operate an aircraft in flight

"pilot"

DEF={human|人:HostOf={Occupation|职位},
{guide|引导:patient={ship|船},
ResultEvent={VehicleGo|驶},agent={~}}}

Cf. natural language definition:

a person qualified to conduct a ship into and out of port or through dangerous waters.

"clinical thermometer"

DEF={tool|用具:{measure|测量:content={Temperature|温度:
host={AnimalHuman|动物}},instrument={~}}}

Cf. natural language definition:

a mercury thermometer used to measure the temperature of the human body, especially a small glass thermometer designed with a narrowing above the bulb so that the mercury column stays in position when the instrument is removed from the body.

"florist shop"

DEF={InstitutePlace|场所:domain={commerce|商业},
{buy|买:location={~},possession={FlowerGrass|花草}},
{sell|卖:agent={~},possession={FlowerGrass|花草}}}

Cf. natural language definition:

a shop where flowers and ornamental plants are sold

Note: The definition of "florist shop" indicates that a florist shop is a commercial place where people can buy flowers and the shop as the agent sells flowers. It is very similar to the definition in natural language, but it is non-ambiguous and thus computable by the computer.

(4) Situational expressions

The class of "things" includes situational expressions such as "Good morning", "Sorry". A special way of defining is regulated, which is focused on the purpose for using the expression, e.g.

W_C=对不起
G_C=EXPR [dui4 bu4 qi3]
E_C=
W_E=Sorry
G_E=EXPR
E_E=
DEF={expression|词语:{express|表示:content={~},time={apologize|道歉}}}

W_C=早安
G_C=EXPR [zao3 an1]
E_C=
W_E=good morning
G_E=EXPR
E_E=
DEF={expression|词语:{express|表示:content={~},time={SayHello|问候:time={time|时间:TimeSect={morning|晨}}}}}

Note: The definitions for "Sorry" and "Good morning" are not explanations of the words, instead they denote that they are the expressions which are the content one uses to express when he is sorry or he is saying hello to someone in the morning.

8.3.2.2. *Regulations for defining events*

(1) Simple concepts of events

A simple concept of events is defined with only one categorial sememe which belongs to the event taxonomy, e.g.

"lie"

DEF={LieDown|躺卧}

Cf. natural language definition:

be lying, be prostrate, be in horizontal position

"lie"

DEF={deceive|欺骗}

Cf. natural language definition:

tell an untruth, pretend with intent to deceive

(2) Concepts value-restrictive

A complex concept of events is defined with certain value(s), in most cases they express the manner of the events, e.g.

"mumble"

DEF={speak|说:manner={LowVoice|低声}}

Cf. natural language definition:

talk indistinctly, usually in a low voice

"lead astray"

DEF={guide|引导:manner={wrong|误}}

Cf. natural language definition:

lead someone in the wrong direction or give someone wrong directions

(3) Concepts function-restrictive

A concept is defined with its specific functions. The functions may be represented by various semantic roles, e.g.

"program"

DEF={compile|编辑:ContentProduct={software|软件}}

Cf. natural language definition:

write a computer program

"profiteer"

DEF={seek|谋取:possession={wealth|钱财}}

Cf. natural language definition:

make an unreasonable profit, as on the sale of difficult to obtain goods

"fish"

DEF={catch|捉住:patient={fish|鱼}}

Cf. natural language definition:

catch or try to catch fish or shellfish

"shoplift"

DEF={steal|偷:source=
{InstitutePlace|场所:domain={commerce|商业},
{buy|买:location={~}},{sell|卖:agent={~}}}}

Cf. natural language definition:

to steal from a store

Note: It should be reminded that this sort of definitions can be done only when the words or expressions themselves actually contain the concept that the semantic role denotes. To take the "shoplift" as an example, the word "shoplift" intrinsically contains the concept "shop" which serves as the semantic role "source".

8.3.2.3. *Regulations for defining components*

In defining concepts of components, no simple concepts are allowed. Any concepts of components must be defined with the sememe "component|部分", or, in most cases, its hyponymous sememes "part|部件" and "fittings|配件" as its categorial sememe and with its *whole* as the indispensable semantic role. For example:

"act"

DEF={part|部件:whole={shows|表演物}}

Cf. natural language definition:

a subdivision of a play or opera or ballet

"scene"

DEF={part|部件:whole={part|部件:whole={shows|表演物}}}

Cf. natural language definition:

a subdivision of an act of a play (the first act has three scenes)

In most cases another semantic roles will be usually added in the definition, which is termed "PartPosition", for example:

"prologue"

DEF={part|部件:PartPosition={head|头},
whole={shows|表演物}}

Cf. natural language definition:

an introduction to a play

In appearance "PartPosition" indicates what position the part defined lies in its whole, but in reality it expresses what role the part defined plays, for instance, PartPosition={heart|心} not only indicates the position but also states that it is the core of its whole, and it is so important that its whole will lose the main function or even will unavoidably collapses once it breaks down. For example: a man will die if his heart ceases to beat; a computer cannot work if its CPU breaks down; an oil lamp will no longer light if it has no more wick. So the words "heart", "CPU", and "wick" are defined as {heart|心} in their definitions:

"heart"

DEF={part|部件:PartPosition={heart|心},
whole={AnimalHuman|动物},
{circulate|循环:instrument={~}}}

"CPU"

DEF={part|部件:PartPosition={heart|心},
whole={computer|电脑}}

"wick"

DEF={part|部件:PartPosition={heart|心},
whole={tool|用具:{illuminate|照射:instrument={~}}}}

8.3.2.4. *Regulations for defining attributes*

(1) "Simple" concepts of attributes

In defining concepts of attributes, no simple concepts are allowed. Any concepts of attributes must be defined with the sememe listed in the taxonomy of attributes as its categorial sememe and with its *host* as the indispensable semantic role. For example:

"size"

DEF={Size|尺寸:host={physical|物质}}

Cf. natural language definition:

the physical magnitude of something (how big it is)

"draft"

DEF={Depth|深度:host={ship|船},
scope={GoInto|进入:LocationFin={waters|水域}}}

Cf. natural language definition:

the depth of a vessel's keel below the surface (especially when loaded)

In the above examples, the semantic role "host" of the HowNet definitions are similar to "of something" and "of a vessel's keel" in the natural language definitions. Again the HowNet definitions are non-ambiguous.

As the semantic role "host" is absolutely necessary in the definitions for attributes, we can regard those that have only one categorial sememe besides "host" as the simple concepts of attribute.

(2) Concepts value-restrictive

A complex concept of attributes is defined with certain value(s), in most cases they express the concrete property. Generally, there are two ways: by means of "modifier" or "scope". The former is used for attribute values; the latter is used for events or other attributes, e.g.

"toxicity"

DEF={Property|特性:
host={physical|物质},modifier={poisonous|有毒}}

"masculinity"

DEF={Sex|性别:host={animate|生物},modifier={male|男}}

"discretion"

DEF={Ability|能力:host={human|人},scope={judge|裁定}}

"contrast"

DEF={Similarity|异同:host={physical|物质},
scope={Brightness|明暗}{Color|颜色}}

Note: "Modifier" or "scope" gives a certain restriction to the attribute defined, for instance: "discretion" is an ability which belongs to human being (its host) when he judges.

Cf. Natural language definition:

the trait of judging wisely and objectively (a man of discretion)

(3) Concepts of unit of measurement

Concepts of unit of measurement are divided into three subclasses in HowNet: units in general (Unit|单位), units for measuring events (ActUnit|动量), and units for measuring things (NounUnit|名量). Among the three the last two are mainly used in Chinese. For example:

"unit"

DEF={Unit|单位:host={Measurement|量度}}

Cf. natural language definition:

any division of quantity accepted as a standard of measurement or exchange

"ft"

DEF={Unit|单位:belong="UK|英国",
host={Distance|距离}{Length|长度}{Width|宽度}}

"glassful"

DEF={NounUnit|名量:host={inanimate|无生物}}

Cf. natural language definition:

the quantity a glass will hold

"piece"

DEF={NounUnit|名量:host={inanimate|无生物}}

Cf. natural language definition:

a serving that has been cut from a larger portion; "a piece of pie" "drop"

DEF={NounUnit|名量:host={liquid|液}}

Cf. natural language definition:

a small quantity (especially of a liquid)

"round"

DEF={ActUnit|动量:host={event|事件}}

Cf. natural language definition:

an interval during which a recurring sequence of events occurs

8.3.2.5. *Regulations for defining attribute-values*

(1) Simple concepts of attribute-values

A simple concept of attribute-values is defined with only one categorial sememe which belongs to the attribute-values taxonomy, e.g.

W_C=曲
G_C=ADJ [qv1]
E_C=
W_E=crooked
G_E=ADJ
E_E=crooked coutry roads
DEF={curved|弯}

W_C=歪歪扭扭
G_C=ADJ [wai1 wai1 niu3 niu3]
E_C=
W_E=crooked
G_E=ADJ
E_E=crooked teeth
DEF={slanted|歪}

W_C=贼
G_C=ADJ [zei2]
E_C=那人~眉鼠眼的不是什么好东西，~头~脑
W_E=crooked

G_E=ADJ
E_E=
DEF={wicked|歹}

(2) Concepts value-restrictive or scope-restrictive

A complex concept of attribute-values is defined with certain value(s). Generally, there are two ways: by means of "degree" or "scope", e.g.

"light brown"
DEF={brown|褐:degree={light|淡}}

"brand-new"
DEF={new|新:degree={most|最}}
Cf. natural language definition:
completely new

"impalpable"
DEF={difficult|难:scope={understand|领会:content={$}}}
Cf. natural language definition:
difficult to perceive or grasp by the mind

"inspiring"
DEF={able|能:scope={urge|促使:
ResultEvent={excited|激动}}}
Cf. natural language definition:
tending to arouse or exalt

8.3.2.6. *Regulations for defining time*

(1) Simple concepts of time

A simple concept of time is defined with only one categorial sememe, that is, {time|时间}, e.g.

"time"
DEF={time|时间}
Cf. natural language definition
the continuum in which events occur in apparently irreversible succession from the past through the present to the future.

(2) Time restricted by time section and time feature

Time has its own section line and its special features. They are specified in the secondary features list. Most of the time concepts are defined with {TimeSect|时间段} or {TimeFeature|时间特性}, e.g.

"year"

DEF={time|时间:TimeSect={year|年}}

Cf. natural language definition:

a period of time containing 365 or 366 days

"day"

DEF={time|时间:TimeSect={day|日}}

Cf. natural language definition:

time for Earth to make a complete rotation on its axis

"Tuesday"

DEF={time|时间:TimeSect={day|日:whole={week|周}}}

Cf. natural language definition:

the third day of the week

"beginning"

DEF={time|时间:TimeFeature={beginning|始}}

Cf. natural language definition:

the time at which something begins or is begun

"end"

DEF={time|时间:TimeFeature={ending|末}}

Cf. natural language definition:

the point in time at which something ends

"year-end"

DEF={time|时间:TimeFeature={ending|末},
TimeSect={year|年}}

Cf. natural language definition:

the end of a calendar year

"Christmas Eve"

DEF={time|时间:TimeFeature={festival|节},
TimeSect={night|夜},domain={religion|宗教},
modifier={ProperName|专}}

Cf. natural language definition:

The evening before Christmas

(3) Concepts value-restrictive

A complex concept of time is defined with certain value(s), e.g.

"long time"

DEF={time|时间:modifier={TimeLong|长时间}}

Cf. natural language definition:

a prolonged period of time

"golden age"

DEF={time|时间:modifier={flourishing|兴}}

Cf. natural language definition:

A period of great peace, prosperity, and happiness

(4) Concepts function-restrictive

A concept of time is defined with its specific functions. The functions may be represented by various semantic roles, e.g.

"wedding day"

DEF={time|时间:TimeSect={day|日},
{GetMarried|结婚:time={~}}}

Cf. natural language definition:

the day of a wedding

"bedtime"

DEF={time|时间:{sleep|睡:time={~}}}

Cf. natural language definition:

the time one goes to bed

8.3.2.7. *Regulations for defining space*

As aforesaid, the "space" is an abstract concept. It does not include any concrete things which may imply space, such as "land", "sky", "sea", "buildings", "organizations". The "space" is classified into two categories: "direction|方向" and "location|位置".

(1) Simple concepts of space

A simple concept of space is defined with only one categorial sememe which is either "space|空间", "direction|方向", or "location|位置", e.g.

"room"

DEF={space|空间}

Cf. natural language definition:

a space that is or may be occupied

"direction"

DEF={direction|方向}

Cf. natural language definition:

the spatial relation between something and the course along which it points or moves

(2) Concepts space-restrictive

Many concepts of space, including direction and location, are defined by a categorial sememe with a restrictive of something or certain space attached, e.g.

"wind direction"

DEF={direction|方向:belong={wind|风}}

Cf. natural language definition:

the direction of wind

"bull's eye"

DEF={location|位置:belong={tool|用具:{AimAt|定向:
patient={~},time={drill|练习:content={firing|射击}}}}}

Cf. natural language definition:

the center of a target

(3) Concepts function-restrictive

A concept of space is defined with its specific functions or affected by a specific function, e.g.

"tear"

DEF={location|位置:{split|破开:location={~}}}

Cf. natural language definition:

an opening made forcibly as by pulling apart

"destination"

DEF={location|位置:{arrive|到达:LocationFin={~}}}

Cf. natural language definition:

the place designated as the end (as of a race or journey)

"course"

DEF={direction|方向:{SelfMoveInManner|方式性自移:
direction={~}}}

Cf. natural language definition:

general line of orientation

8.4. Principles of Defining Concepts

After the detailed description of KDML, we would like to have some deep-going discussion about the principles of defining concepts. We will show the way from concept definition to the visualization of the relations among concepts and the relations among the concept attributes.

Concept definitions are the basis of HowNet. The computation of meaning in HowNet is based on the concept definitions. In a sense, the concept definitions govern the senses or meanings denoted by the words and expressions. Besides, HowNet has verified that the concept definitions are language-independent. The relations between words and meanings in HowNet can be depicted as shown in Fig. 8.1, according to the latest statistics of the data in knowledge dictionary.

In practice, the the computation of meaning of HowNet is not based on words and expressions, but on the concept definitions.

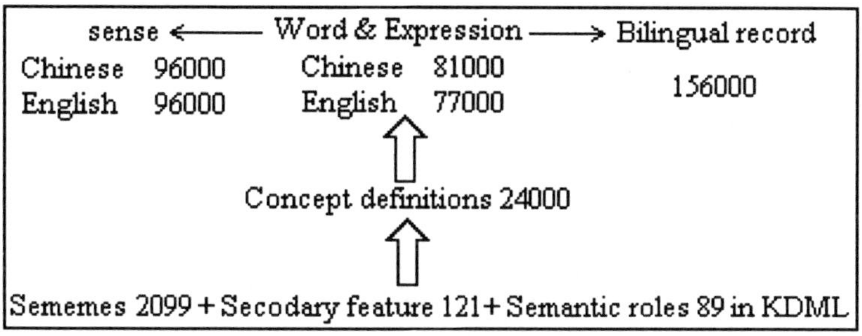

Fig. 8.1. Relations between words and meanings in HowNet.

8.4.1. *Static defining and dynamic activating*

The defining of concepts in HowNet is featured by its static and isolated way. When we are defining a concept, we need not care its possible connections with other concepts. In HowNet most of the concept relations are not coded manually. In practice it is impossible to do so, as HowNet is bilingual and the correspondence between two languages is in a many-to-many way. Most of the concept relations are visualized by automatic computation. How can we achieve this then? What we should do in developing HowNet is:

(1) to define concepts in a static and isolated way;
(2) to develop the devices of computation of meaning which are instructed to dynamically activate various kinds of relations.

By the way of static and isolated defining, we mean that when we define a concept, we only focus on the meaning of the concept to be defined itself, we need not care for its possible relations with other concepts. For example:

"fire"

DEF={fire|火}

Cf. natural language definition:

the process of combustion of inflammable materials producing heat, light, and smoke

"fire"

DEF={mishap|劫难:cause={fire|火}}

Cf. natural language definition:

the event of something burning (often destructive)

"fire engine"

DEF={LandVehicle|车:
{remove|消除:instrument={~},patient={fire|火}}}

Cf. natural language definition:

any large motor vehicles that carry firefighters and equipment to the site of a fire and support extinguishing operations

"fire door"

DEF={part|部件:PartPosition={mouth|口},
whole={building|建筑物},
{obstruct|阻止:instrument={~},patient={fire|火}}}

Cf. natural language definition:

a door made of fire-resistant material that can be closed to prevent the spread of fire

All the above concepts are defined in a static and isolated way. However, in reality they are closely interrelated in meaning. Maybe the concept "fire" will be a stimulant. Thus when we use one of the secondary resources of HowNet — Concept Relevance Calculator to check the relevance of the word "fire fighting", all the above words and phrases are evoked in the list of relevance.

8.4.2. *Uniformity in various levels of language structure*

The mechanism of defining concepts in HowNet proves to be very effective to various structural levels of the language. The mechanism guarantees the best uniformity in the levels of words, phrases, even sentences. We can successfully use HowNet KDML based on sememes and semantic roles to represent all kinds of structures of the language. For example:

(1) Word level

W_C=劫持
G_C=V [jie2 chi2]
E_C=
W_E=hijack
G_E=N
E_E=
DEF={control|控制:manner={fierce|暴}{guilty|有罪}}

(2) Phrase level

"W_C=劫机
G_C=V [jie2 ji1]
E_C=
W_E=hijack a plane
G_E=V
E_E=
DEF={control|控制:manner={fierce|暴}
{guilty|有罪},patient={aircraft|飞行器}}"

W_C=女劫机犯
G_C=N [jie2 ji1 fan4]
E_C=
W_E=woman hijacker
G_E=N
E_E=
DEF={human|人:modifier={female|女},
{control|控制:agent={~},manner={fierce|暴}
{guilty|有罪},patient={aircraft|飞行器}}}

W_C=落网
G_C=V [luo4 wang3]
E_C=
W_E=be caught
G_E=V
E_E=
DEF={suffer|遭受:content={catch|捉住}}

(3) Sentence level

W_C=女劫机犯落网
G_C=V [luo4 wang3]
E_C=
W_E=the woman hijacker was caught
G_E=V
E_E=
DEF={suffer|遭受:content={catch|捉住},
experiencer={human|人:modifier={female|女},
{control|控制:agent={~},manner={fierce|暴}
{guilty|有罪},patient={aircraft|飞行器}}}}

W_C=女劫机犯昨天在福州落网
G_C=V [luo4 wang3]
E_C=
W_E=the woman hijacker was caught in Fuzhou yesterday
G_E=V
E_E=
DEF={suffer|遭受:content={catch|捉住},
experiencer={human|人:modifier={female|女},
{control|控制:agent={~},manner={fierce|暴}
{guilty|有罪},patient={aircraft|飞行器}}},
location={place|地方:
PlaceSect={city|市},belong="China|中国",
modifier={ProperName|专}},
time={time|时间:TimeSect={day|日},
modifier={past|过去}}}

In this sense the HowNet scheme of the sememes and semantic roles is suitable to be used for semantic annotation of texts.

8.4.3. *Language-independent*

The defining of concepts in HowNet is independent of languages. We are confident that the scheme of sememes and semantic roles and KDML are undoubtedly suitable to any languages. This has been fully verified by the bilingual knowledge dictionary and the secondary resources that HowNet itself contains.

Chapter 9

REVELATION OF RELATIONS IN HOWNET

The essence of a computer-oriented knowledge system lies in the revelation of the relations among concepts and the relations among the attributes of concepts. The fundamental task of HowNet, as a knowledge system, is to unveil the relations. In terms of the depth that the computation of meaning reaches, the relations are classified into two types: explicit relations and implicit relations. The former is mainly computed and represented by HowNet browser while the latter by HowNet secondary resources.

9.1. Explicit Relations

There are 11 types of explicit relations in HowNet. They are the relations of synonym, synclass, antonym, converse, hypernym, hyponym, part-to-whole, value-to-attribute, attribute-to-host, cognate role-frame, semantic-roles-to-event. Linguistically, the last four types among them are cross-parts-of-speech relations.

9.1.1. *Synonym*

The synonymous relation represented by HowNet is not manually coded but is computed when the following rules are satisfied among the words and expressions:

(1) they have one and the same concept definitions (DEF item);
(2) they share an identical translation or an identical set of translations;
(3) they share the same part-of-speech when an English synonymous set is searched.

For example, the word “photo” has the words “photograph” and “picture” as its synonyms, because (1) they share one and the same definition:

DEF={image|图像:{TakePicture|拍摄:LocationFin={~}}};

and (2) they share a set of their Chinese equivalents: “像片”, “照片”, “图片”, “影”, “照”; and (3) they share the same part-of-speech. Meanwhile all the Chinese words listed here are synonyms too because they share one and the same definition and share a set of their English equivalents: “photo”, “photograph” and “picture”. Hence we acquire two synonymous sets that correspond to each other in Chinese and English. They are computed according to the above rules and acquired from the following records (only related parts shown below) in the knowledge dictionary.

W_C=像片
G_C=N [xiang4 pian4]
W_E=photo
G_E=N
DEF={image|图像:{TakePicture|拍摄:LocationFin={~}}}

W_C=照片
G_C=N [zhao4 pian4]
W_E=photo
G_E=N
DEF={image|图像:{TakePicture|拍摄:LocationFin={~}}}

W_C=图片
G_C=N [tu2 pian4]
W_E=photograph
G_E=N
DEF={image|图像:{TakePicture|拍摄:LocationFin={~}}}

W_C=像片
G_C=N [xiang4 pian4]
W_E=photograph
G_E=N
DEF={image|图像:{TakePicture|拍摄:LocationFin={~}}}

W_C=影
G_C=N [ying3]
W_E=photograph
G_E=N
DEF={image|图像:{TakePicture|拍摄:LocationFin={~}}}

W_C=照
G_C=N [zhao4]
W_E=photograph
G_E=N
DEF={image|图像:{TakePicture|拍摄:LocationFin={~}}}

W_C=照片
G_C=N [zhao4 pian4]
W_E=photograph
G_E=N
DEF={image|图像:{TakePicture|拍摄:LocationFin={~}}}

W_C=影
G_C=N [ying3]
W_E=picture
G_E=N
DEF={image|图像:{TakePicture|拍摄:LocationFin={~}}}

W_C=照
G_C=N [zhao4]
W_E=picture
G_E=N
DEF={image|图像:{TakePicture|拍摄:LocationFin={~}}}

W_C=照片
G_C=N [zhao4 pian4]
W_E=picture
G_E=N
DEF={image|图像:{TakePicture|拍摄:LocationFin={~}}}

A question may be raised: "Does the way HowNet acquire synonyms means that the synonyms of one language depend on another language?" Our answer is no. The way HowNet acquires synonyms is just a clever technical treatment to avoid manual coding. It would be extremely difficult to acquire bilingual synonyms if they are coded manually. In addition, theoretically synonyms are not based on the relation among *concepts* but are based on the relation among *words*, because a synonymous set is of the same concept. In other words, synonyms are based on the level of words rather than the level of concepts, so the equivalents between different languages can offer a useful way to acquire synonyms. The latest version of HowNet totally acquires over 13,000 Chinese synonymous sets and 18,000 English synonymous sets, for instance:

English synonymous sets:

①photo; photograph; picture;

②BSE, bovine spongiform encephalitis, mad cow disease;

③automobile; car; limo; limousine; motor vehicle; sedan;

④admission; entrance; entry; incoming; ingress;

⑤come; come in; enter; entry; get in; get into; go in; go into; plunge; into; walk in;

⑥attentive; careful; close; conscientious; deliberate; elaborate; meticulous; painstaking; remindful; scrupulous; thorough:

⑦attentively; carefully; conscientiously; deliberately; elaborately; intently; meticulously; painstakingly; thoroughly;

⑧attention; attentiveness;

⑨biology; biological science;

⑩biologic; biological

⑪bootlick; curry favor with; fawn on; flatter; flattery; ingratiate; ingratiate oneself with; laud to the skies; lavish praise on;

lick ... boots; make up to; oversell; play up to; shamelessly flatter; soft-soap; toady; toady to; try to ingratiate oneself with; try to please; try to win ... favor.

Chinese synonymous sets:

①像片; 照片; 图片; 影; 照;
②疯牛病; 疯牛症; 牛海绵状脑病;
③轿车; 汽车; 卧车; 小车; 小轿车; 小汽车; 小卧车;
④步入; 进; 进来; 进门; 进去; 进入; 入; 入场; 扎; 走进; 走入; 钻; 钻进;
⑤把细; 不苟; 当心; 负责; 过细; 紧紧; 精; 精细; 精心; 经心; 经意; 留神; 留意; 密; 密切; 绵密; 腻; 入微; 无微不至; 细; 细密; 细细; 细心; 细致; 详密; 心细; 一笔不苟; 一笔一划; 周密; 周详; 仔细; 仔仔细细; 缜; 缜密;
⑥生物; 生物学;
⑦阿谀; 巴结; 吹捧; 戴高帽; 戴高帽子; 逢迎; 奉承; 奉迎; 溜须; 拍马; 买好; 卖好; 媚; 拍; 拍 ... 马屁; 拍马; 拍马屁; 捧; 捧场; 趋奉; 趋附; 取悦; 抬轿子; 讨好; 献媚; 佞; 谀; 谄; 谄媚; 谄谀.

Why do we have to add one more condition that restricts English synonymous sets to the same part-of-speech? The reason is that English words have grammatical inflections and words of different parts-of-speech may carry the same meaning, and then in HowNet will share one and the same concept definitions. Let's look at the following English sentences:

To *translate* from one language into another by a computer
The *translation* from one language into another by a computer

In the above sentences, the words "translate" as a verb and "translation" as a noun are the same in meaning and their relations between preposition phrases headed by "from", "into" and "by" are also identical. It may be noticed that in LDOCE words of this kind are regarded as "related words listed without explanation" and the ways of showing such words are: "*~ness*", "*~lation*", and "*curliness*" as at the end of "curly".

Therefore, in order to avoid the unreasonable synonymous sets of, say, "compute", "computation", "computational", or "careless", "carelessly", "carelessness" in English, we add part-of-speech restriction to the computing of English synonymous relation. Thus we can see the gap between concepts and English words and phrases. We can also see the peculiarity of the Chinese language.

9.1.2. *Synclass*

Synclass denotes the relation in which words and expressions share the same concept definition. The Synclass relation represented by HowNet is not manually coded either, but is computed when the following rules are satisfied:

(1) they have one and the same definitions;

(2) they share the same part-of-speech when an English synclass set is searched.

The synclass relation is obviously looser than the synonymous relation, for instance, "photo", "photograph" and "picture", "bareheaded photo", "black-and-white photo", "group photo", "group picture", "half-length, bareheaded, full-faced photo", "photo of a person in stage costumes" and "stereo" are of the same class. Their corresponding Chinese translations are naturally of the synclass relation too. They are also computed according to the above-listed rules and acquired out of the following records apart from those above-listed records of the synonyms.

W_C=免冠照
G_C=N [mian3 guan1 zhao4]
W_E=bareheaded photo
G_E=N
DEF={image|图像:{TakePicture|拍摄:LocationFin={~}}}

W_C=黑白照
G_C=N [hei1 bai2 zhao4]
W_E=black-and-white photo

G_E=N
DEF={image|图像:{ TakePicture|拍摄:LocationFin={~}}}

W_C=合影
G_C=N [he2 ying3]
W_E=group photo
G_E=N
DEF={image|图像:{TakePicture|拍摄:LocationFin={~}}}

W_C=合照
G_C=N [he2 zhao4]
W_E=group photo
G_E=N
DEF={image|图像:{TakePicture|拍摄:LocationFin={~}}}

W_C=合影
G_C=N [he2 ying3]
W_E=group picture
G_E=N
DEF={image|图像:{TakePicture|拍摄:LocationFin={~}}}

W_C=半身免冠正面相
G_C=N [ban4 shen1 mian3 guan1 zheng4 mian4 xiang4]
W_E=half-length, bareheaded, full-faced photo
G_E=N
DEF={image|图像:{TakePicture|拍摄:LocationFin={~}}}

W_C=立体照片
G_C=N [li4 ti3 zhao4 pian1]
W_E=stereo
G_E=N
DEF={image|图像:{TakePicture|拍摄:LocationFin={~}}}

Because of the same reason as that in handling English synonymous relation, we add part-of-speech restriction when searching English synclass sets.

9.1.3. *Antonym and converse*

Converse relation can be regarded as a special kind of antonymous relation. In HowNet the converse relation is only related to event concepts while antonymous relation is referred to attribute-value concepts. In HowNet the computation and acquisition of these two kinds of relation need two sets of specifications of antonymous and converse pairs of sememes as shown in Fig. 6.12 and Fig. 6.13.

These two kinds of relation are established when the following three conditions are satisfied:

(1) they should include in their definitions a pair of antonymous sememes or converse sememes which can be found in the antonymous and converse sememes lists;

(2) the rest of their definitions should remain identical;

(3) they share the same part-of-speech when an English antonymous or converse set is searched.

For instance, “young” and “aged” are antonymous, as their definitions include a pair of antonymous sememes: {child|少儿} and {aged|老年} while “child” and “aged” are antonymous too, as their definitions include a pair of antonymous sememes: {child|少儿} and {aged|老年} and the rest part of the definitions remain identical, as shown respectively by the records below.

W_C=幼小
G_C=ADJ [you4 xiao3]
E_C=
W_E=young
G_E=ADJ
E_E=
DEF={child|少儿}

W_C=年老
G_C=ADJ [nian2 lao3]
E_C=
W_E=aged
G_E=ADJ
E_E=
DEF={aged|老年}

W_C=孩童
G_C=N [hai2 tong2]
E_C=
W_E=child

W_C=老年人
G_C=N [lao3 nian2 ren2]
E_C=
W_E=aged

G_E=N
E_E=
DEF={human|人
:modifier={child|少儿}}

G_E=N
E_E=
DEF={human|人:
modifier={aged|老年}}

Similarly, "rise" and "drop" are converse, as their definitions include a pair of converse sememes:{BecomeMore|增多} and {BecomeLess|减少} while "range of rise" and "range of fall" are converse too, as their definitions include a pair of converse sememes:{BecomeMore|增多} and {BecomeLess|减少} while the rest part of the definitions remain identical, as shown respectively by the records below.

W_C=增
G_C=V [zeng1]
E_C=
W_E=rise
G_E=V
E_E=
DEF={BecomeMore|增多}

W_C=降
G_C=V [jiang4]
E_C=价格~了，工资~了半级
W_E=drop
G_E=V
E_E=
DEF={BecomeLess|减少}

W_C=涨幅
G_C=N [zhang3 fu2]
E_C=
W_E=range of rise
G_E=N
E_E=
DEF={Range|幅度:domain={economy|经济},host={Price|价格},
scope={BecomeMore|增多}}

W_C=跌幅
G_C=N [die1 fu2]
E_C=
W_E=range of fall
G_E=N
E_E=
DEF={Range|幅度:domain={economy|经济},host={Price|价格},
scope={BecomeLess|减少}}

Because of the same reason as that in handling English synonymous relation, we add part-of-speech restriction when searching English antonymous sets and converse sets in order to avoid ungrammatical phenomenon that antonyms or converses of different parts-of-speech in English.

9.1.4. *Hypernym*

The hypernym relation is computed and acquired from the taxonomies of HowNet. Figure 9.1 shows the result of retrieving the word "ship" denoting "a watercraft" at HowNet browser. The result is acquired from taxonomy of entity as shown in Fig. 9.2. Figure 9.3 shows the result of retrieving the word "lend" denoting "temporarily give" at HowNet browser. The result is acquired from taxonomy of event as shown in Fig. 9.4.

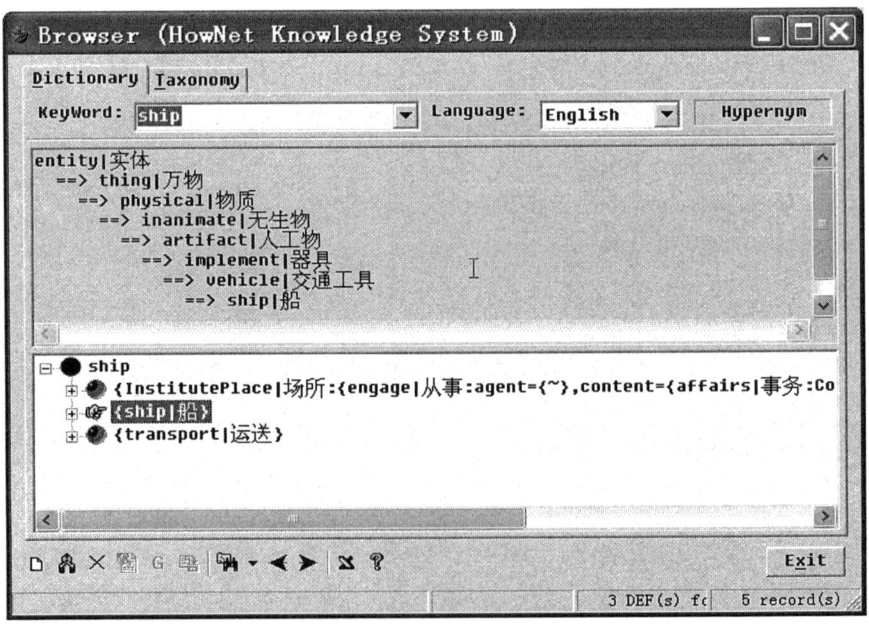

Fig. 9.1. Hypernyms of "ship".

```
- {entity|实体}
   ├ {thing|万物}
   | ├ {physical|物质}
   | | ├ {animate|生物}
   | | | ├ {AnimalHuman|动物}
   | | | | ├ {human|人}
   | | | | └ {animal|兽}
   | | | └ {bacteria|微生物}
   | | ├ {inanimate|无生物}
   | | | ├ {NaturalThing|天然物}
   | | | ├ {artifact|人工物}
   | | | | ├ {implement|器具}
   | | | | | ├ {computer|电脑}
   | | | | | ├ {vehicle|交通工具}
   | | | | | | ├ {LandVehicle|车}
.  | | | | | | ├ {ship|船}
```

Fig. 9.2. Part of Taxonomy of Entity.

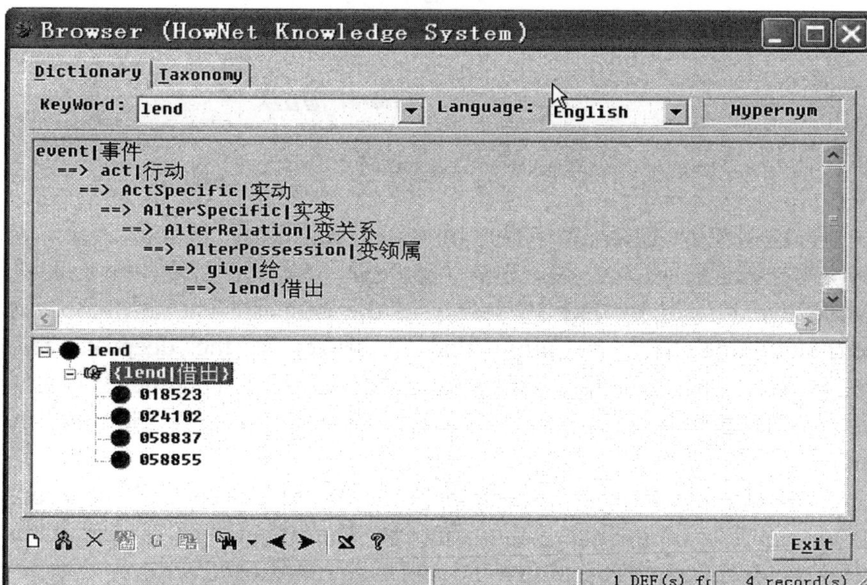

Fig. 9.3. Hypernyms of "lend".

```
- {event|事件}
  ├ {static|静态}
  |  |  ├ {possession|领属关系}
  |  |  |  ├ {own|有}
  |  |  |  ├ {OwnNot|无}
  |  |  |  └ {owe|欠}
  |  └ {state|状态}
  |     ├ {StatePhysical|物理状态}
  |     └ {StateMental|精神状态}
  └ {act|行动}
     ├ {ActGeneral|泛动}
     └ {ActSpecific|实动}
        ├ {AlterGeneral|泛变}
        └ {AlterSpecific|实变}
           ├ {AlterRelation|变关系}
           |  ├ {AlterPossession|变领属}
           |  |  ├ {take|取}
           |  |  ├ {give|给}
           |  |  |  ├ {return|还}
           |  |  |  ├ {sell|卖}
           |  |  |  ├ {lend|借出}
```

Fig. 9.4. Part of Taxonomy of Event.

In HowNet, different types of categories vary in the depth of hypernymous relation levels. Entity category has 8 levels at the deepest while event category has 13 levels at the deepest. The attribute and attribute-value have no more than 5 levels at the deepest. This shallowness results from their nature of dependency. They never can be as independent as entity and event concepts do, because they usually attach to other types of categories.

Let us take "talent" as an example of attribute concept and "talented" as an example of attribute-value concept. Their depths of hypernymous relation levels are shown in Fig. 9.5 and Fig. 9.6 respectively.

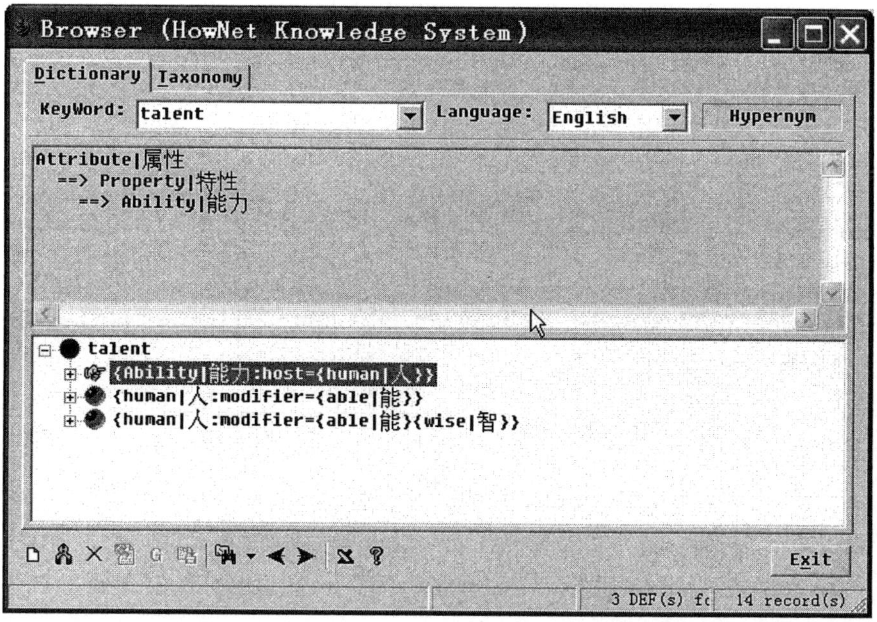

Fig. 9.5. Depth of hypernymous relation levels of "talent".

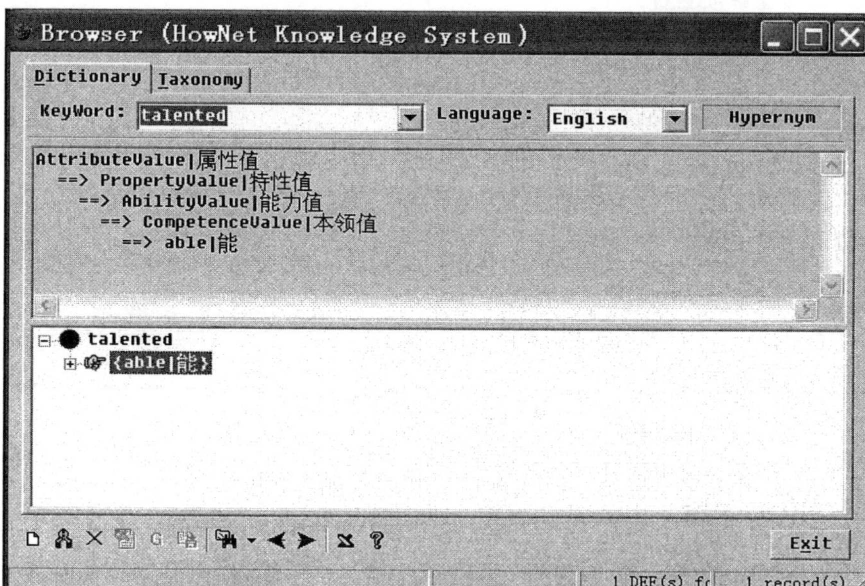

Fig. 9.6. Depth of hypernymous relation levels of "talented".

Speaking of the depth of a taxonomy, which is better, deep one or shallow one? This is a frequently-asked question too. Our answer is: it is hard to say which is better. It is not desirable to evaluate a scheme of taxonomy by its depth. We would like to answer the question in a reversed way. It should not be encouraged to build a taxonomy with an uneven depth, that is, a taxonomy too shallow in one part and too deep in another.

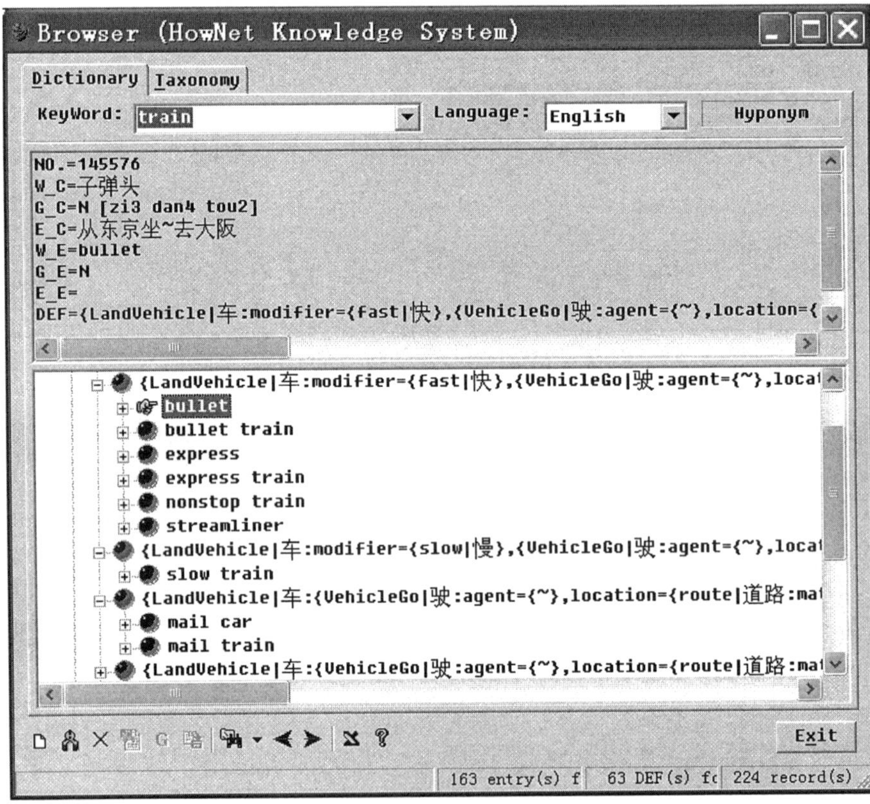

Fig. 9.7. Hyponyms of "train".

9.1.5. *Hyponym*

In HowNet, hyponym is a concept that is more specific than the given concept, including troponym, as conventionally termed.

Unlike the acquisition of hypernyms, the hyponymous relation is computed and acquired on the basis of the concept definitions, or to be accurate, on the basis of the sememes in the concept definitions.

Let us take the hyponyms of "train" meaning "a vehicle of transport" as an example before going to further discussion. Figure 9.7 shows the result that HowNet browser displays.

The hyponymous relation is established when the following is satisfied:

(1) the hyponyms and the given word or expression should share one and the same categorial sememe;
(2) the definitions of the hyponyms should cover the definition of the given word or expression;
(3) the definitions of the hyponyms should have at least one more section than the definition of the given word or expression. We call this part "specific".

Look at the details of the hyponyms of the word "train" meaning "a vehicle of transport". The specific as compared with the definition of the given word "train" is in italic.

"train" — given word
DEF={LandVehicle|车:
{VehicleGo|驶:agent={~},
location={route|道路:material={material|材料:
RelateTo={LandVehicle|车},
material={metal|金属},modifier={linear|线}}}}}

(a) military train
DEF={LandVehicle|车:*domain={military|军}*,
{VehicleGo|驶:agent={~},
location={route|道路:material={material|材料:
RelateTo={LandVehicle|车},
material={metal|金属},modifier={linear|线}}}}}

(b) bullet, bullet train, express, express train, nonstop train, streamliner

DEF={LandVehicle|车:*modifier={fast|快}*,
{VehicleGo|驶:agent={~},
location={route|道路:material={material|材料:
RelateTo={LandVehicle|车},
material={metal|金属},modifier={linear|线}}}}}
{transport|运送:instrument={~},patient={human|人}}}

(c) slow train
DEF={LandVehicle|车:*modifier={slow|慢}*,
{VehicleGo|驶:agent={~},
location={route|道路:material={material|材料:
RelateTo={LandVehicle|车},
material={metal|金属},modifier={linear|线}}}}}
{transport|运送:instrument={~},patient={human|人}}}

(d) mail car, mail train
DEF={LandVehicle|车:
{VehicleGo|驶:agent={~},
location={route|道路:material={material|材料:
RelateTo={LandVehicle|车},
material={metal|金属},modifier={linear|线}}}},
{post|邮寄:instrument={~}}}

(e) boat train, commuter, commuter train, passenger car, passenger train, passenger van
DEF={LandVehicle|车:
{VehicleGo|驶:agent={~},
location={route|道路:material={material|材料:
RelateTo={LandVehicle|车},
material={metal|金属},modifier={linear|线}}}},
{transport|运送:instrument={~},patient={human|人}}}

(f) freight car, freight train, goods train
DEF={LandVehicle|车:
{VehicleGo|驶:agent={~},
location={route|道路:material={material|材料:

RelateTo={LandVehicle|车},
material={metal|金属},modifier={linear|线}}}},
{transport|运送:instrument={~},
patient={physical|物质}}}

(g) morning coach, morning train
DEF={LandVehicle|车:
{VehicleGo|驶:agent={~},
location={route|道路:material={material|材料:
RelateTo={LandVehicle|车},
material={metal|金属},modifier={linear|线}}},
time={time|时间:TimeSect={morning|晨}}}}

(h) night train
DEF={LandVehicle|车:
{VehicleGo|驶:agent={~},
location={route|道路:material={material|材料:
RelateTo={LandVehicle|车},
material={metal|金属},modifier={linear|线}}},
time={time|时间:TimeSect={night|夜}}}}

The definitions of all the 8 hyponym sets have their own unique specifics (in italic), meanwhile they share the definition of the word "train", i.e.

DEF={LandVehicle|车:
{VehicleGo|驶:agent={~},
location={route|道路:material={material|材料:
RelateTo={LandVehicle|车},
material={metal|金属},modifier={linear|线}}},

which carries the meaning: "a train is a vehicle of transport that goes on railroad."

The hyponym relation may cover any categories of concepts only if the concept relations satisfy the above-described conditions. The common feature shared by any categories of concepts such as entity, attribute, event and attribute-value is that all the hyponyms has some specifics compared with the given word or expression. In HowNet, there is no distinction between hyponyms and troponyms. Let us look at some more categories of concepts other than entity.

"temperature" — given word

DEF={Temperature|温度:host={physical|物质}}

(a) critical temperature

DEF={Temperature|温度:*domain={chemistry|化学}{physics|物理}*,host={physical|物质}}

(b) high temperature

DEF={Temperature|温度:host={physical|物质}, *modifier={GreaterThanNormal|高于正常}*}

(c) ultrahigh temperature

DEF={Temperature|温度:host={physical|物质}, *modifier={GreaterThanNormal|高于正常: degree={over|超}}*}

(d) low temperature

DEF={Temperature|温度:host={physical|物质}, *modifier={LessThanNormal|低于正常}*}

(e) ultralow temperature

DEF={Temperature|温度:host={physical|物质}, *modifier={LessThanNormal|低于正常: degree={over|超}}*}

(f) constant temperature

DEF={Temperature|温度:host={physical|物质}, *modifier={constant|恒定}*}

(g) homoiothermy

normal atmospheric temperature

DEF={Temperature|温度:host={physical|物质}, *modifier={normal|正常}*}

(h) boiling point
DEF={Temperature|温度:host={physical|物质},
scope={StateChange|态变:
PatientValue={StateGas|气态},
means={WarmUp|加热}}}

(i) melting point
DEF={Temperature|温度:host={physical|物质},
scope={StateChange|态变:
PatientValue={StateLiquid|液态},
means={WarmUp|加热}}}

(j) condensation point, solidifying point
DEF={Temperature|温度:host={physical|物质},
scope={StateChange|态变:
PatientValue={StateSolid|固态}}}

(k) freezing point
DEF={Temperature|温度:host={physical|物质},
scope={StateChange|态变:
PatientValue={StateSolid|固态},
means={cool|制冷}}}

"walk" — given word (part of hyponyms)
DEF={walk|走}

(a) march, night march, rapid march
DEF={walk|走:*domain={military|军},manner={fast|快}*}

(b) walk alone
DEF={walk|走:*manner={alone|独自}*}

(c) tiptoe, walk gingerly, walk on tiptoe, walk softly
DEF={walk|走:*manner={gentle|柔}*}

(d) go for a stroll, go for a walk, loaf, promenade, ramble, roam, saunter, stroll, take a leisurely walk, take a short walk, take a stroll, take a walk, walk aimlessly, walk with measured steps, wander about unhurriedly

DEF={walk|走:*manner={idle|闲}*}

(e) careen, dodder, limp, limping, lurch, reel, stagger, stumble, swag, walk haltingly, walk unsteadily, wobble, walk unsteadily in a zigzag

DEF={walk|走:*manner={shaky|不稳}*}

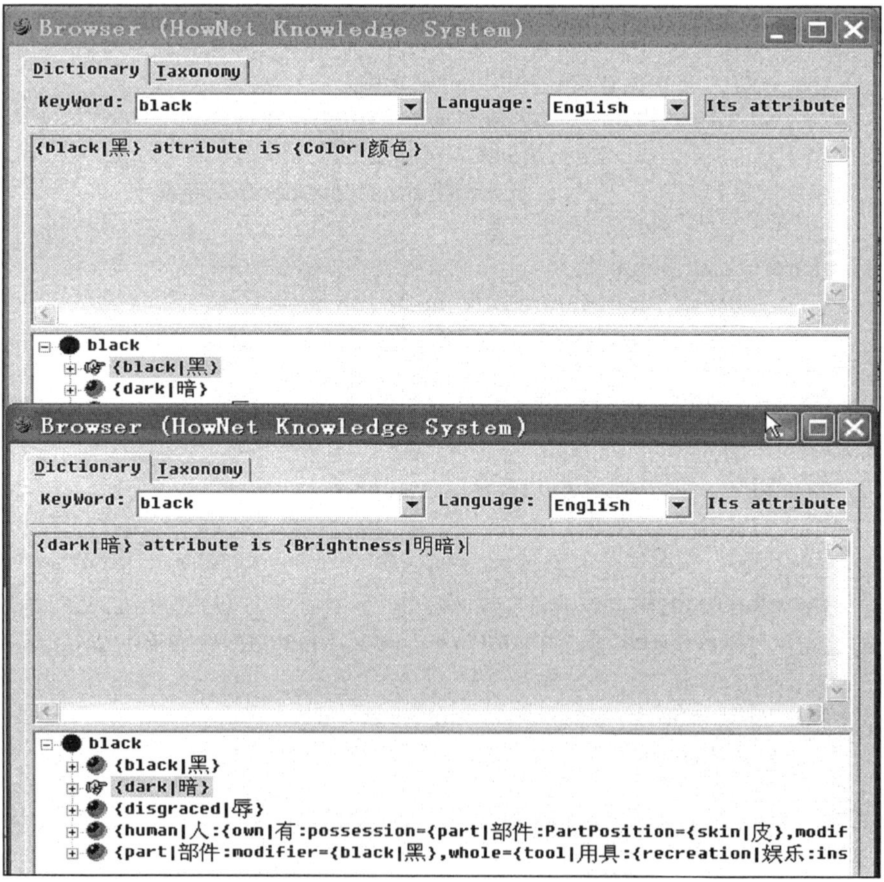

Fig. 9.8. Attribute of the word "black" (two senses).

9.1.6. *Value-to-attribute*

As aforesaid, we consider that any one of attributes should have its corresponding value(s), vice versa, any one of attribute-values should have its corresponding attribute. One of the taxonomies in HowNet specifies the relations between attributes and their corresponding values, see Secs. 6.3 and 6.4.

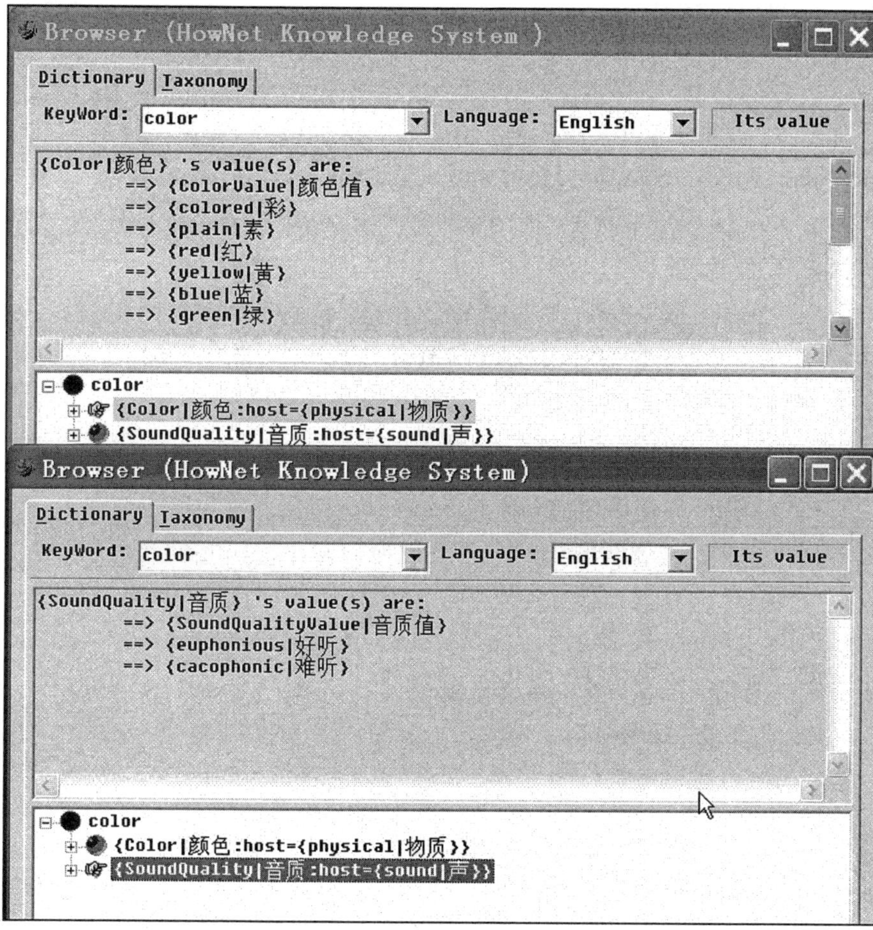

Fig. 9.9. Values of the word "color" (two senses).

Hence the browser can achieve the representation of the value/attribute relations according to the taxonomy. Any sense of a value can retrieve its corresponding attribute as shown by Fig. 9.8 and any sense of an attribute can retrieve its corresponding value(s) as shown by Fig. 9.9.

9.1.7. *Part-to-whole*

As discussed in Chap. 8, when defining a component including part|部件 and fittings|配件, the class of its whole or the definition of its whole should be coded under the role "whole" and the information about its position (function) in the whole should also be coded if possible. Thus a relation of part-to-whole is established by imperative coding. For instance:

"roof"
DEF={part|部件:PartPosition={head|头},
whole={house|房屋}}
house: DEF={house|房屋}

"wing"
DEF={part|部件:PartPosition={wing|翅},
whole={aircraft|飞行器}}
airplane: DEF={aircraft|飞行器}

"wing"
DEF={part|部件:PartPosition={wing|翅},whole={bird|禽}}
bird: DEF={bird|禽}

watchband
DEF={fittings|配件:whole={tool|用具:{tell|告诉:
content={time|时间},instrument={~}}}}
*watch: DEF={tool|用具:{tell|告诉:content={time|时间},
instrument={~}}}*

finger

DEF={part|部件:whole={part|部件:PartPosition={hand|手},
whole={human|人}}}

hand: DEF={part|部件:PartPosition={hand|手},
whole={human|人}}

man: DEF={human|人}

With the help of the way of defining parts or fittings, HowNet browser realizes the representation of the whole-to-part relation, that is, it can acquire the parts of any whole if it owns. For example, when we retrieve the parts and fittings of "watch" denoting "timepiece" using icon "whole" in Sec. 3 of Search mode 3, the browser will return the following: "watchband", "watch chain", "balance wheel", "crystal", "dial plate", "hour hand", "minute hand", etc. Similarly, the browser will return "wheel" as a part if the word "car" is the query, and "rim", "spoke", "tyre", etc. as the parts if the word "wheel" is the query.

9.1.8. *Attribute-to-host*

Again as discussed in Chap. 8, in defining an attribute, the class of its host or the definition of its host must be coded under the role "host". Thus a relation of attribute-to-host is established by imperative coding. For instance:

"learnedness"

DEF={Learning|学问:host={human|人}}

man: DEF={human|人}

"curative effect"

DEF={Effectivity|效果:domain={medical|医},
host={medicine|药物}{method|方法},
scope={doctor|医治}}

medicine: DEF={medicine|药物}

therapy: DEF={method|方法:domain={medical|医},
{doctor|医治:method={~}}}

"shade"

DEF={Hue|浓淡:host={Color|颜色}}

color: DEF={Color|颜色:host={physical|物质}}

With the help of the way of defining attributes, HowNet browser realizes the representation of the host-to-attribute relation, that is, it can acquire the attributes of any host if it owns. For example, when we retrieve the attributes of the word "drug" denoting "medicine" using icon "host" in Sec. 3 of Search mode 3, the browser will return the following: "dosage", "curative effect", "aftereffect", "indication", "form of a drug", "property of a medicine", "compatibility of medicines", etc. as shown in Fig. 9.10.

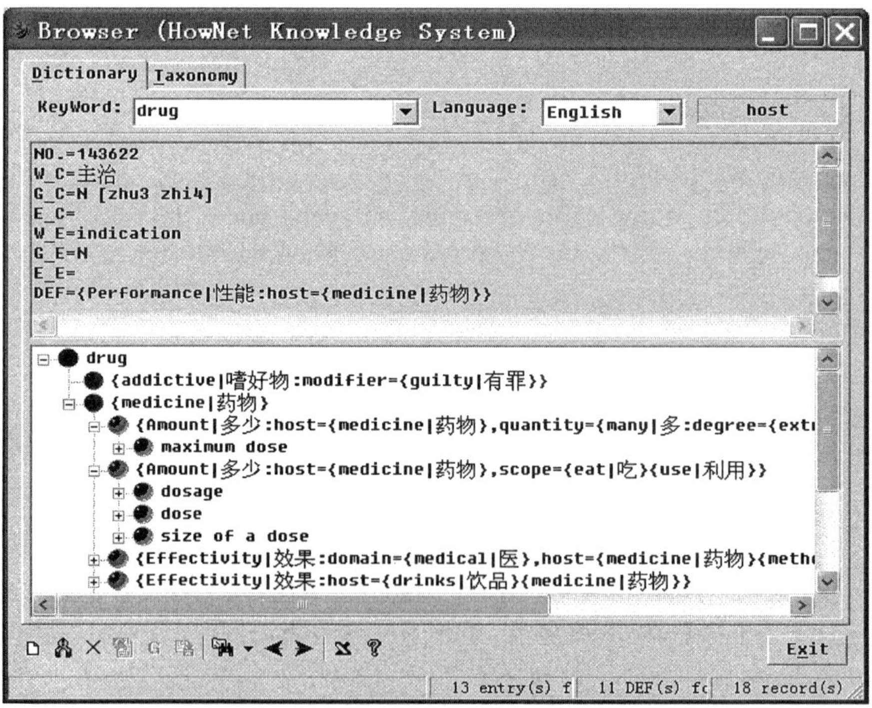

Fig. 9.10. Attributes of the word "drug".

9.1.9. *Semantic-roles-to-event*

Previously we gave full elaboration of semantic roles specified in HowNet. If the part-to-whole relation and the attribute-to-host relations are coded deliberately and forcibly, the semantic-role-to-event relations are coded naturally as needed in defining concepts, for instance:

"doctor"

DEF={human|人:HostOf={Occupation|职位},
domain={medical|医},{doctor|医治:agent={~}}}

"hospital"

DEF={InstitutePlace|场所:domain={medical|医},
{doctor|医治:content={disease|疾病},location={~}}}

"patient"

DEF={human|人:domain={medical|医},
{SufferFrom|罹患:experiencer={~}},
{doctor|医治:patient={~}}}

"be hospitalized"

DEF={reside|住下:location={InstitutePlace|场所:
domain={medical|医},{doctor|医治:
content={disease|疾病},location={~}}}}

"major operation"

DEF={fact|事情:CoEvent={doctor|医治},
domain={medical|医}}

"postoperative"

DEF={time|时间:{doctor|医治:TimeAfter={~},
domain={medical|医}}}

The definitions of the above examples show clearly the semantic-role relations between the entity concepts of "doctor", "hospital", "patient", etc. and the event concepts of "give medical treatment" and "suffer".

What is more, the relatedness among the entity concepts themselves will also be naturally established via the related sememes.

9.1.10. *Cognate role-frame*

Borrowing from the term of "cognate object", we use "Cognate Role-Frame" to reveal a kind of semantic relations between an event concept and its derivationally related entity concepts like "hate" and "hatred", "fight" and "war", "protect" and "plant protection", etc.

The relation of Cognate Role-Frame is manually coded with a role identifier "CoEvent" (meaning event coreference) in HowNet. For example:

W_C=仇怨
G_C=N
E_C=
W_E=hatred
G_E=N
E_E=
DEF={emotion|情感:CoEvent={hate|仇恨}}

W_C=憎恨
G_C=V
E_C=
W_E=hate
G_E=V
E_E=
DEF={hate|仇恨}

As the Cognate Role-Frame specifies, the concept denoted by the noun "hatred" shares the same role frame of the verb "hate". That is to say, syntactically "hatred" is a noun and "hate" is a verb, but semantically they are in common. As specified in the event taxonomy, the class {hate|仇恨} has the following role frame: experiencer={*},target={*},degree={*},cause={*}}. This role frame means that whenever the event "hate" occurs, the following essential roles must participate in it: experiencer (who hates), target (whom or what is hated), degree (degree one hates), and cause (the reason why one hates). We can easily see that the word "hatred", as denoting "a strong feeling of dislike", seems to have the same roles that participate in whenever the feeling occurs, for instance, experiencer (who cherish the feeling), target (toward whom or what the feeling directs), degree (how strong the feeling is), and cause (who or what lead to the feeling). The unique discovery of the Cognate Role-frame relation is of great significance in the computation of meaning.

The relation of Cognate Role Frame mainly falls into the following concept classes: {affairs|事务}, {fact|事情}, {phenomena|现象}, {emotion|情感} and {aspiration|意愿}, etc. For instance:

W_C=电信
G_C=N
E_C=
W_E=telecommunication
G_E=N
E_E=
DEF={affairs|事务:CoEvent={disseminate|传播:
content={information|信息}}}

W_C=保健
G_C=N [bao3 jian4]
E_C=
W_E=health care
G_E=N
E_E=
DEF={affairs|事务:CoEvent={maintain|保养},
domain={medical|医}}

W_C=婚姻
G_C=N
E_C=
W_E=marriage
G_E=N
E_E=

DEF={fact|事情:CoEvent={GetMarried|结婚}}

W_C=暴行
G_C=N [bao4 xing2]
E_C=
W_E=atrocity
G_E=N
E_E=
DEF={fact|事情:CoEvent={MakeBad|加害:manner={fierce|暴}}}

W_C=房荒
G_C=N
E_C=
W_E=housing shortage
G_E=N
E_E=
DEF={phenomena|现象:CoEvent={lack|缺少:
scope={house|房屋}}}

W_C=恶梦
G_C=N [e4 meng4]
E_C=
W_E=nightmare
G_E=N
E_E=
DEF={phenomena|现象:CoEvent={dream|做梦},
modifier={able|能:scope={urge|促使:
ResultEvent={fear|害怕}}}}

W_C=怒
G_C=N
E_C=
W_E=rage
G_E=N
E_E=
DEF={emotion|情感:CoEvent={angry|生气}}

W_C=负罪感
G_C=N [fu4 zui4 gan3]
E_C=
W_E=guilty conscience
G_E=N
E_E=
DEF={emotion|情感:CoEvent={bear|承担:content={blame|埋怨}}}

W_C=心声
G_C=N
E_C=
W_E=aspiration
G_E=N
E_E=
DEF={aspiration|意愿:CoEvent={expect|期望}}

9.2. Implicit Relations

In general, explicit relations are established on the basis of a single and relatively explicit sememe connection. For example, synonymous relation is based on the identical concept definitions; semantic-role/event relation is based on the semantic role of the entity specified.

In contrast with explicit relations, the implicit relations are acquired with more complexity. They are established on the basis of a complex and relatively implicit connections of sememes. Currently HowNet represents mainly two kinds of implicit relations, that is, the relation of concept relevance and the relation of concept similarity. The relations in HowNet are dynamic and interrelated in a net rather than a tree. Figure 9.11 displays the two types of relations.

Let us take the relation of concept relevance as an example to illustrate the implicitness we are discussing. We use HowNet's Concept Relevance Calculator (CRC) and test it with "pen" meaning a writing tool as the keyword. We can then get as the result a list of 290 words and expressions which are related to "pen". In the list the following are found:

paper, paper pulp, blackboard, tablet-armed chair, ink, ballpoint pen, postcard, copybook, literate, illiterate, calligraphist, typist, take up the pen, rewrite, spell, fill in, written translation, prescribe, stationery, pen-holder, nib, pencil lead, refill, pencil box, poor handwriting, agraphia, anorthography, lower margin ...

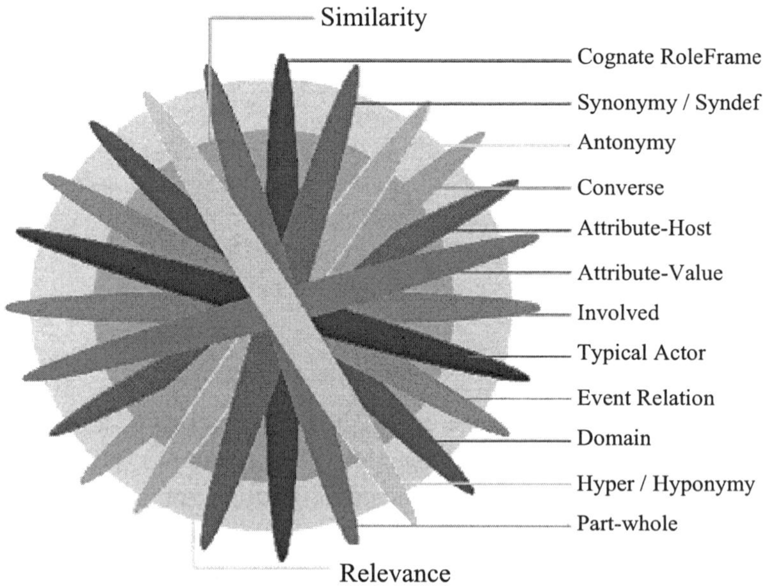

Fig. 9.11. Types of relations revealed in HowNet.

Then let us take the relation of concept similarity by using HowNet's Concept Similarity Measure (CSM) which can compute and give a figure that represents the similarity of any two senses of any words or expressions that HowNet includes. Table 9.1 shows the similarity that HowNet computes.

As aforesaid, in contrast to explicit relations, the implicit relations are not based on a single sememe or simple connection between event and its roles, but based on complicated or multi-layer connections of sememes.

The mechanism of the two devices of computation of meaning will be presented in detail in Chap. 11.

Table 9.1. Concept similarity.

concept-1	concept-2	similarity
president (of a firm)	CEO	0.946154
president (of a firm)	technologist	0.340000
president (of a firm)	college student	0.287500
president (of a republic)	CEO	0.480000
president (of a republic)	college student	0.307692

9.3. Axiomatic Relation of Events and Role Shifting

The axiomatic relation, also known as inferential relation, is based on the logic reasoning among events. In HowNet the axiomatic relations are ensured by the document named "Axiomatic relation of events and role shifting", see Part II, Appendix.

Axiomatic relation of events and role shifting is composed of inferential sets of events as follows:

{earn|赚} ←→ {obtain|得到} [consequence];
agent OF {earn|赚}=possessor OF {obtain|得到};
possession OF {earn|赚}=possession OF {obtain|得到}.

{hold|拿} [precondition] ←→ {CauseToMove|他移};
agent OF {hold|拿}=agent OF {CauseToMove|他移};
patient OF {hold|拿}=patient OF {CauseToMove|他移}.

Each inferential set contains a pair of event sememes. The set describes one axiomatic relation between the two event sememes. Special attention should be paid to the regulation: the relation between the two event sememes should have reasonable connection, for example:

{sell|卖} ←→ {lose|失去} [consequence];
agent OF {sell|卖}=possessor OF {lose|失去};
possession OF {sell|卖}=possession OF {lose|失去}.

{compete|比赛} ←→ {defeat|战胜} [possible consequence];
agent OF {compete|比赛}=agent OF {defeat|战胜};
partner OF {compete|比赛}=experiencer OF {defeated|输掉}.

The Axiomatic relations of events are categorized into:

{axiomatic relation & role shifting}
├ {cause}
├ {consequence}
├ {hypernym}
├ {implication}
├ {interchangeable}
├ {mutual implication}
├ {mutual precondition}
├ {possible consequence}
└ {precondition}

Each set should be specified with one of the relations above-listed, for example:

{earn|赚} ←→ {obtain|得到} [consequence];

which means that {obtain|得到} is the consequence of {earn|赚};

{hold|拿} [precondition] ←→ {CauseToMove|他移};

which means that {hold|拿} is the precondition of {CauseToMove|他移}.

If the two sememes share one and the same semantic role of the principal category, such as agent, possessor, experiencer, no indication signs will be given. If the two sememes have different semantic roles of the principal category, (X) and (Y) will be used, for example:

{deceive|欺骗} (X) ←→ {misunderstand|误信} (Y) [consequence];
target OF {deceive|欺骗}=experiencer OF {misunderstand|误信};
content OF {deceive|欺骗}=content OF {misunderstand|误信}.

Here the principals of {deceive|欺骗} and {misunderstand|误信} are not the same entities, that is (X) deceives and (Y) is misled.

In addition, each set includes the reasoning in role shifting. Let us look at some more sets.

(a) {buy|买} ←→ {obtain|得到} [consequence];
agent OF {buy|买}=possessor OF {obtain|得到};
possession OF {buy|买}=possession OF {obtain|得到}.

In (a) the agent of {buy|买} will shift to the possessor of {obtain|得到} and possession of {buy|买} to the possession of {obtain|得到}. It implies that someone who buys will obtain, and what one buys is what one will obtain.

(b) {SufferFrom|罹患} (X) [cause] ←→{doctor|医治} (Y) ;
experiencer OF {SufferFrom|罹患}=patient OF {doctor|医治};
content OF {SufferFrom|罹患}=content OF {doctor|医治}.

In (b) the experiencer of {SufferFrom|罹患}(be ill) will shift to the patient of {doctor|医治} and the content of {SufferFrom|罹患} will shift to the content of {doctor|医治}. It implies that someone who suffers from illness will receive medical treatment, and the disease one suffers from will be something that is given medical treatment.

The document of "Axiomatic relation of events and role shifting" can contribute further to inference, for example:

{buy|买} ←→ {obtain|得到} [consequence];
agent OF {buy|买}=possessor OF {obtain|得到};
possession OF {buy|买}=possession OF {obtain|得到}.

{buy|买} ←→ {obtain|得到} [consequence];
beneficiary OF {buy|买}=possessor OF {obtain|得到};
possession OF {buy|买}=possession OF {obtain|得到}.

{lose|失去} ←→ {obtain|得到} [mutual precondition];
possessor OF {lose|失去}=possessor OF {obtain|得到};
possession OF {lose|失去}=possession OF {obtain|得到}.

Hence it may be applied to the solution to the deep-level problems such as ellipsis, anaphora, etc. From the document we can retrieve inferential sets of axiomatic relation of events. Look at the following sentence:

"My brother bought for his son a lot of imported toys when he was a child. It is really too bad he lost nearly all of them."

This is a typical problem of anaphora. The determination of the pronoun "he" in the second sentence should be solved. Does it refer to "my brother" or "his son"?

The determination can be done according to the above inferential sets:

beneficiary OF {buy|买}=possessor OF {obtain|得到};
possessor OF {lose|失去}=possessor OF {obtain|得到};

Hence as "his son" is the "beneficiary" of "buy", "his son" "obtains"; as "his son" "obtains", "his son" "loses". We imagine that a computer can infer this way.

Chapter 10

BROWSER — HOWNET'S DEVICE OF COMPUTATION OF MEANING

The browser for HowNet is a show window through which the full set of data can be browsed and the computation of meaning especially of explicit relations among the concepts denoted by Chinese and English words and expressions is implemented. Through the browser the users not only can take a comprehensive look around HowNet but also can export the data in various ways. Meanwhile the browser serves as a handy tool for users to maintain and update the data of HowNet when necessary.

The browser for HowNet is composed by two pages as a friendly interface with its users: the dictionary page shown in Fig. 10.1 and the taxonomy page shown in Fig. 10.28.

10.1. Dictionary Page

Whenever the browser is run, dictionary page will appear automatically. You can deliberately switch to the dictionary page by clicking the tab of Dictionary.

10.1.1. *Layout of dictionary page*

The dictionary page is composed by: Title, Keyword combo box, Language combo box, Search mode bar, Edit box, Tree view, Right key menu, Toolbar, Exit button, Status bar.

The dictionary page has the following functions: Search, Addition, Deletion, Modification, Save, Export, Statistics.

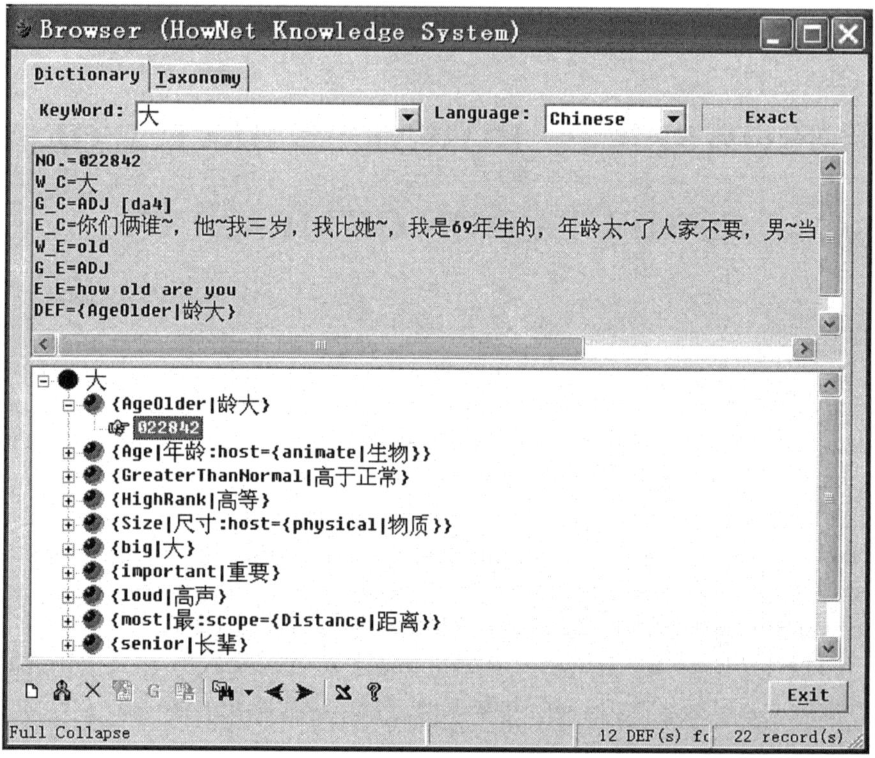

Fig. 10.1. Layout of dictionary page of the browser.

Title

Title shows the version of HowNet to which the browser belongs.

Keyword combo box

Keyword combo box is used to input the keyword. It can save ten latest searches. The type of the input keyword can be the following:

Chinese word or expression

English word or phrase

A sememe between a set of curly braces

A definition or part of definition

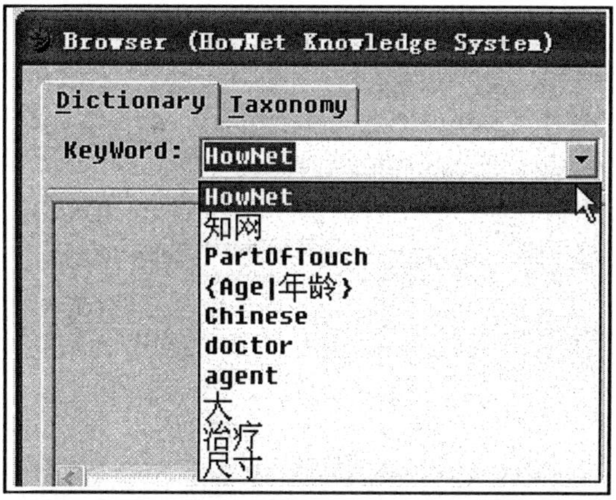

Fig. 10.2. Keyword combo box.

Language combo box

There are three choices in Language combo box. They are: Chinese, English, and Feature.

Note: The type of keyword must correspond to the search language. When the keyword is a Chinese word or expression, the search language should be "Chinese"; when the keyword is an English word or phrase, the search language should be "English". When the keyword is a sememe, part of a definition or a full definition, the search language should be "Feature" (at the same time, the search mode should be either "Exact", "First" or "Fuzzy").

Fig. 10.3. Language combo box.

Edit box

Edit box is used to display a whole record of a search. When you search a word or expression, the Edit box is read-only and its color remains gray. When you are adding a record or modifying a record, the Edit box will become editable and its color will turn white.

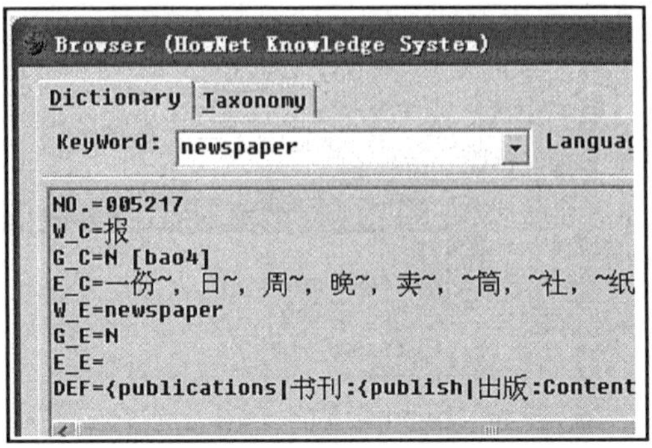

Fig. 10.4. Edit box (read-only).

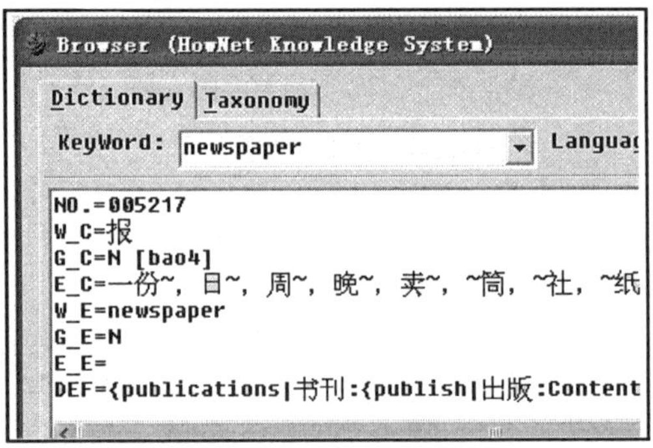

Fig. 10.5. Edit box (editable).

Tree View

All the search result will be shown in tree view.

Fig. 10.6. Tree view.

Right Key Menu

The following functions are splayed and shown when you click the right key of the mouse:

```
Full Expand
Full Collapse
-------------------------------------------
Export HowNet
Export by Conception
Export Definitions
-------------------------------------------
Export Chinese Word List
Export English Word List
-------------------------------------------
Export Chinese Synset
Export Chinese Antonym
Export Chinese Converse
-------------------------------------------
Export English Synset
Export English Antonym
Export English Converse
-------------------------------------------
Export Search Result (Full)
Export Search Result (Chinese Words)
Export Search Result (English Words)
```

Fig. 10.7. Right key menu.

Full Expand: to fully expand the tree view;

Full Collapse: to fully collapse the tree view;

Export HowNet: to export the database of HowNet;

Export by Concept: to export the database of HowNet by the concept sequence;

Export Definitions: to export the DEF items;

Export Chinese Word List: to export all the Chinese entries, i.e. unique forms of words and expressions;

Export English Word List: to export all the English entries, i.e. unique forms of words and phrases;

Export Chinese Synset: to export all the Chinese synonymous sets;

Export Chinese Antonym: to export all the Chinese antonymous sets;

Export Chinese Converse: to export all the Chinese converse sets;

Export English Synset: to export all the English synonymous sets;

Export English Antonym: to export all the English antonymous sets;

Export English Converse: to export all the English converse sets;

Export Search Result (Full): to export the search result, in full record form;

Export Search Result (Chinese Words): to export the search result, in Chinese word list form;

Export Search Result (English Words): to export the search result, in English word list form.

Toolbar

The toolbar of the dictionary page plays an important role in various functions of the Browser. There are eleven functions in the toolbar. They are addition, modification, deletion, save current, give up, save to file, search, previous record, next record, statistics and help, shown as follows.

Addition
Modification
Deletion
Save-Current: to save after addition or modification is done
Give-Up: to give up after addition or modification is done
Save-to-File
Search: three Search Modes to choose by clicking the arrow beside the button
Previous record: to check the record before the current record
Next record: to check the record after the current record
Statistics
Help

Status Bar

Status bar has four sections which are used to display the following statistics: the prompt information, the number of entries found, the number of definitions found, and the number of records found. Figure 10.8 shows that when we search the synonyms of English word "chair", 3 entries, 2 definitions and 8 records are found.

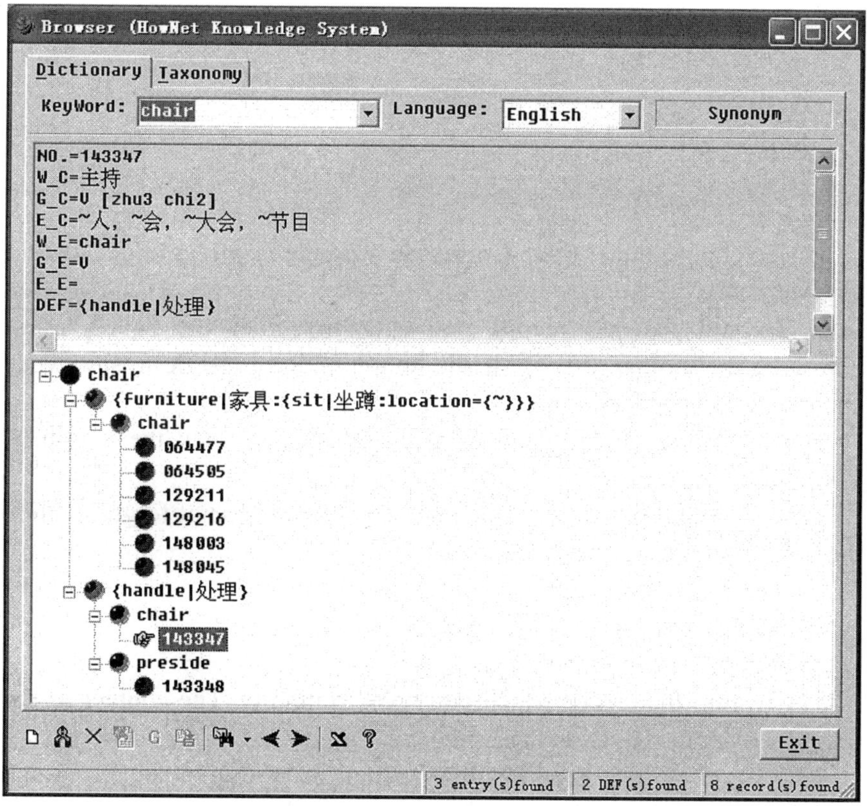

Fig. 10.8. Status bar.

10.1.2. *Functions of dictionary page*

Addition

The addition procedure is as follows:

(1) To click the append button on the toolbar, you can see that the Edit box become editable. At the same time, a blank record as below will appear, and you may fill in the items.

NO.=000000
W_C=
G_C=
E_C=
W_E=
G_E=
E_E=
DEF=

(2) To choose either Save-Current to save the new record or Give-up to give it up.

a. To save the new record, you must first click the Save-Current button on the toolbar, then click the button of Save-to-File to save your changes to the index file.

b. To give up your operation, you just need to click the button of Give-Up on the toolbar.

Note: Every time when you append one record, do not forget to click the button of Save-Current or Give-Up

Modification

The modification procedure is as follows:

(1) To find the record which you want to modify. The content of the record will be displayed in the Edit box;

(2) To click the modification button on the toolbar. To make modifications when the Edit box becomes editable.

(3) To save the modified record or give it up.

a. To click the Save-Current button on the toolbar to save the modified record, and then to save the modified record to the index file by clicking the Save-to-File button.

b. To clicking the Give-Up button to give up your operation

Note: Every time when you finish modifying a record, remember to save your current operation or give it up by clicking the respective button.

Deletion

The deletion procedure is as follows:

(1) To find the record which you want to delete. The record will be displayed in the Edit box.

(2) To click the deletion button on the toolbar to finish deleting a record. Remember the deletion has not really been done if you do not save your changes to the index file by clicking the Save-to-File button on the toolbar.

(3) To save your operation to the index file. It can be realized by clicking the Save-to-File button on the toolbar.

Note: As long as you have clicked this button, the record you have just deleted cannot be restored any more.

Save

There are two ways of saving a record:

(1) To use Save-current; It can be achieved by clicking the button of Save-Current on the toolbar.

(2) To use Save-to-File; After clicking the Save-to-File button on the toolbar, you save to the index file the data you have just modified. If you want to apply your new data, you must do this operation.

Statistics of Data

The statistics dialog is displayed by clicking the statistics button on the toolbar. There are three pages in the statistics dialog as shown in Fig. 10.9, Fig. 10.10 and Fig. 10.11.

The first page shows seven items: Chinese Character, Chinese word and expression, English word and expression, Chinese meaning, English meaning, DEF, and Record.

The second page shows eight items of semantic information: pure entity, event, attribute, attribute-value, thing (entity), time (entity), space (entity), component (entity).

The last page shows the syntactic information, twenty parts-of-speech in all: adjective (ADJ), adverb (ADV), auxiliary (AUX), classifier (CLAS), conjunction (CONJ), coordinate (COOR), echo (ECHO), expression (EXPR), infinitive sign (INFSIGN), noun (N), numeral (NUM), prepositional phrase (PP), prefix (PREFIX), preposition (PREP), pronoun (PRON), punctuation (PUNC), structure words (STRU), suffix (SUFFIX), verb (V), character (cha).

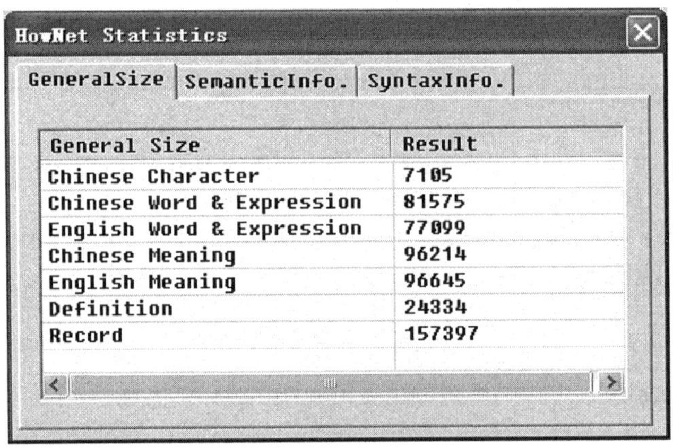

General Size	Result
Chinese Character	7105
Chinese Word & Expression	81575
English Word & Expression	77099
Chinese Meaning	96214
English Meaning	96645
Definition	24334
Record	157397

Fig. 10.9. HowNet statistics (1).

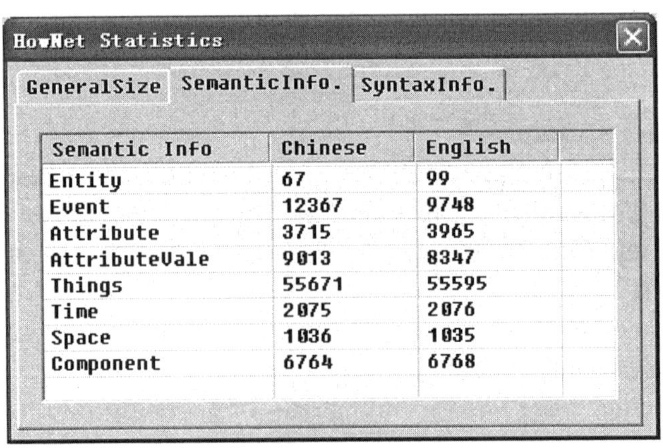

Semantic Info	Chinese	English
Entity	67	99
Event	12367	9748
Attribute	3715	3965
AttributeVale	9013	8347
Things	55671	55595
Time	2075	2076
Space	1036	1035
Component	6764	6768

Fig. 10.10. HowNet statistics (2).

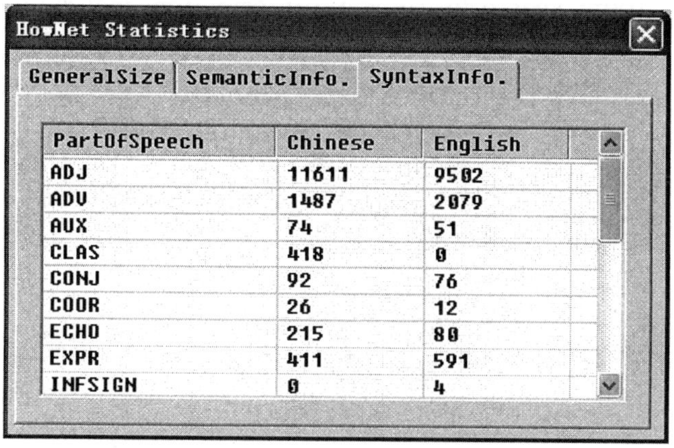

PartOfSpeech	Chinese	English
ADJ	11611	9502
ADV	1487	2079
AUX	74	51
CLAS	418	0
CONJ	92	76
COOR	26	12
ECHO	215	80
EXPR	411	591
INFSIGN	0	4

Fig. 10.11. HowNet statistics (3).

10.1.3. *Search modes of dictionary page*

You can find the search mode by clicking the arrow beside the search button on the toolbar.

There are three groups in the search mode: FirstGroup, SecondGroup and ThirdGroup.

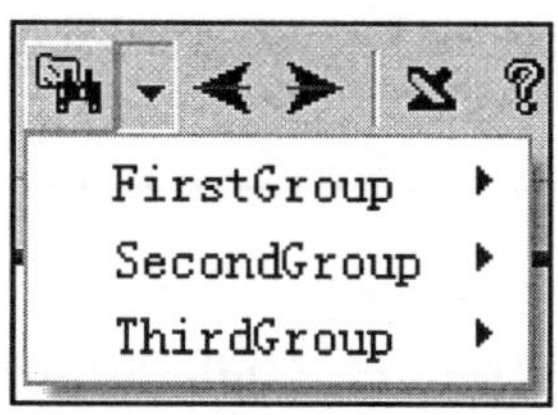

FirstGroup: Search by the keyword, including Exact, First, Fuzzy, Fuzzy Abbr, Fuzzy Jump, Last.

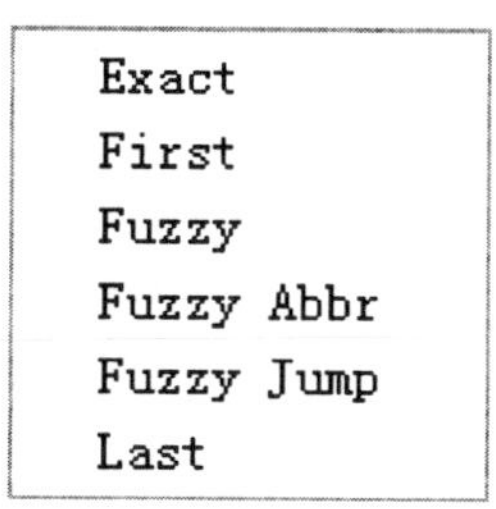

SecondGroup: Search by semantic information, including Antonym, Converse, Synonym, SynClass, Hypernym, Hyponym, Its value, Its attribute.

```
Antonym
Converse
Synonym
SynClass
Hypernym
Hyponym
Its value
Its attribute
```

ThirdGroup: Search by semantic roles of an event, including all kinds of semantic roles of the event, see Chap. 5.

(1) FirstGroup

Exact

(1) To search with the exact character, words or expressions either in Chinese or in English you key in KeyWord box. The search result will be displayed in the tree view, e.g. the English word "book" as shown in Fig. 10.12.

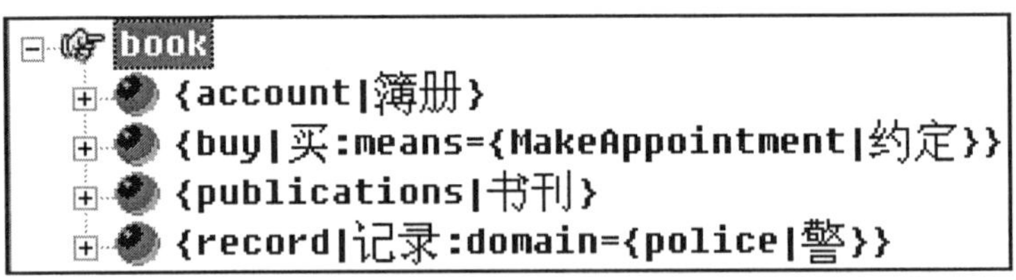

Fig 10.12. Exact search result for "book".

(2) To search with a sememe in a set of curly braces to find the words and expressions or phrases whose DEFs contain the sememe you key in KeyWord Box as the only categorial sememe. The search result will be shown in the tree view, e.g. "{FondOf|喜欢}" as shown in Fig. 10.13.

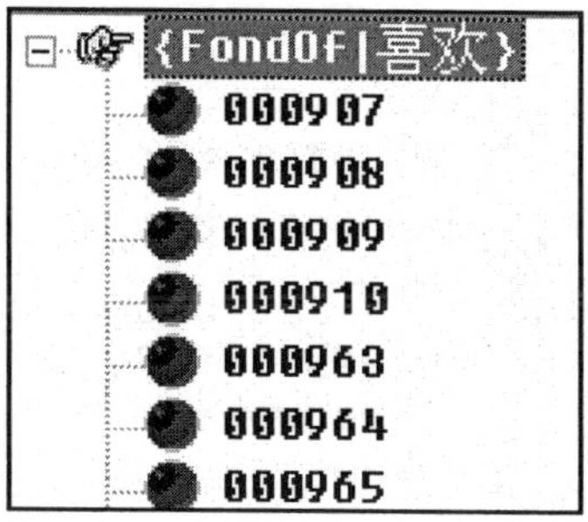

Fig. 10.13. Exact search for sememe "{FondOf|喜欢}".

First

(1) To search with the first character(s) (in Chinese words or expressions) or the first word(s) (in English phrases) you key in KeyWord box. The search result will be displayed in the tree view, e.g. the English word "book" as shown in Fig. 10.14.

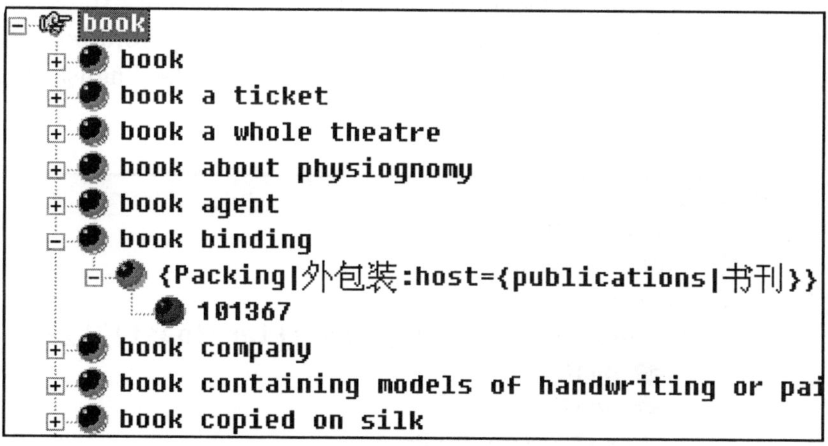

Fig. 10.14. First search for "book".

(2) To search with a sememe in a set of curly braces to find all the words and expressions or phrases whose DEFs contain the sememe you key in KeyWord Box. The search result will be shown in the tree view, e.g. "{FondOf|喜欢}" as shown in Fig. 10.15.

Fig. 10.15. First search for sememe "{FondOf|喜欢}".

Last

To search with the last character(s) (in Chinese words or expressions) or the last word(s) (in English phrases) you key in KeyWord box. The search result will be displayed in the tree view, e.g. the English word "book" as shown in Fig. 10.16.

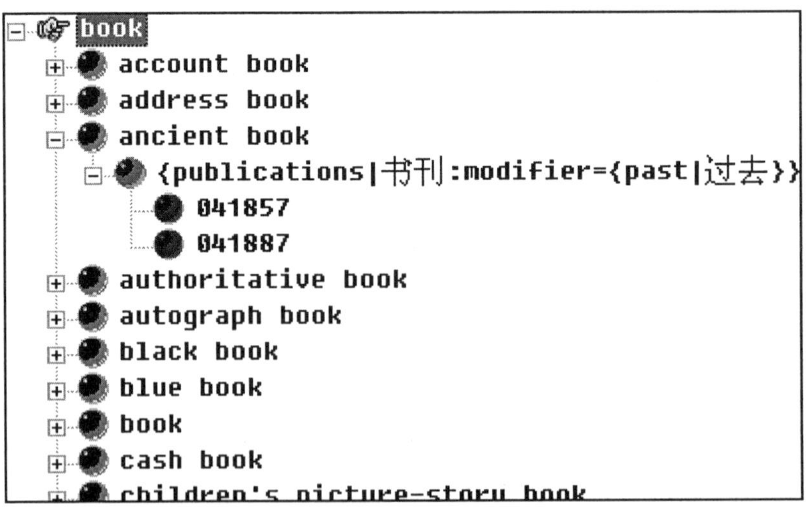

Fig. 10.16. Last search for "book".

Fuzzy

(1) To search with character(s) (in Chinese words or expressions) or word(s) (in English phrases) to find the words and expressions or phrases which contain the character(s) or word(s) you key in KeyWord box. The search result will be shown in the tree view, e.g. the English word "book" as shown in Fig. 10.17.

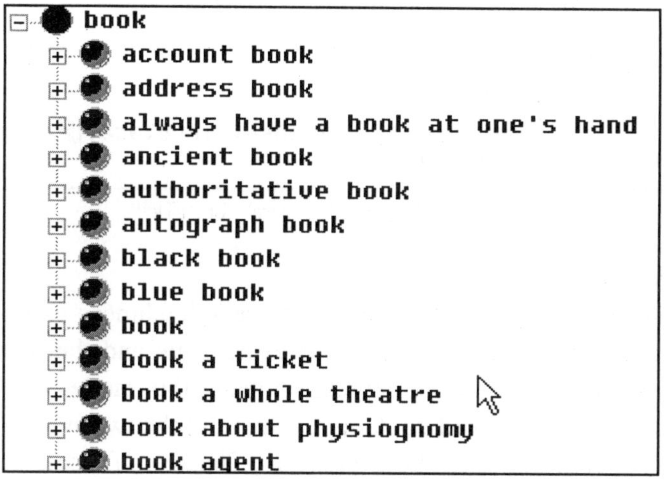

Fig. 10.17. Fuzzy search of "book".

(2) To search with a sememe in a set of curly braces to find the words and expressions or phrases whose DEFs contain the sememe you key in KeyWord Box. The search result will be shown in the tree view, e.g. "{FondOf|喜欢}" as shown in Fig. 10.18.

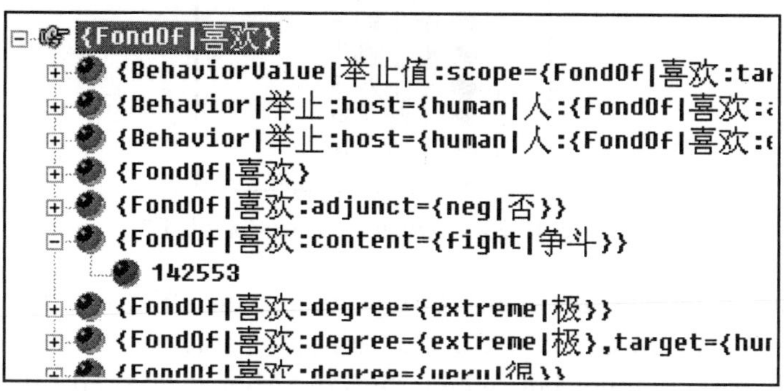

Fig. 10.18. Fuzzy search for sememe "{FondOf|喜欢}".

Fuzzy Abbr

This search mode can only be used to search Chinese expressions. The language mode should be in Chinese. Using this function we can search with a Chinese abbreviation which may be out of vocabulary. The search result will be the full form of the abbreviation, for example:

With “刑释”, we can get “刑满释放”; with “婚介”, we can get “婚姻介绍所” and with “巡展”, we can get “巡回展览” etc.

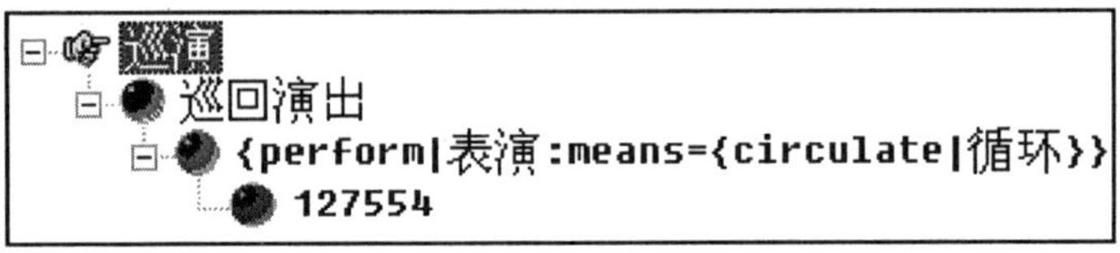

Fig. 10.19. Fuzzy abbr. search for “巡展”.

Fuzzy Jump

This search mode can only be used to search Chinese expressions. If we just know some parts of a Chinese expression, and the parts are not continuous. We may find the expression using this mode. For example, we just know that the word contains “大小” and the two words “大” and “小” are not continuous in the expression. The search result will be “半大不小”, “不大不小”, “大材小用” and “大惊小怪” etc. Figure 10.20 take “上下” as an example.

Fig. 10.20. Fuzzy jump search for “上下”.

The difference between “Fuzzy Jump” and “Fuzzy Abbr.” lies in: when “Fuzzy Jump” is used, the Chinese characters in the expressions found are separate but when “Fuzzy Abbr.” is used, the Chinese characters in the expressions found may be either separate or adjacent. For example, we take the Chinese abbreviation "国企" as an example.

When the search mode is "Fuzzy Jump", the result is "国营企业", "国有企业". The characters "国" and "企" are separated.

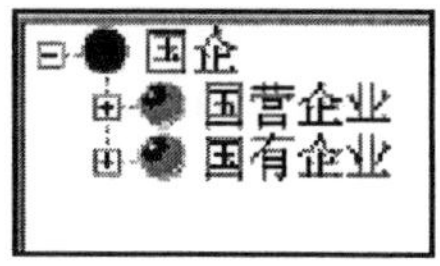

Fig. 10.21. Fuzzy jump search for "国企".

When the search mode is "Fuzzy Abbr.", the word "跨国企业" will be added to the result. The character "国" and "企" are adjacent.

Fig. 10.22. Fuzzy abbr. search for "国企".

SecondGroup

Synonym

To search all the synonyms of the given word or expression. The result will be displayed as follows: all the concept definitions of the keyword are shown first and all the synonymous entries based on each of the concept definitions are shown next.

Antonym

To search all the antonyms of the given word or expression. The result will be displayed as follows: all the concept definitions of the keyword are shown first and all the antonymous entries based on each of the concept definitions are shown next.

Converse

To search all the converses of the given word or expression. The result will be displayed as follows: all the concept definitions of the keyword are shown first and all the converse entries based on each of the concept definitions are shown next.

SynClass

To search all the SynClass words and expressions of the given word or expression. The result will be displayed as follows: all the concept definitions of the keyword are shown first and all the SynClass entries based on each of the concept definitions are shown next.

Hypernym

We can find the hypernym-hyponym relation of a concept in the Taxonomy by this search mode. Let us find the hypernym of the word "doctor" using "Hypernym" search mode.

(1) DEF={doctor|医治}

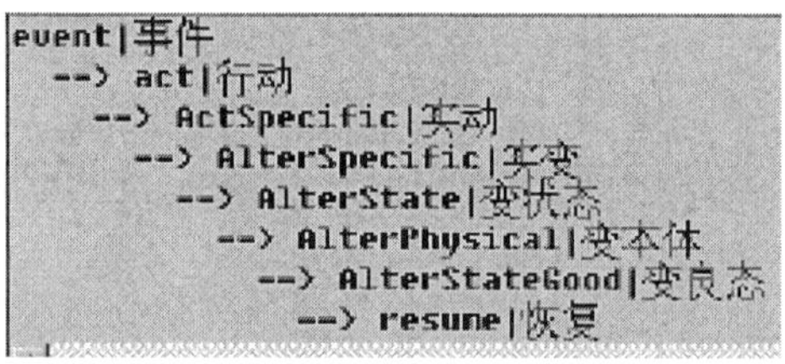

Fig. 10.23. Hypernym of sememe "{doctor|医治}".

(2) DEF={human|人:HostOf={Occupation|职位},
domain={medical|医},{doctor|医治:agent={~}}}

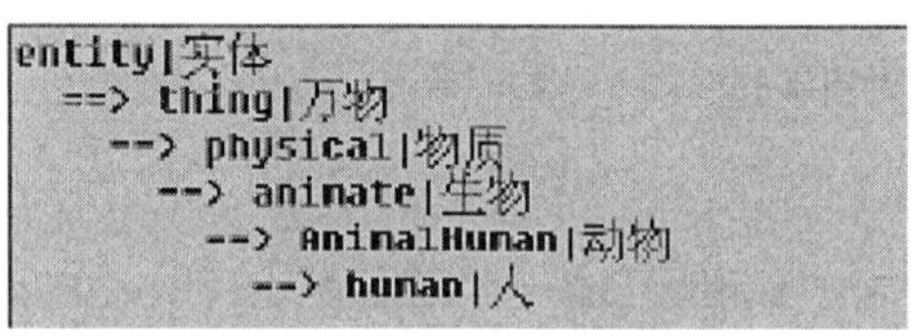

Fig. 10.24. Hypernym of sememe "{human|人}".

Hyponym

We can find the hyponyms of any concept of the given word or expression. For example, The word "doctor" has three senses, two of which are human. Let us find the hyponyms of these two using "Hyponym" search mode.

(1) DEF={human|人:HostOf={Occupation|职位},
domain={medical|医},{doctor|医治:agent={~}}}

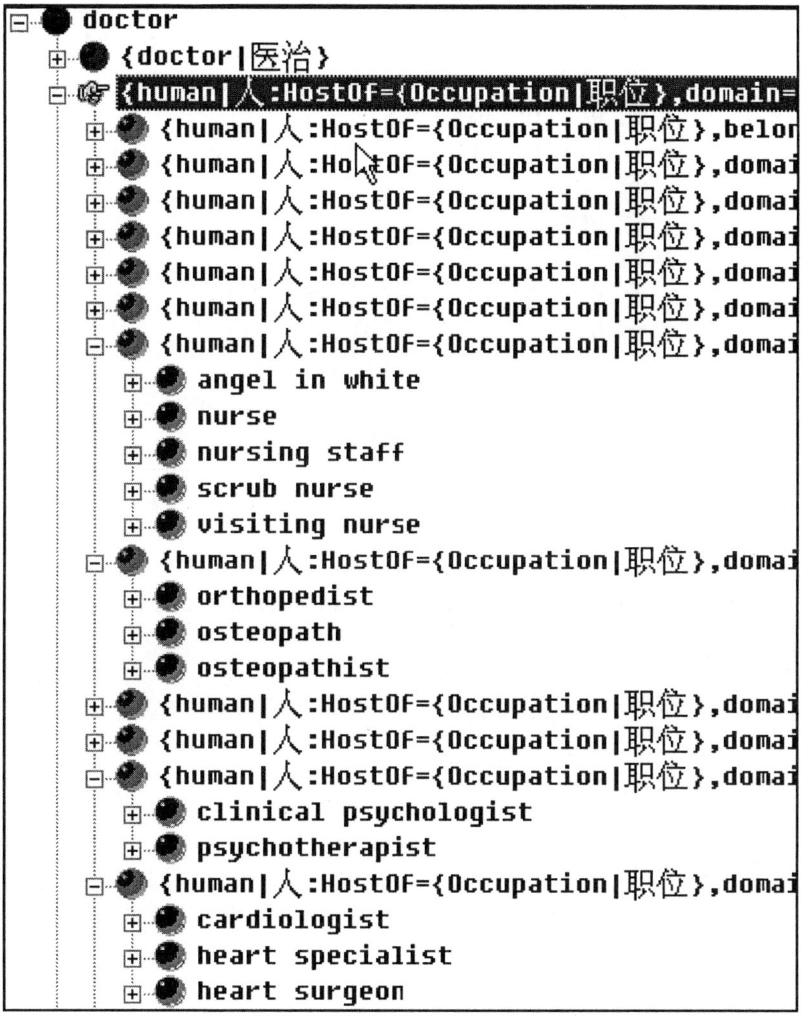

Fig. 10.25. Hyponym search result of "doctor" (1).

(2) DEF={human|人:{own|有:possession={Status|身分:
domain={education|教育},modifier={HighRank|高等:
degree={most|最}}},possessor={~}}}

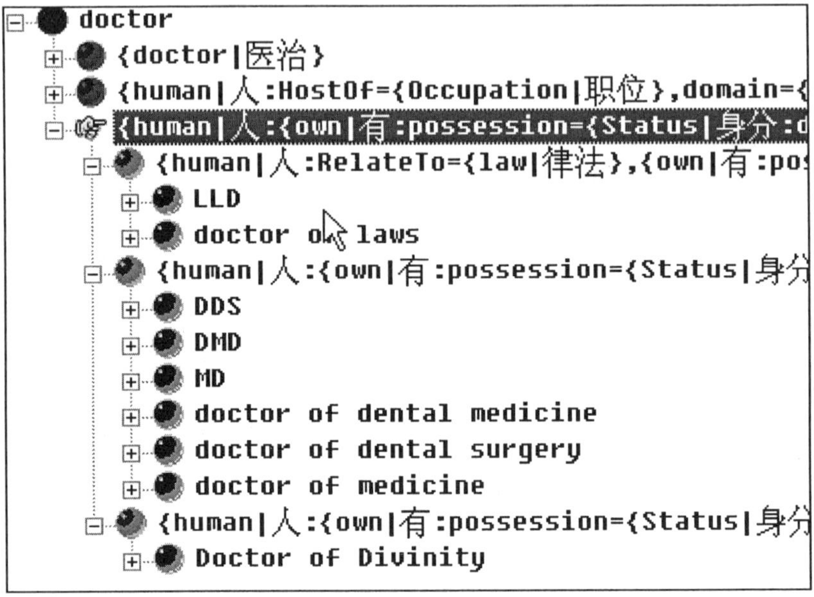

Fig. 10.26. Hyponym search result of "doctor" (2).

Its value

To find all the attribute-values that an attribute corresponds to, e.g. "age". The search result is:

{Age|年龄} 's value(s) are:
==> {AgeValue|年龄值}
==> {aged|老年}
==> {MiddleAge|中年}
==> {adult|成年}
==> {young|青年}
==> {child|少儿}
==> {AgeOlder|龄大}
==> {AgeYounger|龄小}

Its attribute

To find the attribute that an attribute-value corresponds to. The search result is as shown in Table 10.1.

Table 10.1. Sample of the attribute of attribute-values.

attribute value	its attribute
DEF={NotHeavy|轻}	Weight|重量
DEF={gentle|柔}	Friendliness|友善性
DEF={noncritical|轻微}	Seriousness|严重性
DEF={small|小}	Size|尺寸
DEF={unimportant|不重要}	Importance|重要性
DEF={young|青年}	Age|年龄

(2) ThirdGroup

To search semantic roles of an event, such as CoEvent, LocationIni, RelateTo, TimeFin, agent, cause, target etc.

10.2. Taxonomy Page

10.2.1. *Layout of taxonomy page*

You can switch to this page by clicking the tab of taxonomy. This page is made up by Keyword Combo Box, Semantic Feature Combo Box, View, Right Key Menu, Toolbar, the exit button and Status Bar, as shown in Fig. 10.28. The function of the page includes: to search, to export, and to show Tooltips.

Semantic Feature Combo Box

The combo box contains Event, Entity, Attribute, Attribute Value, Secondary Feature, Event Role & Features, Syntax, ProperNoun, Sign, Antonym, Converse.

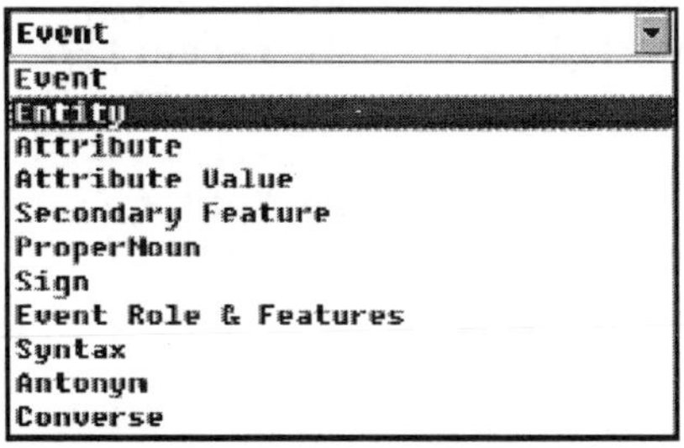

Fig. 10.27. Semantic feature combo box.

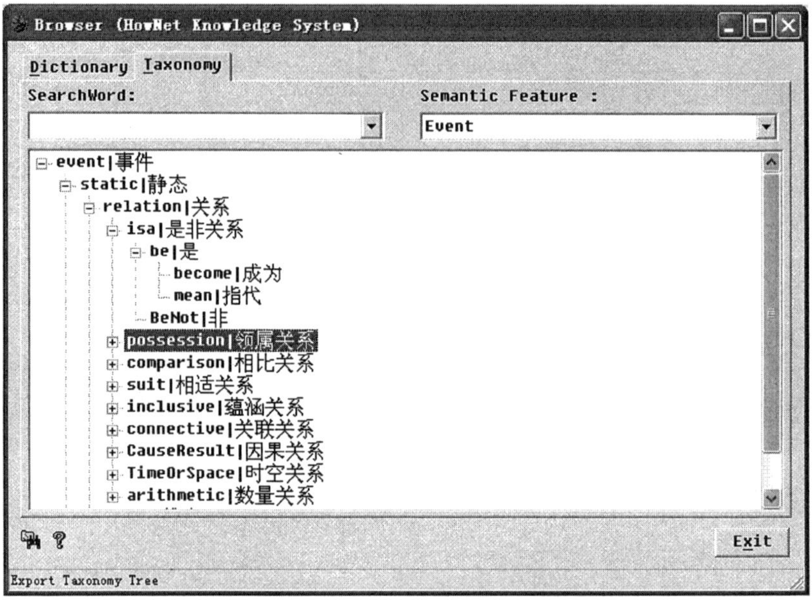

Fig. 10.28. Layout of taxonomy page of the browser.

Keyword Combo Box

Keyword Combo Box is used to input your search keyword. It can save ten words of the latest search. The input keyword can be a whole sememe, the English part of a sememe or the Chinese part of a sememe.

View

The antonym and the converse are displayed in a list table.

aged|老年	child|少儿
alien|外来	original|原
alike|似	different|异
all|全	pieced|片
alone|独自	together|共同
already|已经	NotYet|尚未
always|总是	never|从不
amiable|友善	unfriendly|不友善

Fig. 10.29. List view of antonym.

The other sememes are displayed in a tree view.

Fig. 10.30. Tree view of sememes.

Right Key Menu

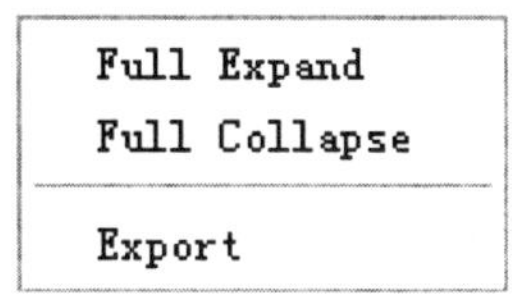

The right key menu will be shown when you click the right key of the mouse. The function includes:

Full Expand: to fully expand the sememe tree;

Full Collapse: to fully collapse the sememe tree;

Export: to export the database

Toolbar

There are two functions in its toolbar.

Search: to search specific sememe, feature or role

Help

Status Bar

There is only one part in the status bar of this page. The number of the sememes will be shown in it.

The above graph shows that there are 230 nodes in the list.

ToolTips

When you put your mouse on the taxonomy tree for a moment, the tooltips will appear, which show the DEF or the event frame of each sememe.

```
Relation:
{OwnNot|无:possessor={*},possession={*}}

Comment:
```

Fig. 10.31. Tooltips of sememe.

Chapter 11

SECONDARY RESOURCES — HOWNET'S DEVICES OF COMPUTATION OF MEANING

As discussed in Chap. 9, in terms of reaching the depth of the computation of meaning, the relations in HowNet are classified into two types: explicit relations and implicit relations. The former is mainly computed and represented by HowNet browser while the latter by HowNet secondary resources, which include Concept Relevance Calculator (CRC), Concept Similarity Measure (CSM) and Query Expansion Tool (QET). The purpose of developing the secondary resources is to make HowNet approach to practical applications and to serve as testing tools for evaluating the quality of HowNet knowledge data and HowNet's capability of the computation of meaning.

11.1. Concept Relevance Calculator (CRC)

Related concepts field is a group of words and expressions which are closely related in multiple sememe connections. They are acquired and represented by a specially-designed device named Concept Relevance Calculator (CRC) in HowNet. The device is capable to give a related concepts field of any senses of any words and expressions both in English and Chinese included in HowNet. For example, when the word "bus" is keyed in as a query, 2 groups of related words and expressions corresponding to the 2 senses of "bus" will be displayed respectively by the tool:

(a) Sense 1: a vehicle carrying many passengers:

carrying capacity
transport capacity
transport mileage
bus company
bus service
transfer post
first bus
last bus
minibus
tram
trolley
autobus
bus
double-decker
long-distance bus
omnibus
subway train
tourist coach
regular bus
lorry
truck
dumpcart
by bus
carrying trade
public traffic
transport service
transportation
regular bus service
give a lift
land transportation
pick up
transportation
traffic
carry passenger
take on passengers

(b) Sense 2: an electrical conductor:

CPU
central processing unit
microprocessor
processor
CD drive
CD driver
bus
computer hardware
disc drive
drive
driver
floppy disk driver
keyboard
hardware
light pen
mouse
monitor
external memory
floppy disk drive
hard disc
inner memory
main memory
memory
memory board
electronic pen
enter key
save

11.1.1. *Algorithm of CRC*

The algorithm of CRC includes the following steps:

Step 1. To take the DEF of the given word as the keyword and make a fuzzy search to extract all the words and expressions with the same segment as the DEF, including synclass, synonyms, hyponyms, etc.

Let us take "programming" as the given word. Its DEF is: DEF={compile|编辑:ContentProduct={software|软件}}. When we make a fuzzy search with this DEF as the keyword, we find three DEFs which involve {compile|编辑:ContentProduct={software|软件}}, and as a result we extract the following words and phrases:

> ALGOL, FORTRAN, Java, LISP, Prolog, algebraic language, algorithmic language, application-oriented language, program, assembly language, programmer, etc.

Step 2. To extract all the antonymous or converse words and expressions. For example, the DEF of "pauper" is: DEF={human|人:modifier={poor|穷}}.

The antonyms of "pauper" are:

> billionaire, boss, countrified moneybag, financial magnate, great riches, landlord, magnate, man of wealth, millionaire, money bags, moneybag, multimillionaire, plutocrat, rich man, potbellied merchant, rich merchant, rich person, tycoon, zillionaire, etc.

Step 3. To extract all the words and expressions with the same values of domain and "RelateTo" as that of the given word if it has, using fuzzy search with the domain value and "RelateTo" value. For example,

"jump ball"

DEF={phenomena|现象:domain={basketball|篮球}}

The result of extracting with the same domain value includes:

> backboard, basketball, basketball backboard, basketball circle, basketball court, basketball game, basketball league, basketball match, basketball player, basketball team, guard, holding, jump ball,

men's basketball, professional basketball, rebound, rim, tap-off, tip-off, women's basketball;

"homepage"
DEF={readings|读物:RelateTo={internet|因特网}}

The result of extracting with the same RelateTo value includes:
Internet courting, in the internet, e-mail address, log off, WWW, web, upload, chat room, off line, mass email, email, spam

Step 4. To deal with the given word or expression according to different categorial sememes (entity, event, attribute and attribute-value).

Step 4.1. Entity category

Step 4.1.1. To treat the roles "CoEvent" and "time"

If the roles "CoEvent" or "time" is found in the DEF of the given word or expression, we extract all the words and expressions which contain the same values of "CoEvent" and "time". Suppose we take "metrorrhagia" as the given word, whose DEF is: DEF={disease|疾病:CoEvent={bleed|出血}}. Then we extract all the words and expressions which contain {bleed|出血} in their DEFs:
bleeding, nosebleed, uterine bleeding, hemorrhagic, shed blood, massive haemorrhage, bleed, internal haemorrhage, lose blood, spit blood, have a hemorrhage, hemorrhage

Step 4.1.2. To take the segment headed by an event sememe as a keyword to make a fuzzy search and extract all the words and expressions containing the segment, if the entity's DEF contains event sememe (s). Let's take "savings bank" as an example. Its DEF is:

DEF={InstitutePlace|场所:domain={finance|金融},
{SetAside|留存:location={~},possession={money|货币}},
{TakeBack|取回:location={~},possession={money|货币}}}

In this DEF we find two segments headed by event sememes, "SetAside|留存" and "TakeBack|取回". We take the description node "location={~}" out of the two segments, use the remaining parts,

{SetAside|留存:possession={money|货币}} and {TakeBack|取回:possession={money|货币}}, and make a fuzzy search to extract all the words and expressions with these two remaining segment. So we can get the following result:

Bank of China, DBS Bank, Federal Reserve Bank, HSBC Bank, bank corruption, commercial bank, credit card, deposit book, domestic branch, overseas branch, etc.

Step 4.1.3. To take the complex segment of a "whole" from the DEF of an entity as the keyword to make a fuzzy search and extract all the words and expressions whose DEF contain the whole segment. For example, the DEF of "finger" is:

DEF={part|部件:whole=
{part|部件:PartPosition={hand|手},whole={human|人}}}

We take the complex segment, {part|部件:PartPosition={hand|手},whole={human|人}}, to make a fuzzy search and the result is:

wave, applaud, beckon, clapping, clench, click, finger tip, fist, forefinger, hand, palm, script, snap, thumb, win, etc.

Step 4.1.4. To take some specific segments in the DEF of the given word's categorial sememe in the taxonomy. If in the DEF we can find an event sememe, we will select the following semantic roles under the event sememe: ContentProduct, location, content, instrument. Let us take the word "small fish" as an example. Its DEF is: DEF={fish|鱼:modifier={small|小}}, and its categorial sememe is {fish|鱼}; and in the taxonomy we find its DEF is:

{animal|兽:{alive|活着:experiencer={~},location={waters|水域}},{swim|游:agent={~}},{eat|吃:patient={~}},MaterialOf={edible|食物}}

In this DEF we find an event sememe, "alive|活着" and two semantic roles under it: "experiencer" and "location", and we select {waters|水域}

in location={waters|水域} to make a fuzzy search. So we can extract the following words and expressions:

yellow sea, oceanic trench, offshore, draft, voyage, dive, sink, tide, water level, seascape, sheepshead etc.

It should be noted that this step is conducted only for Rank 3.

Step 4.2. Event category

Step 4.2.1. To take a specific segment or sememe in the DEF of the given word or expression and make a fuzzy search to extract all the relevant words and expressions. Let us take "treat a disease" as an example. Its DEF is: DEF={doctor|医治:content={disease|疾病},domain={medical|医}}.

Taking "{disease|疾病}" as the keyword and making a fuzzy search, we get the following result:

AIDS, Alzheimer's disease, BSE, Balkan Syndrome, Black Death, CDC, Down syndrome, Down's syndrome, E.N.T. department, ER, Ebola virus disease, German measles, Graves' disease, Gulf War Syndrome, HNC, Hodgkin's disease, etc.

Step 4.2.2. To take one of the sememes in the event frame of the categorial sememe of the given word and expression and make a fuzzy search to extract all the relevant words and expressions. Let us take "steal" as an example. Its DEF is: DEF={steal|偷} and its event frame is: {take|取:agent={*},possession={*},source={*},manner={covert|隐秘}}

We take {covert|隐秘} as the keyword and make a fuzzy search and extract all the relevant words and expressions as follows:

abscond, abscondment, argot, assassinate, assassination, backstage, be hermit, call secretly, caucus, clandestine, concealed, conclave, confidential talk, covert place, decampment, dubious, eavesdrop, enigmatic, enigmatically, furtive, etc.

Step 4.3. Attribute category

Step 4.3.1. To take all the attribute-values corresponding to the categorial sememe of the given word and expression as the keywords and make an exact search and extract all the words and expressions. To take the word "health" as an example, its DEF is:{Health|健康:host={AnimalHuman|动物}}, and its categorial sememe is: {Health|健康}, whose corresponding attribute-values are:

{HealthValue|健康值}

==> {healthy|康健}

==> {unhealthy|不健}

After making an exact search using {healthy|康健} and {unhealthy|不健} as the keywords, we get the result as follows:

full of sap, full of vigour and vitality, hale and hearty, healthily, healthy, healthy and vigorous, healthy and well, healthy in old age, in good health, in one's prime, in the prime of life, strong, delicate, sick and weak, sickly

Step 4.3.2. To treat semantic role "scope". Let us take the word "hearing" as an example. Its DEF is:{Ability|能力:host={AnimalHuman|动物},scope={listen|听}}. By taking {listen|听} and making a fuzzy search, we get the following result:

acute hearing, audiology, listen, listen in, turn a deaf ear to, bug, eavesdrop, overhear, take in, telephone tapping, wiretap, etc.

Step 4.4. Attribute-value category

Step 4.4.1. To take the attribute corresponding to the categorial sememe of the given word and expression as the keyword and make a fuzzy search and extract all the words and expressions. To take the word "pink" as an example, its DEF is:{red|红:degree={light|淡}}. And its categorial sememe is: {red|红}, whose corresponding attribute is:{Color|颜色}.

After making a fuzzy search using {Color|颜色} as the keyword, we get the result as follows:

aberration, black race, chroma, chromatogram, color, color property, complexion contrast, cool colour, cryptic coloration, dark colors, deep or light, design and colour, discolour, dithered color, fade, filter, food color, harmonize colours, look, lose colour, magenta, match colours, mauve, melanin, mix colours, palette, pure color, red race, shade, spectroscopy, spectrum, tarnish, tone, tricolor, warm tones, etc.

Step 4.4.2. To treat semantic role "scope". Let us take the word "decorative" as an example. Its DEF is:{{able|能:scope={decorate|装饰}}. By taking {decorate|装饰} and making a fuzzy search, we get the following result:

anklet, artificial flower, azurite, backdrop, background, bracelet, breast pin, bric-a-brac, brooch, canopy, carpet, casket, curtain, deck, decorations, dress up, embellishment, frontlet, garland, garniture, handicraft, jade article, jewelry, necklace, necklet, etc.

Finally, let us introduce an important function which is most frequently used in CRC for taking a specific part out of a DEF.

void Capture_Def (const S_DEF* ApsDef , S_DEF* ApsRlt , int AnCurNode)

parameters:	ApsDef	source DEF
	ApsRlt	buffer for extracted results
	AnCurNode	initial node of segment
return value :	None	

The function is used to taking out of a DEF the segment which we find the key feature and to use the segment to extract all the words and expressions from HowNet knowledge database.

Let us take the word "hospital" as an example. Its DEF is:

DEF={InstitutePlace|场所:domain={medical|医}, {doctor|医治:content={disease|疾病},location={~}}}

If we want to take the second segment out of the DEF, by using the function we intend to take {doctor|医治:content={disease|疾病}}, rather than {doctor|医治:content={disease|疾病},location={~}}, because the segment with {~} is not grammatical in KDML. When using this function and making a search with the keyword of {doctor|医治:content={disease|疾病}, we can extract much more correct words and expressions.

11.2. Concept Similarity Measure (CSM)

Concept Similarity Measure (CSM) is able to measure the similarity between any senses of any words and expressions in HowNet. In HowNet the measurement of similarity is based on the concept, it proves to achieve a very high accuracy. Table 11.1 displays the results of the similarity between the concept "doctor" denoting "licensed medical practitioner" and some other concepts related to medical domain respectively.

Table 11.1.

concept1	**concept2**	**similarity value**
doctor	physician	1.000000
doctor	surgeon	0.950000
doctor	nurse	0.883333
doctor	pharmacist	0.550000
doctor	anesthetist	0.340000
doctor	patient	0.203636
doctor	symptom	0.021053
doctor	disease	0.018605
doctor	therapy	0.018605

When discussing relevance and similarity, it is significant for us to have a clear distinction between (1) similarity and relevance in meaning; (2) similarity and co-occurrence in context, and (3) similarity and collocation in usage. The similarity defined in HowNet is based on the meaning; it has nothing to do with relevance, for example, "doctor" and "dentist" are of high similarity — 0.883333, as shown in Fig. 11.1, but "doctor" and "fever" are of very low similarity — 0.001247 as shown in Fig. 11.2 — in fact they have no similarity in meaning, but they are of high relevancy. Collocation in essence is a question of usage of words and particularly of idiom in a language, for example, the words "watch" and "TV" collocate but the words "see" and "TV" do not, though "see" and "watch" are close synonymous.

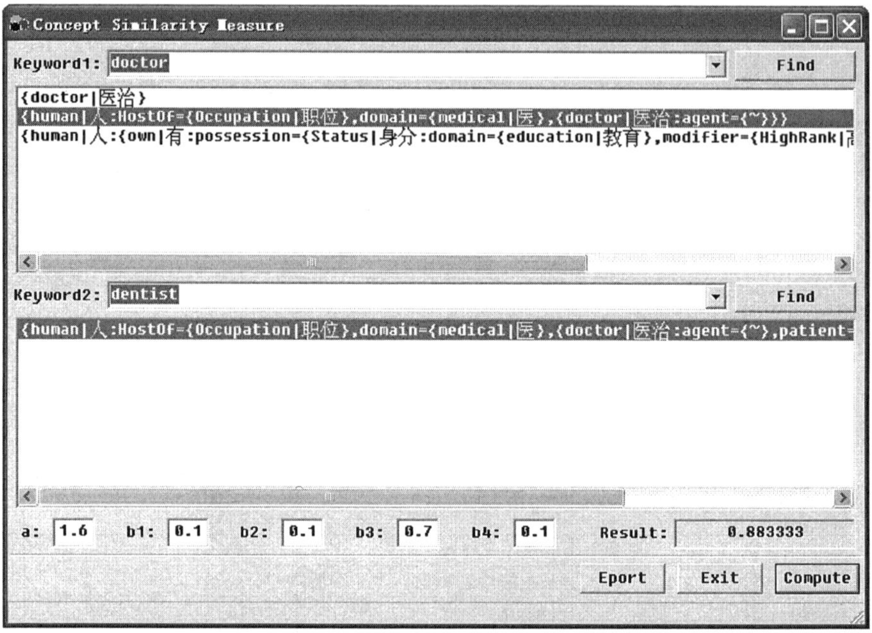

Fig. 11.1. Result of the similarity measurement (1).

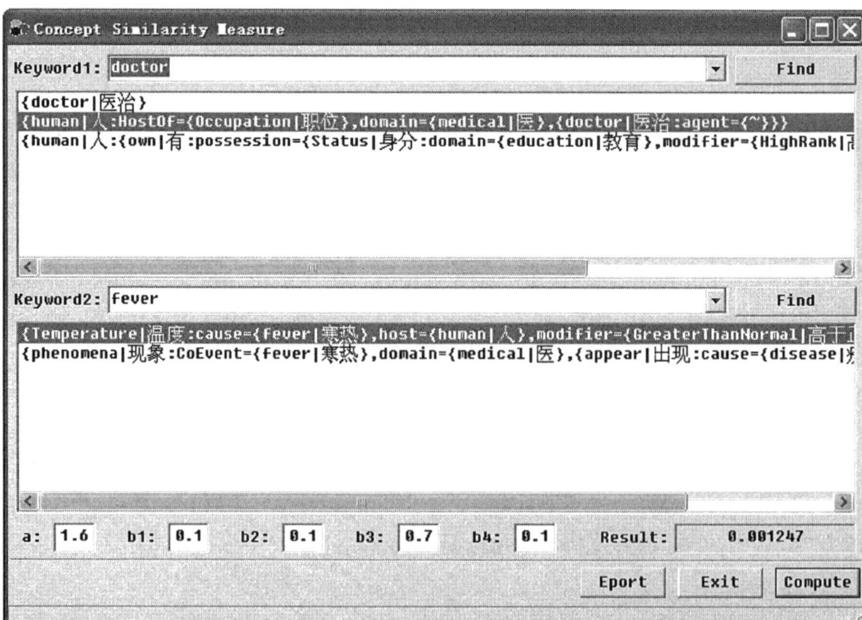

Fig. 11.2. Result of the similarity measurement (2).

Besides, the similarity defined by HowNet is irrelevant with syntactic features and the usage of the words and expressions. A comparison between the different senses of the words "treat" and "treatment" is shown in Table 11.2.

Table 11.2. Result of the similarity measurement (3).

concept1	concept2	similarity value
treat {doctor|医治}	treatment{doctor|医治}	1.000000
treat {doctor|医治}	treatment {treat|对待}	0.018605
treat {treat|对待}	treatment{doctor|医治}	0.018605
treat {treat|对待}	treatment {treat|对待}	1.000000

11.2.1. *Algorithm of CSM*

The algorithm of CSM includes the following steps:

Step 1. To check the two given concepts: if they are synonyms, then the similarity is 1.000000. For example, the concepts "doctor" denoting "licensed medical practitioner" and "doc" are synonyms, their similarity is 1.000000, that is, S(c1,c2) = 1.000000.

Step 2. To check the two given concepts: if they are of synclass, then the similarity is 0.950000. For example, the concepts "doctor" denoting "licensed medical practitioner" and "surgeon" are of synclass, their similarity is 0.950000, that is, S(c1,c2) = 0.950000.

Step 3. To check the two given concepts: if they are antonyms or converse, then the similarity is 0.000000. For example, the concepts "poor man" and "rich man" are antonyms, their similarity is 0.000000, that is, S(c1,c2) = 0.000000; the concepts "agree" and "disagree" are converse, their similarity is 0.000000, that is, S(c1,c2) = 0.000000.

Step 4. To compute based on the following special semantic roles: CoEvent and MaterialOf by taking the values of these semantic roles as the DEF of the concepts. For example, the DEF of "charity" is:

DEF={affairs|事务:CoEvent={TakeCare|照料:manner=
{voluntary|自愿}}{help|帮助:manner={voluntary|自愿}}}

When computing the similarity of "charity", we regard its DEF as:

{TakeCare|照料:manner={voluntary|自愿}}{help|帮助:
manner={voluntary|自愿}}

The DEF of the concept "paper pulp" is:

DEF={material|材料:MaterialOf={material|材料:
{wrap|包扎:instrument={~}},{write|写:LocationFin={~}}}}

When computing the similarity of "paper pulp", we regard its DEF as:

{material|材料:
{wrap|包扎:instrument={~}},{write|写:LocationFin={~}}}

Step 5. To check the two given concepts: if they do not fit the cases in the above steps 1~3, some refined computing should be conducted.

Step 5.1. To check the two given concepts to see if their DEFs are mutually including or not, then a value of p1 will be given. If the two DEFs are mutually including, then p1=1.000000; if not, then p1=0.000000. Let us look at the DEFs of the concepts "psychotherapist" and "doctor":

"psychotherapist":
DEF={human|人:HostOf={Occupation|职位},
domain={medical|医},{doctor|医治:agent={~},
content={disease|疾病:cause={mental|精神}}}}

"doctor":
DEF={human|人:HostOf={Occupation|职位},
domain={medical|医},{doctor|医治:agent={~}}}

The DEF of "doctor" is imbedded in the DEF of "psychotherapist", then p1= 1.000000.

Step 5.2. To check the categorial sememes (the first unit of DEF) of the two given concepts to see the similarity between them, and p2 will be given. As all the sememes are organized into a hierarchy representing hypernymous/hyponymous relations, we can compute the semantic distance between the two sememes. Suppose the distance of the two sememes is d, and is based on formula (1).

$$p2 = \alpha/(d + \alpha). \quad (1)$$

d is the distance between the categorial sememe of the first concept and the categorial sememe of the second concept in the sememe hierarchy, which is a positive integer. we specify $\alpha = 1.6$.

Let us look at the computing of the distance between the sememes "human|人" and "tree|树" as an example.

The hypernym tree of "human|人" is:

entity|实体
==> thing|万物
  ==> physical|物质
    ==> animate|生物
      ==> AnimalHuman|动物
        ==> human|人

and the hypernym tree of "tree|树" is:

entity|实体
==> thing|万物
  ==> physical|物质
    ==> animate|生物
      ==> plant|植物
        ==> tree|树

We find that the common hypernym of the two sememes is "animate|生物" and the length between the two sememes and their hypernym is two steps respectively, so the distance between the two sememes is 4 steps, that is, $d = 4$.

$$\begin{aligned} p2 &= \alpha/(d + \alpha) \\ &= 1.6/(4+1.6) \\ &= 1.6/5.6 \\ &= 0.285714. \end{aligned}$$

Step 5.3. To check the similarity in description node between the two DEFs, then p3 is given. The computation is based on formula (2):

$$p3 = Ns*2/(Nc1+Nc2). \quad (2)$$

Note: Description node is a combination made by "semantic role = sememe" or "ZeroRole = sememe".

Ns denotes the number of the same description nodes in the DEFs of the given two concepts;

Nc1 denotes the number of description nodes in the DEF of the first given concept;

Nc2 denotes the number of description nodes in the DEF of the second given concept.

Let us compare the description nodes of the following two concepts and show the result of comparison in Table 11.3.

"private instructor"
DEF={human|人:{teach|教:agent={~},
location={family|家庭}}}
"assistant"
DEF={human|人:HostOf={Occupation|职位},
{teach|教:agent={~}}}

Table 11.3. Result of comparison between description nodes (1).

4 description nodes of "private instructor"	4 description nodes of "assistant"
ZeroRole={human|人}	*ZeroRole={human|人}*
	HostOf={Occupation|职位}
ZeroRole={teach|教}	*ZeroRole={ teach|教}*
agent={~}	*agent={~}*
location={family|家庭}	

Table 11.3 shows "private instructor" and "assistant" have three same description nodes (in italic). The similarity in this stage is computed as follows:

p3(private instructor，assistant) = 3*2/(4+4)
= 6/8
= 0.750000.

One more comparison between the description nodes of the following two concepts and show the result of comparison in Table 11.4.

"senior student"
DEF={human|人:
{study|学习:agent={~},location={InstitutePlace|场所:
domain={education|教育},
{study|学习:location={~}},{teach|教:location={~}}}}}

"headmaster"
DEF={human|人:HostOf={Occupation|职位},
modifier={official|官},{manage|管理:agent={~},
patient={InstitutePlace|场所:domain={education|教育},
{study|学习:location={~}},{teach|教:location={~}}}}}

Table 11.4. Result of comparison between description nodes (2).

9 description nodes of "senior student"	11 description nodes of "headmaster"
ZeroRole={human|人}	*ZeroRole={human|人}*
	HostOf={Occupation|职位}
	modifier={official|官}
ZeroRole={study|学习}	ZeroRole={manage|管理}
agent={~}	agent={~}
location={InstitutePlace|场所}	patient={InstitutePlace|场所}
domain={education|教育}	domain={education|教育}
ZeroRole={study|学习}	ZeroRole={study|学习}
location={~}	location={~}
ZeroRole={ teach|教}	ZeroRole={ teach|教}
location={~}	location={~}

It seems that these two concepts have 7 same description nodes, but in fact they have only one same node (in italic), for apart from the first node {human | 人}, the rest six are governed by different father nodes: {study|学习} in "senior student" and {manage|管理} in "headmaster". Thus the similarity in this stage is as follows:

p3(senior student， headmaster) = 1*2/(9+11)
= 2/20
= 0.100000.

Step 5.4. In the hierarchy of the HowNet entity taxonomy, each sememe class has a definition, for instance, "human|人" has a definition as follows:

{AnimalHuman|动物:HostOf={Ability|能力}{Name|姓名}{Wisdom|智慧},{speak|说:agent={~}},{think|思考:agent={~}}}

As a sememe class is defined in the same form as a concept in the knowledge dictionary, Step 5.4 does the same computation as Step 5.3, that is, checking the similarity in description node between the definitions of the two sememe class, then p4 is given.

Step 5.5. Final computing of the similarity will be based on:

$$S(c1,c2) = (p1*\beta_1 + p2*\beta_2 + p3*\beta_3 + p4*\beta_4)*\gamma. \qquad (3)$$

β_1, β_2, β_3, β_4 are the weights for the different stages of computing. Their relation will be $\beta_1 + \beta_2 + \beta_3 + \beta_4 = 1$ and their respective values are: $\beta_1 = 0.1$, $\beta_2 = 0.1$， $\beta_3 = 0.7$， $\beta_4 = 0.1$

When two given concepts have the same event sememe at the same level and if there exists a contrastive pair of semantic roles under the event sememe in Table 11.5, then a penalty factor γ should be applied to the solution of Formula (3), we specify $\gamma = 0.35$. On the contrary, we specify $\gamma = 1.0$.

Table 11.5. Contrastive pairs of roles.

principal semantic roles	affected semantic roles
agent	patient
experiencer	target
relevant	content
existent	partner
possessor	PatientProduct
	PatientContent
	possession

Let us first look at the computing of similarity between "doctor" and "nurse". The DEFs of the two words are:

"doctor"

DEF={human|人:HostOf={Occupation|职位},
domain={medical|医},{doctor|医治:agent={~}}}

"nurse"

DEF={human|人:HostOf={Occupation|职位},
domain={medical|医},{TakeCare|照料:agent={~}}}

According to Step 5.1, the result is: p1 = 0.000000.

According to the formula (1) of Step 5.2, the result is:

$p2 = \alpha/(d + \alpha)$
$= 1.6/(0 + 1.6)$
$= 1.000000.$

Then the computation according to p3 = Ns*2/(Nc1+Nc2) of Step 5.3 is conducted:

According to Table 11.6, Ns = 3, Nc1 = 5, Nc2 = 5

p3 = Ns*2/(Nc1+Nc2)
= 3*2/(5+5)
= 6/10
= 0.600000.

Table 11.6. Result of comparison between description nodes (3).

5 description nodes of "doctor"	5 description nodes of "nurse"
ZeroRole={{human|人}	*ZeroRole={{human|人}*
HostOf={Occupation|职位}	*HostOf={Occupation|职位}*
domain={medical|医}	*domain={medical|医}*
ZeroRole={doctor|医治}	ZeroRole={TakeCare|照料}
agent={~}	agent={~}

Then Step 5.4 is followed. The categorial sememes of "doctor" and "nurse" are the same: "human|人", whose DEF in the taxonomy is: {AnimalHuman|动物:HostOf={Ability|能力}{Name|姓名}{Wisdom|智慧},{speak|说:agent={~}},{think|思考:agent={~}}}

Table 11.7. Description nodes of "human|人".

8 description nodes of "human|人"
ZeroRole={ AnimalHuman|动物}
HostOf={Ability|能力}
HostOf={Name|姓名}
HostOf={Wisdom|智慧}
ZeroRole={ speak|说}
agent={~}
ZeroRole={ think|思考}
agent={~}

The result is:

p4 = Ns*2/(Nc1+Nc2)
 = 8*2/(8+8)
 = 1.000000.

As the two given words have the same event sememe at the same level and there do not exist a contrastive pair of semantic roles under the event sememe in Table 11.5, $\gamma = 1.0$.

Finally the similarity between "doctor" and "nurse" is:

$S(doctor,nurse) = (p1*\beta_1 + p2*\beta_2 + p3*\beta_3 + p4*\beta_4)*\gamma$
= (0.000000*0.1+1.000000*0.1+0.600000*0.7+1.000000*0.1)*1.0
= (0.000000+0.100000+0.420000+0.10000)*1.0
= 0.620000.

Let us see what the similarity between "doctor" and "patient" is then. The DEFs of "doctor" and "patient" are:

"doctor"
DEF={human|人:HostOf={Occupation|职位},
domain={medical|医},{doctor|医治:agent={~}}}

"patient"
DEF={human|人:domain={medical|医},{SufferFrom|罹患:
experiencer={~}},{doctor|医治:patient={~}}}

The computation according to Step 5.1 gives the result: p1 = 0.000000, and according to the formula (1) in Step 5.2, the computation is:

p2 = $\alpha/(d + \alpha)$
= 1.6/(0+1.6)
= 1.000000.

Then we come to Step 5.3, the computation according to the formula:
p3 = Ns*2/(Nc1+Nc2).
According to Table 11.6, we can get: Ns = 3, Nc1 = 5, Nc2 = 5
p3 = Ns*2/(Nc1+Nc2)
= 3*2/(5+6)
= 6/11
= 0.545455.

Table 11.6. Result of comparison between description nodes (4).

5 description nodes of "doctor"	6 description nodes of "patient"
ZeroRole={{human|人}	*ZeroRole={{human|人}*
HostOf={Occupation|职位}	
domain={medical|医}	*domain={medical|医}*
ZeroRole={doctor|医治}	*ZeroRole={doctor|医治}*
agent={~}	patient={~}
	ZeroRole={ SufferFrom|罹患}
	experiencer={~}

Then Step 5.4 is followed. The categorial sememes of "doctor" and "patient" are the same: "human|人", whose DEF in the taxonomy is:

{AnimalHuman|动物:HostOf={Ability|能力}{Name|姓名}{Wisdom|智慧},{speak|说:agent={~}},{think|思考:agent={~}}}

The result is:
p4 = Ns*2/(Nc1+Nc2)
= 8*2/(8+8)
= 1.000000.

As the two given words have the same event sememe at the same level and there exists a contrastive pair of semantic roles under the event sememe in Table 11.5, $\gamma = 0.35$.

ZeroRole={doctor|医治}	ZeroRole={doctor|医治}
agent={~}	patient={~}

According to Step 5.5:

$S(doctor,patient) = (p1*\beta_1 + p2*\beta_2 + p3*\beta_3 + p4*\beta_4)*\gamma$

$= (0.000000*0.1+1.000000*0.1+0.545455*0.7+1.000000*0.1)*0.35$

$= (0.000000+0.100000+0.3818185+0.100000)*0.35$

$= 0.5818185*0.35$

$= 0.203636.$

To sum up, our intuition tells us that the similarity between "doctor" and "patient" should differ from that between "doctor" and "nurse". It should be believed that the following result given by HowNet CSM is reasonable and acceptable:

similarity between "doctor" and "nurse" is 0.620000.

similarity between "doctor" and "patient" is 0.203636.

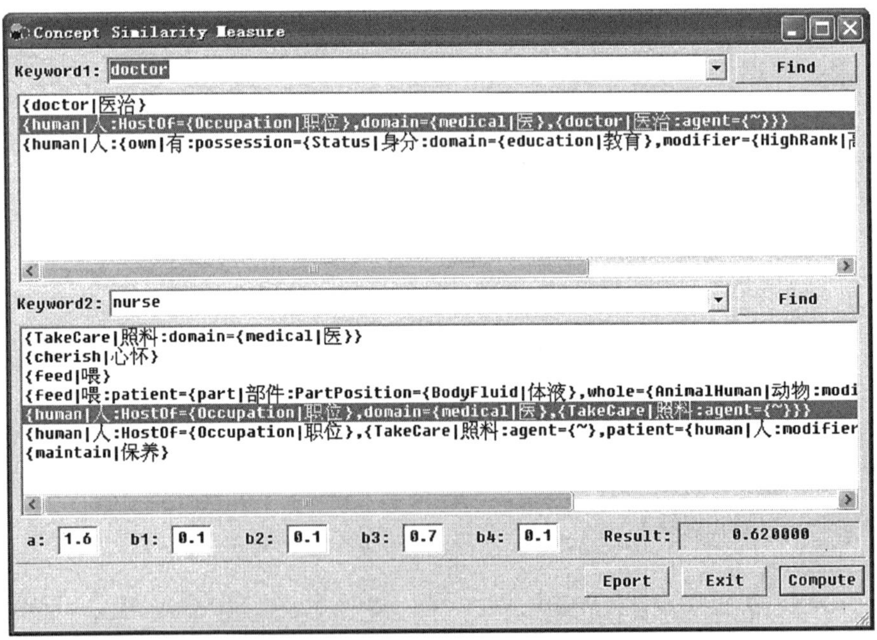

Fig. 11.3. Result of the similarity measurement (3).

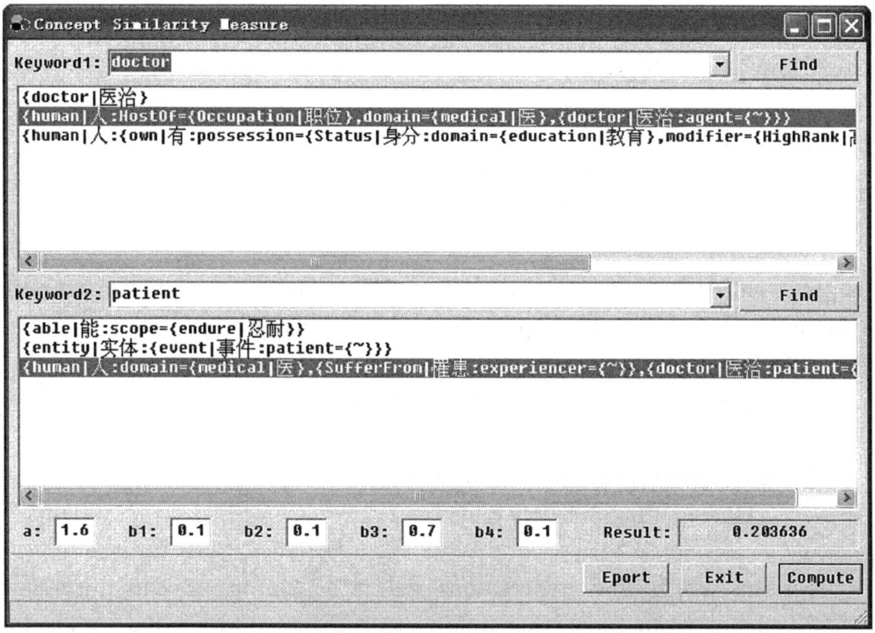

Fig. 11.4. Result of the similarity measurement (4).

11.3. Query Expansion Tool (QET)

The HowNet-based query-expansion tool is designed to be used in an interactive for a search engine.

11.3.1. *Three ranks*

The tool is mainly based on three types of semantic relations: (1) synonymous words and expressions as the first-rank expansion, (2) synclass words and expressions as the second rank expansion, and (3) part of hyponymous words and expressions as the third-rank expansion. To take English word "TV" as an example:

(a) First-rank expansion (2 entries):
TV, television

(b) Second-rank expansion (7 entries):

TV, TV program, TV show, satellite TV, stage photo, television, television program

(c) Third-rank expansion (9 entries):
MTV, TV, TV program, TV show, music TV, satellite TV, stage photo, television, television program

The words and expressions of the first-rank and the second-rank usually have the same concept definitions, for instance:

"TV" (first-rank)
DEF={image|图像:RelateTo={shows|表演物}}

"television program" (second-rank)
DEF={image|图像:RelateTo={shows|表演物}}

But the words and expressions that are peculiar to the third-rank usually differ from those that belong to the first and second ranks, for instance:

"MTV"
DEF={image|图像:RelateTo={music|音乐}{shows|表演物}}

Let us take "teacher" as one more example. Its first-rank expansion includes four words: educator, instructor, school teacher, teacher. The results of its second-rank and third-rank expansions are shown in Fig. 11.5 and Fig. 11.6.

11.3.2. *Cross-language*

When the query expansion tool is applied as an interactive in a search engine, it can be used in a cross-language way. Through the dialogue box the user may choose the function which can automatically shift from one language, say, English to the other, say, Chinese. Let us take the English word "teacher" again as an example. When we input it as a query and if we give a positive answer to the cross-language dialogue box of the interactive, the interactive may provide us the expansion selections in both the languages, for example, from "teacher" to the Chinese equivalent "教师", and thus provides the three-rank expansion in Chinese, as shown as follows:

(a) First-rank expansion (8 entries), as shown in Fig. 11.7:
教师, 教书匠, 教书先生, 教员, 老师, 师长, 先生, 园丁

(b) Second-rank expansion (25 entries), as shown in Fig. 11.8:
班主任, 博导, 博士生导师, 大学讲师, 导师, 恩师, 夫子, 副教授, 级主任, 讲师, 教师, 教授, 教书匠, 教书先生, 教员, 客座教授, 老师, 师长, 实习教师, 硕导, 先生, 业师, 园丁, 正教授, 助教

(c) Third-rank expansion (29 entries), as shown in Fig. 11.9:
班主任, 博导, 博士生导师, 大学讲师, 导师, 督学, 恩师, 夫子, 副教授, 级主任, 讲师, 教师, 教授, 教书匠, 教书先生, 教员, 客座教授, 老师, 名师, 女校长, 师长, 实习教师, 硕导, 先生, 校长, 业师, 园丁, 正教授, 助教

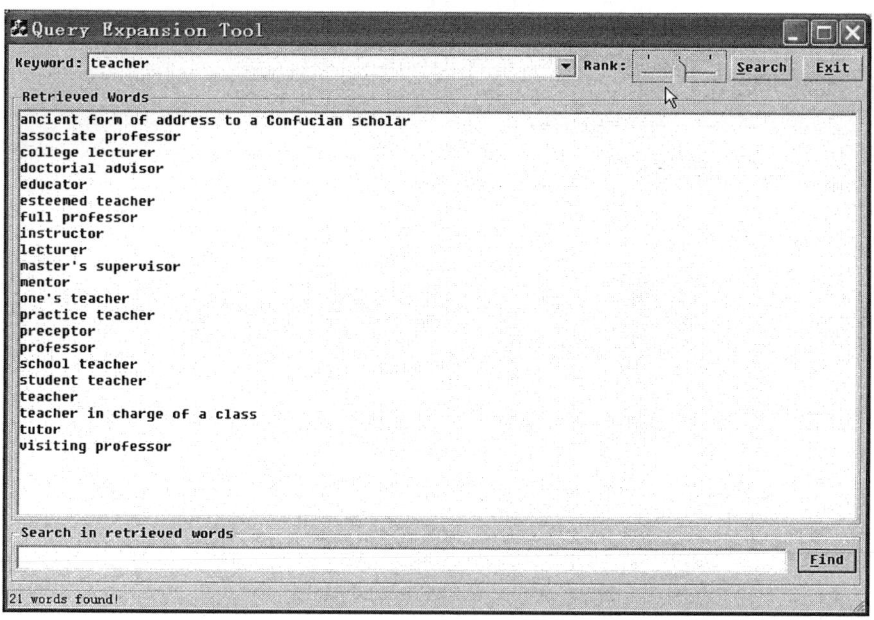

Fig. 11.5. Result of query expansion (1).

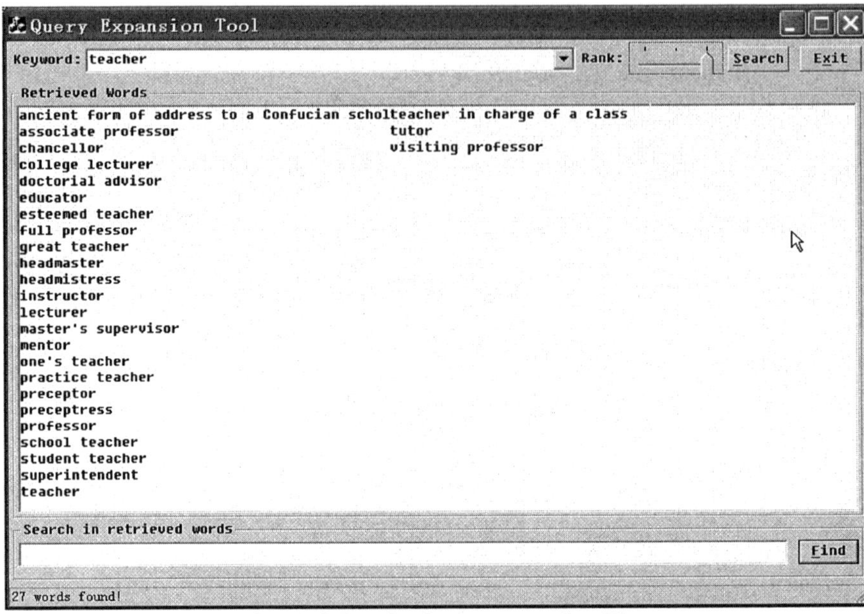

Fig. 11.6. Result of query expansion (2).

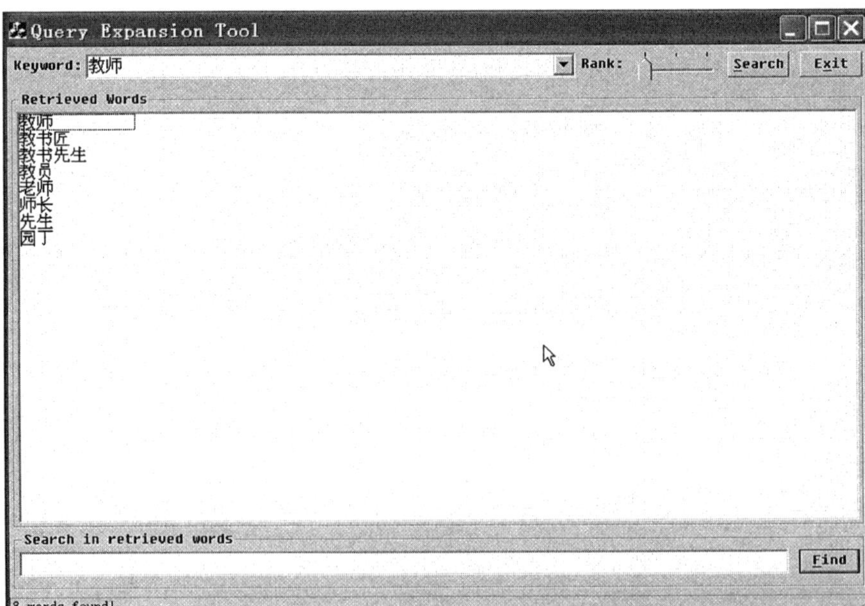

Fig. 11.7. Result of query expansion (3).

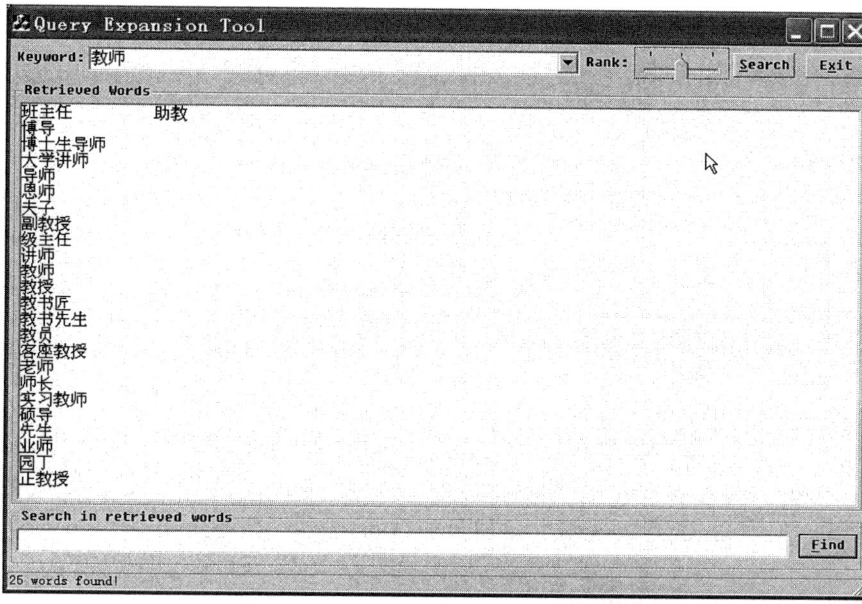

Fig. 11.8. Result of query expansion (4).

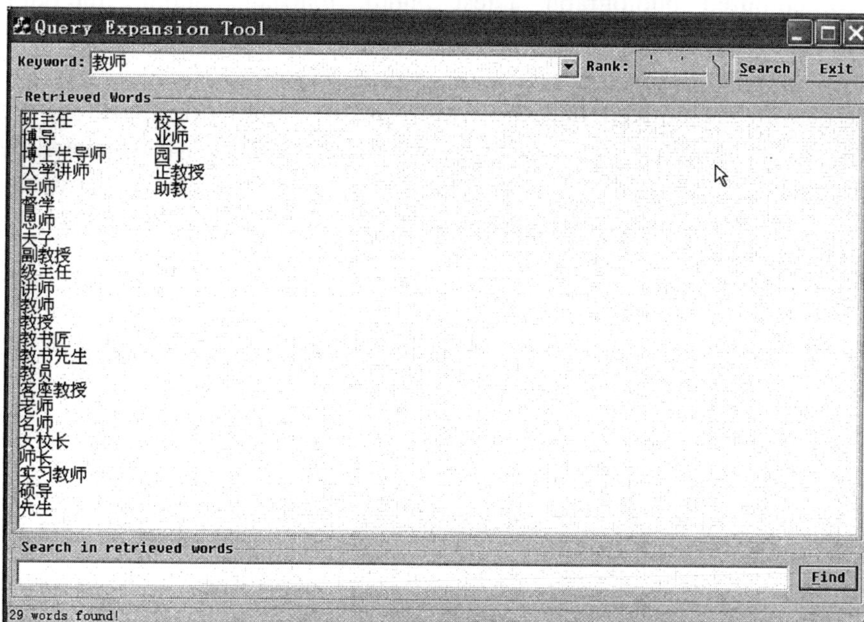

Fig. 11.9. Result of query expansion (5).

11.3.3. *Restraint of over-expansion*

In query expansion, one of the most crucial issues is how to avoid over-expansion, that is, over-generation of the queries that the tool may provides. It would be easy for HowNet to restrain over-expansion by the sense count of the word or expression if it is chosen as a query. For example, if we choose the English word "photo" as a query, the expansion results that the tool gives is as follows:

first-rank: (2 entries)
photo, photograph

second-rank: (10 entries)
bareheaded photo, black-and-white photo, group photo, photo, group picture, half-length bareheaded photograph, stereoscopic photograph, stereoscopic picture, full-faced photo, stereo

third-rank: (23 entries)
coloured photograph, latest photo, marriage photo, microdot, phlebogram, microphotograph, ...

It may be noticed that the word "picture" does not appear in the expansion although it is one of the synonyms of "photo". It is deleted by the tool because it has 6 senses in the knowledge dictionary of HowNet. A rule is set in the query expansion tool that any word should not be taken as a query or an expansion if it has 3 or more than 3 senses.

Chapter 12

HOWNET AS A SOFTWARE

As discussed previously, the goal of HowNet system is strongly computer-oriented. In the previous chapters we illustrated how HowNet recognizes the world, how HowNet describes knowledge, and how HowNet intends to make the computation of meaning. Nevertheless, if we just kept the elaboration and description as some static theory, it would be meaningless to computer and HLT. The computer-orientation needs to activate the static or isolated knowledge that HowNet provides and make it computable in concept relations and concept attribute relations. As we pointed out previously that most concept relations and attribute relations expressed by HowNet are not pre-coded manually and pre-stored in the system, instead they are computed on-line and in real time. How can HowNet achieve this? This chapter will give the answer and present HowNet as a software.

12.1. Data Construction

12.1.1. *Basic principles of programming*

The programming of HowNet software observes the following basic principles:

(1) To benefit the language engineers in developing and updating data. HowNet is characterized by its very large-scale volume of knowledge data and its very comprehensive and complex computation of meanings. The development of HowNet requires close collaboration between software

engineers and language engineers. In terms of software, its design achieves the separation between knowledge data construction and the implementation of software. The language engineers of HowNet can easily represent and edit the knowledge data in KDML needless to care about operation of software.

(2) The data management tool of HowNet guarantees highly consistency of the knowledge data and detection of redundancy or duplication of data. As all the knowledge data in HowNet are manually coded, it is critical to maintain their consistency.

(3) Speed and effectiveness of HowNet programs are crucial. Users can feel its speed when they test HowNet browser and secondary tools of computation of meaning.

12.1.2. *Different types of database in HowNet*

As aforesaid, HowNet is not an on-line bilingual dictionary, but a very complex knowledge system. The construction of data is not merely a static storage of data, but should form various complicated relations. This is the reason why we do not adopt any current database. The data of HowNet are divided into two parts: Taxonomy database and Dictionary database.

(1) Taxonomy database

HowNet Taxonomy database includes 11 files, which all take pure text form.

Firstly, we should construct 9 files: Event, Entity, Attribute, AttributeValue, Sencondary Feature, Proper, Event Role & Feature, Sign, Part of speech. In these files, every line represents a node, with which a tree-structured relation is established.

Secondly, after constructing the 9 files, we would construct the rest of the two files. They are Antonymous sememes list and Converse sememes list, in which all the sememes exist as correspondent pairs.

Finally, we should construct the relations among Taxonomy files.

(2) Dictionary database

HowNet dictionary is a very large-scale database, which currently contains over 150,000 data records with 80,000 Chinese and English words and expressions respectively. Moreover the database undergoes very frequent modification and updating. Therefore its management tool should be of very high efficiency.

Firstly, we should check the records in their grammatical correctness.

(a) Record format checking: in constructing dictionary, every record should be checked in its format as well as its content. As aforesaid in HowNet dictionary each record is composed of 8 items: Record serial number, Chinese word or expression, Chinese grammatical information, Chinese examples, English word or phrase, English grammatical information, English examples, Concept definition.

(b) KDML grammar checking: in Chap. 8 KDML was presented in detail. In this step the management tool check every item of the record to guarantee its grammatical correctness. Besides the tool will compile KDML.

(c) Deduplicating: after grammar checking of KDML for each item of the record, the tool will detect record duplications and remove them if any.

Secondly, we should digitalize the records.

Finally, we index Chinese word or expression, English word or expression and DEF of each record respectively.

12.1.3. *KDML compilation*

(1) To select all the sememes and semantic roles out of the DEF in pure text and put them in a buffer, and record the amount;

(2) To check the level and the match between left and right braces;

(3) To spell check every sememe and semantic role;

(4) To check the punctuations used in the record;

(5) To check DEF for its reasonableness to avoid the following errors:

a. coordinate ZeroRole

wrong:

{human|人:{doctor|医治:agent={~}}{discharge|开除:patient={~}}}

right:
{human|人:{doctor|医治:agent={~}},{discharge|开除:patient={~}}}

b. with the exception of categorial sememe, any non-event sememes preceded by no semantic role
wrong:
{human|人:{Occupation|职位},{doctor|医治:agent={~}}}
right:
{human|人:HostOf={Occupation|职位},{doctor|医治:agent={~}}}

c. any duplications of segment
wrong:
{human|人:{doctor|医治:agent={~}},{doctor|医治:agent={~}}}
right:
{human|人:{doctor|医治:agent={~}}}

d. any duplications of semantic role
wrong:
{human|人:domain={medical|医},domain={economy|经济}}
right:
{human|人:domain={medical|医}{economy|经济}}

e. omission of referent relation by swung-dash in braces:{~}
wrong:
{human|人:HostOf={Occupation|职位},{doctor|医治}}
right:
{human|人:HostOf={Occupation|职位},{doctor|医治:agent={~}}}

f. non-attribute-value for the semantic role modifier
wrong:
{human|人:modifier={economy|经济}}
right:
{human|人:modifier={female|女}}

g. omission of "host" for a categorial sememe of attribute
wrong:

{Color|颜色}
right:
{Color|颜色:host={physical|物质}}

h. referent relation by swung-dash in braces: {~} with no precedent governing event sememe
wrong:
{human|人:agent={~}}
right:
{human|人:{teach|教:agent={~}}}

(6) To sort: Sorting of the records in HowNet dictionary observes the following guidelines:

a. according to the order of their categorial sememes;

b. according to the alphabetical order of their semantic roles if the order of the categorial sememes are the same;

c. according to the alphabetical order of the values of their semantic roles if the orders of the categorial sememes and semantic roles are the same;

(7) To store the DEF that has been checked and sorted into a self-defined structure(S_DEF) which contains three items: number of segments, number of sememes and content of segments.

```
struct S_DEF
{
    BYTE        NodeNum;              //   number of segments
    BYTE        SemeNum;              //   number of sememes
    S_DEF_NODE  Node[Max_Num];        //   content of segments
};
struct S_DEF_NODE
{
    WORD Domai;   //   semantic role in digital code
    WORD Class;   //   value of the semantic role in digital code
    char        Fathe;   //   parent segment ID
    char        Exten;   //   extend ID
    char        Layer;   //   segment layer
```

```
    char        S_Off;  //    segment ID of first son
};
```

12.2. Application Program Interface (API) of HowNet

HowNet provide users not only the database but also many APIs. We will introduce some important APIs of HowNet in this section.

(1) bool HowNet_Initial (void)

Function Description: To initialize the data in HowNet;

Return Value: The function returns true if the initialization is successful, otherwise returns false;

Parameters: None.

Remarks: The function should be called before all other functions. The function needs the indexing file "hownet.idx". The absence of the file leads to failure of initialization.

Sample Code:

*/*To initialize the data of HowNet system. If it fails, gives the error message. */*

```
#include "HowNet.h"
CHOWNET_API cHowNet_Api;

if(!cHowNet_Api.HowNet_Initial())
{
MessageBox(cHowNet_Api.HowNet_Get_ErrMsg(), "Warning",
MB_OK);
}
```

(2) DWORD HowNet_GetUnitNum(void)

Function Description: To get the total number of the records in HowNet dictionary;

Return Value: Total number of records in HowNet dictionary;

Parameters: None.

Remarks: As described in Chap. 7, the knowledge dictionary of HowNet is composed by the records each of which contains 8 items as shown below:

NO.= Record serial number
W_C= Chinese word or expression
G_C= Chinese POS, phonetic transcription
E_C= Chinese examples
W_E= English word or phrase
G_E= English POS
E_E= English examples
DEF= Concept definition

Sample Code:

*/*To get the total number of the records in HowNet dictionary*/*

```
#include "HowNet.h"
CHOWNET_API cHowNet_Api;

/*To initialize the data of HowNet system*/
if(!cHowNet_Api.HowNet_Initial())
   return;

/*To get the total number of the records in HowNet dictionary*/
DWORD dwUnitNum = cHowNet_Api.HowNet_GetUnitNum()
```

(3) WORD HowNet_Search_Keyword
(char* ApStr, S_HOWNET_SEARCHMODE AsSearchMode)

Function Description: To search according to the given keyword;

Return Value: To return the number of the records that have been searched;

Parameters:

ApStr	the given keyword
AsSearchMode	ways of searching

Remarks:

"sHowNet_SearchMode" is a structure which is defined as follow:

```
struct S_HOWNET_SEARCHMODE
{
BYTE language;        //    search languages
WORD mode;            //    search modes
};
```

a. Parameter "language" has three values to be selected:
HOWNET_LANGUAGE_CHINESE: to search in Chinese;
HOWNET_LANGUAGE_ENGLISH: to search in English;
HOWNET_LANGUAGE_FEATURE: to search in KDML;

b. Parameter "mode" has six values to be selected:

HowNet_SearchMode_Exact:	exact search
HowNet_SearchMode_First:	initial word search
HowNet_SearchMode_Fuzzy:	fuzzy search
HowNet_SearchMode_Fuzzy_Abbr:	fuzzy abbr search
HowNet_SearchMode_Fuzzy_Jump:	fuzzy jump search
HowNet_SearchMode_Last:	ending word search

Using this function we can get the search result according to the specific search mode and the given keyword. Normally we use it together with the following functions in order to get the specific search result we expect:

HowNet_Get_SearchResult,
HowNet_Get_Unit_Item

In this case, function HowNet_Search_Keyword will be first called to get the number of the records found; then function HowNet_Get_SearchResult will be called afterwards to get the array of the serial numbers of the searched records; finally function HowNet_Get_Unit_Item will be called to get the specific record that is expected.

It should be cautioned that the search mode and the search language should be well-matched, otherwise the search will fail. Table 12.1 shows the match between the search mode and the search language.

Table 12.1. Match between the search mode and the search language.

Search mode	Available language
HowNet_SearchMode_Exact HowNet_SearchMode_Fuzzy HowNet_SearchMode_First	HOWNET_LANGUAGE_CHINESE HOWNET_LANGUAGE_ENGLISH HOWNET_LANGUAGE_FEATURE
HowNet_SearchMode_Last	HOWNET_LANGUAGE_CHINESE HOWNET_LANGUAGE_ENGLISH
HowNet_SearchMode_Fuzzy_Abbr HowNet_SearchMode_Fuzzy_Jump	HOWNET_LANGUAGE_CHINESE

Sample Code:

```
/*To search English word "big" in fuzzy search mode*/

#include "HowNet.h"
CHOWNET_API cHowNet_Api;

/*To initialize the data of HowNet system*/
if(!cHowNet_Api.HowNet_Initial())
    return;

char szRecordContent[2048];
/*To assign English to the language mode; to assign Fuzzy to the
search mode*/
S_HOWNET_SEARCHMODE sSearchMode;
sSearchMode.language   = HOWNET_LANGUAGE_ENGLISH;
sSearchMode.mode       = HowNet_SearchMode_Fuzzy;

/*To get the number of the records searched*/
WORD wCount = cHowNet_Api.HowNet_Search_Keyword("big",
sSearchMode);

/*To get all the serial numbers of the records searched*/
DWORD* pdwSuccessID
= cHowNet_Api.HowNet_Get_SearchResult();
for( WORD i = 0; i < wCount; i ++ )
{
/*To put the content of the records searched into szRecordContent*/
```

```
    cHowNet_Api.HowNet_Get_Unit_Item(pdwSuccessID [i],
HOWNET_ITEM_ID_ALL, szRecordContent);
}
```

(4) WORD HowNet_Search_Relation (DWORD AdwUnitID, S_HOWNET_SEARCHMODE AsSearchMode)

Function Description: To search the relations according to serial number;

Return Value: The number of the records that have been searched;

Parameters:

AdwUnitID	serial number
AsSearchMode	ways of searching

Remarks:

"sHowNet_SearchMode" is a structure which is defined as follow:

```
struct S_HOWNET_SEARCHMODE
{
    BYTE language;        //  search languages
    WORD    mode;         //  search modes
};
```

a. Parameter "language" has two values to be selected:

HOWNET_LANGUAGE_CHINESE: to search in Chinese;
HOWNET_LANGUAGE_ENGLISH: to search in English;

b. Parameter "mode" has 95 values to be selected in two categories.

First category: To search according to semantic relations

HowNet_SearchMode_Antonym:	to search antonyms
HowNet_SearchMode_Converse:	to search converse
HowNet_SearchMode_Synonym:	to search synonyms
HowNet_SearchMode_SynClass:	to search SynClass
HowNet_SearchMode_Hyponym:	to search hyponyms

Second category: To search according to semantic-role/event relations. See Chap. 5.

HowNet_SearchMode_AccordingTo
HowNet_SearchMode_CoEvent

HowNet_SearchMode_ContentCompare
HowNet_SearchMode_ContentProduct
HowNet_SearchMode_DurationAfterEvent
HowNet_SearchMode_DurationBeforeEvent
HowNet_SearchMode_EventProcess
HowNet_SearchMode_HostOf
HowNet_SearchMode_LocationFin
HowNet_SearchMode_LocationIni
HowNet_SearchMode_LocationThru
HowNet_SearchMode_MaterialOf
HowNet_SearchMode_OfPart
HowNet_SearchMode_PartOfTouch
HowNet_SearchMode_PatientAttribute
HowNet_SearchMode_PatientPart
HowNet_SearchMode_PatientProduct
HowNet_SearchMode_PatientValue
HowNet_SearchMode_QuantityCompare
HowNet_SearchMode_RelateTo
HowNet_SearchMode_ResultContent
HowNet_SearchMode_ResultEvent
HowNet_SearchMode_ResultIsa
HowNet_SearchMode_ResultWhole
HowNet_SearchMode_SincePeriod
HowNet_SearchMode_SincePoint
HowNet_SearchMode_SourceWhole
HowNet_SearchMode_StateFin
HowNet_SearchMode_StateIni
HowNet_SearchMode_TimeAfter
HowNet_SearchMode_TimeBefore
HowNet_SearchMode_TimeFin
HowNet_SearchMode_TimeIni
HowNet_SearchMode_TimeRange
HowNet_SearchMode_accompaniment
HowNet_SearchMode_agent
HowNet_SearchMode_and
HowNet_SeachMode_aspect

HowNet_SearchMode_belong
HowNet_SearchMode_beneficiary
HowNet_SearchMode_besides
HowNet_SearchMode_but
HowNet_SearchMode_cause
HowNet_SearchMode_coagent
HowNet_SearchMode_comment
HowNet_SearchMode_concerning
HowNet_SearchMode_concession
HowNet_SearchMode_condition
HowNet_SearchMode_content
HowNet_SearchMode_contrast
HowNet_SearchMode_cost
HowNet_SearchMode_degree
HowNet_SearchMode_descriptive
HowNet_SearchMode_direction
HowNet_SearchMode_distance
HowNet_SearchMode_duration
HowNet_SearchMode_emphasis
HowNet_SearchMode_except
HowNet_SearchMode_existent
HowNet_SearchMode_experiencer
HowNet_SearchMode_frequency
HowNet_SearchMode_host
HowNet_SearchMode_instrument
HowNet_SearchMode_isa
HowNet_SearchMode_location
HowNet_SearchMode_manner
HowNet_SearchMode_material
HowNet_SearchMode_means
HowNet_SearchMode_method
HowNet_SearchMode_modifier
HowNet_SearchMode_or
HowNet_SearchMode_partner
HowNet_SearchMode_patient
HowNet_SearchMode_possession

HowNet_SearchMode_possessor
HowNet_SearchMode_purpose
HowNet_SearchMode_quantity
HowNet_SearchMode_range
HowNet_SearchMode_relevant
HowNet_SearchMode_restrictive
HowNet_SearchMode_result
HowNet_SearchMode_scope
HowNet_SearchMode_sequence
HowNet_SearchMode_source
HowNet_SearchMode_succeeding
HowNet_SearchMode_target
HowNet_SearchMode_time
HowNet_SearchMode_times
HowNet_SearchMode_transition
HowNet_SearchMode_whole

Similar to function HowNet_Search_Keyword, with this function we can get the number of the records according to the specific search mode and the given keyword. Normally we use it together with the following functions in order to get the specific search result we expect:

HowNet_Get_SearchResult.

In this case, function HowNet_Search_Relation will be called to get the number of the records found, then function HowNet_Get_SearchResult will be called to get the array of the serial numbers of the record found. When using a keyword to search a word or expression, as most of them may have more than one meaning, so function HowNet_Search_Keyword should be first called to search in mode "exact" to get all the meanings and all the serial numbers of the meanings. Hence the relations of concepts will be searched when words or expressions are retrieved in HowNet.

Sample Code:

*/*To search the antonyms of the word "big" and get all the antonymous words and expressions*/*

```
#include "HowNet.h"
CHOWNET_API cHowNet_Api;

/*To initialize the data of HowNet system*/
if(!cHowNet_Api.HowNet_Initial())
    return;

/*As the word "big" is a polysemy, we should get all its meanings by
exact search first so as to get the antonyms for each meaning.*/
/*To assign English to the language mode; to assign exact to the
search mode*/
S_HOWNET_SEARCHMODE sSearchMode;
sSearchMode.language   = HOWNET_LANGUAGE_ENGLISH;
sSearchMode.mode       = HowNet_SearchMode_Exact;

/*To get the number of the records searched*/
WORD wDefCount = cHowNet_Api.HowNet_Search_Keyword
("big", sSearchMode);

/*To get all the serial numbers of the records searched*/
DWORD* pdwTempDefID =
cHowNet_Api.HowNet_Get_SearchResult();

DWORD* pdwSuccessDefID = new DWORD[wDefCount];
memcpy(pdwSuccessDefID, pdwTempDefID,
wDefCount*sizeof(DWORD));

/*To assign sorting mode and sort pdwSuccessDefID in DEF*/
S_HOWNET_SORT_ID  sSortId;
sSortId.content[0] = HOWNET_ITEM_ID_DEF;
sSortId.num = 1;
cHowNet_Api.HowNet_Sort_Unit
(pdwSuccessDefID, wDefCount, sSortId);
```

/*By Function HowNet_Sort_Unit, the sorting of the content of array pdwSuccessDefID has been done, but deduplication has not yet been done. After a function of deduplication is called, we can then get the count (wDefCount) of all the meanings of the word "big" and the array (pdwSuccessDefID) of the meaning. The function of deduplication is omitted here.*/

```
......

char szRecordContent[2048];
WORD wCount;
DWORD* pdwSuccessID;
```

*/*To assign English to the language mode; to assign antonym to the search mode*/*

```
sSearchMode.language  = HOWNET_LANGUAGE_ENGLISH;
sSearchMode.mode = HowNet_SearchMode_Antonym;
```

*/*To assign the sorting mode*/*

```
sSortId.content[0] = HOWNET_ITEM_ID_W_E;
sSortId.num = 1;
```

*/*To get all the antonyms of each concept of the word "big"*/*

```
for(WORD i = 0; i < wDefCount; i ++)
{
wCount=cHowNet_Api.HowNet_Search_Relation
(pdwSuccessDefID [i] , sSearchMode);
if(wCount > 0)
{
pdwSuccessID=cHowNet_Api.HowNet_Get_SearchResult();
cHowNet_Api.HowNet_Sort_Unit
(pdwSuccessID, wCount, sSortId);
```

*/*In order to get the antonyms of "big", we sort the above search result pdwSuccessID using function HowNet_Sort_Unit. Then we deduplicate the array pdwSuccessID to make the result unique in Chinese forms. Here we omit the program of deduplication and*

```
  /*suppose the wCount and pdwSuccessID to be the count and array
  after deduplication.*/
  ……

  for(WORD j = 0; j < wCount; j++)
  {
    /*To get all the antonyms of "big", and place the content into
    szRecordContent*/
  cHowNet_Api.HowNet_Get_Unit_Item
  (pdwSuccessID[j], HOWNET_ITEM_ID_W_E, szRecordContent);
  }
  }
  }
  delete[] pdwSuccessDefID;
```

(5) void HowNet_Sort_Unit(DWORD* ApdwBase, long AlNum, S_HOWNET_SORT_ID AsSortID)

Function Description: To sort;

Return Value: None;

Parameters:

ApdwBase	the array of the serial numbers
AlNum	the number used by array "ApdwBase"
AsSortID	sorting mode

Remarks:

Parameter "ApdwBase" is obtained by function HowNet_Get_SearchResult, when function HowNet_Search_Keyword or function HowNet_Search_Relation is called.

Parameter "S_HOWNET_SORT_ID" is a structure which is defined as follow:

```
struct S_HOWNET_SORT_ID
{
    BYTE content[8];    //   the content for sorting
    BYTE num;           //   the number used by array "content"
};
```

Parameter "content" has eight values to be selected:

HOWNET_ITEM_ID_N_O:	sort by serial number
HOWNET_ITEM_ID_W_C:	sort by Chinese word
HOWNET_ITEM_ID_G_C:	sort by POS of Chinese word
HOWNET_ITEM_ID_E_C:	sort by example of Chinese word
HOWNET_ITEM_ID_W_E:	sort by English word
HOWNET_ITEM_ID_G_E:	sort by POS of English word
HOWNET_ITEM_ID_E_E:	sort by example of English word
HOWNET_ITEM_ID_DEF:	sort by DEF

In searching, we use functions HowNet_Search_Keyword or HowNet_Search_Relation to get the number of the records searched, and use function HowNet_Get_SearchResult to get the array of the serial numbers. It should be noted that the records in the array have not been sorted and deduplicated. For example, presently there are 7 exact matches of the word "big", but there are only 3 concepts. This means that one word or expression may correspond to many records (there is some other difference among the records). Hence we can use this function to sort the searched records.

Sample Code: See HowNet_Search_Relation.

(6) char* HowNet_Get_Unit_Item(const DWORD AdwUnitID, const BYTE AbtItemID, char* ApRlt)

Function Description: To get a specific part of a specific record;

Return Value: To return a specific part, otherwise return NULL;

Parameters:

AdwUnitID	serial number
AbtItemID	specific part of the record
ApRlt	content of the record

Remarks:

The value of Parameter "AdwUnitID" ranges from 0 ~ the total of record (the total can be obtained by function HowNet_GetUnitNum).

Parameter "AbtItemID" has the following values to be selected:

HOWNET_ITEM_ID_N_O:

for the serial number of the specific record (NO.=).

HOWNET_ITEM_ID_W_C:

for the Chinese word or expression of the specific record (W_C=).

HOWNET_ITEM_ID_G_C:

for the POS of Chinese word or expression of the specific record (G_C=).

HOWNET_ITEM_ID_E_C:

for the example of Chinese word or expression of the specific record (E_C=).

HOWNET_ITEM_ID_W_E:

for the English word or phrase of the specific record (W_E=).

HOWNET_ITEM_ID_G_E:

for the POS of English word or phrase of the specific record (G_E=).

HOWNET_ITEM_ID_E_E:

for the example of English word or phrase of the specific record(E_E=).

HOWNET_ITEM_ID_DEF:

for the DEF of the specific record (DEF).

HOWNET_ITEM_ID_P_Y:

for the phonetic transcription Chinese word or expression of the specific record.

HOWNET_ITEM_ID_ALL:

for the whole of the specific record.

HOWNET_ITEM_ID_HYP:

for the hypernymous relation of a concept of the specific record.

HOWNET_ITEM_ID_ATT:

for the attribute of the specific record which corresponds to the attribute-value in HowNet taxonomy.

HOWNET_ITEM_ID_VAL:

for all the attribute-values of the specific record which correspond to the attribute in HowNet taxonomy.

As aforesaid, in HowNet knowledge base, all the concepts are classified into four categories: event, entity, attribute, attribute-value. The categorial sememe of each DEF implies the category which the concept belongs to and it can lead to its hypernyms in the HowNet taxonomies. In addition, an attribute concept can lead to its corresponding attribute-values, vice versa, an attribute-value can lead to its corresponding attribute in the taxonomies.

Sample Code:

```
/*To get a full record whose serial number is 1000*/

 #include "HowNet.h"
 CHOWNET_API cHowNet_Api;

/*To initialize the data of HowNet system*/
 if(!cHowNet_Api.HowNet_Initial())
    return;

/*To specify the serial number 1000*/
 DWORD dwUnitID = 1000;

/*To extract a full record*/
 BYTE btItemID = HOWNET_ITEM_ID_ALL;

 char szRecordContent[2048];

/*To get the full record whose serial number is 1000*/
 char *p = cHowNet_Api.HowNet_Get_Unit_Item(dwUnitID ,
btItemID , szRecordContent);
 if(p != NULL)
    MessageBox(szRecordContent, "The record is:", MB_OK);
```

(7) WORD HowNet_Get_Sememe_Code
(const char *ApKeyword)

Function Description: To get the code of a sememe in HowNet taxonomies;

Return Value: If the specified sememe exits, return its sememe code. Else, return 0xffff.

Parameters:

ApKeyword the string form of a specific sememe. Full string should be the input.

Sample Code:

```
/*To get the code of the sememe "mean|指代"*/

 #include "HowNet.h"
 CHOWNET_API cHowNet_Api;

/*To initialize the data of HowNet system*/
 if(!cHowNet_Api.HowNet_Initial())
    return;

/*To get the code of the sememe "mean|指代", the code is 1954*/
 WORD wSememeCode =
 cHowNet_Api.HowNet_Get_Sememe_Code("mean|指代");
```

(8) WORD HowNet_Get_Concept_Relevance
(DWORD AdwUnitID, BYTE AbtLanguageID, BYTE AbtLevelID)

Function Description: To obtain the relevant concept field of a specified concept;

Return Value: The number of the words and expressions in the relevant concept field;

Parameters:

AdwUnitID	serial number of the searched record
AbtLanguageID	search language.
AbtLevelID	rank specified

Remarks:

Parameter "AbtLanguageID" has two values:

HOWNET_LANGUAGE_CHINESE:	for Chinese
HOWNET_LANGUAGE_ENGLISH:	for English

Parameter "AbtLevelID" has three values:

HOWNET_RELEVANCE_LEVEL1:	Rank 1
HOWNET_RELEVANCE_LEVEL2:	Rank 2
HOWNET_RELEVANCE_LEVEL3:	Rank 3

Only the number of words and expressions in the relevant concept field can be obtained when this function is called. If we want to display the words and expressions in full, we should call the following functions:

HowNet_Get_SearchResult,
HowNet_Sort_Unit,
HowNet_Get_Unit_Item

Sample Code:

```
/*To search the relevant concept field of the word "football" whose
DEF is DEF={SportTool|运动器材:domain={football|足球}}*/

#include "HowNet.h"
CHOWNET_API cHowNet_Api;

/*To initialize the data of HowNet system*/
if(!cHowNet_Api.HowNet_Initial())
   return;

char szRecordContent[2048];
WORD wCount;
DWORD* pdwSuccessID;
/*To search the relevant concept field of the word "football" whose
DEF is DEF={SportTool|运动器材:domain={football|足球}}, (its
serial number is 142787)*/
```

```
wCount = cHowNet_Api.HowNet_Get_Concept_Relevance
(142787,
HOWNET_LANGUAGE_CHINESE,
HOWNET_RELEVANCE_LEVEL2);

/*To get the serial numbers of the searched words*/
pdwSuccessID   = cHowNet_Api.HowNet_Get_SearchResult();
for(WORD i = 0; i < wCount; i++)
{
  /*To place the content searched into szRecordContent*/
cHowNet_Api.HowNet_Get_Unit_Item
(pdwSuccessID[i], HOWNET_ITEM_ID_W_E, szRecordContent);
}
```

(9) bool HowNet_InitialSynAtnCon (void)

Function Description: To initialize the data of synonymous, antonymous and converse words and expressions;

Return Value: Return true, if successful; otherwise return false.

Parameters: None.

Remarks: This function is used to initialize the data of synonymous, antonymous and converse words and expressions. When we want to call a function relevant to the similarity measurement, we should first call this function. This function needs file "HowNet_Synset.idx". The initialization will fail if the file does not exist.

Sample Code:

*/*To initialize the data of synonymous, antonymous and converse words and expressions; if it fails, it gives error message*/*

```
#include "HowNet.h"
CHOWNET_API cHowNet_Api;

if(!cHowNet_Api.HowNet_InitialSynAtnCon())
{
MessageBox(cHowNet_Api.HowNet_Get_ErrMsg(), "Warning",
MB_OK);
}
```

(10) BYTE HowNet_Get_Smemme_Distance
**(WORD AwSem				emeCodeA, WORD AwSememeCodeB)**

Function Description: To measure the distance between two sememes;

Return Value: If the two sememes to be measured are in the same tree of the hierarchy, return the distance, otherwise, return 0xff;

Parameters:

AwSememeCodeA:	code of first sememe
AwSememeCodeB:	code of second sememe

Remarks: The code of a sememe in the Taxonomy can be obtained by using function HowNet_Get_Sememe_Code(). The distance between two sememes implies the number of the steps from one sememe to another. For example, the distance between sememe "receive|收受" and sememe "become|成为" is six steps.

The measurement will proceed as follows: "receive|收受"→(1) "own|有" → (2) "possession|领属关系" → (3) "relation|关系" → (4) "isa|是非关系" → (5) "be|是" → (6) "become|成为".

```
- {event|事件}
  ├ {static|静态}
  │  ├ {relation|关系}
  │  │  ├ {isa|是非关系}
  │  │  │  ├ {be|是}
  │  │  │  │  ├ {become|成为}
  │  │  │  │  └ {mean|指代}
  │  │  │  └ {BeNot|非}
  │  │  ├ {possession|领属关系}
  │  │  │  ├ {own|有}
  │  │  │  │  ├ {obtain|得到}
  │  │  │  │  └ {receive|收受}
```

Sample Code:

*/*To get the distance between sememes "crop|庄稼" and "ice|冰"*/*

```
#include "HowNet.h"
CHOWNET_API cHowNet_Api;

/*To initialize the data of HowNet system*/
if(!cHowNet_Api.HowNet_Initial())
   return;

/*To get the numbers of  sememes "crop|庄稼" and "ice|冰"*/
WORD wSememeCodeA =
cHowNet_Api.HowNet_Get_Sememe_Code("crop|庄稼");
WORD wSememeCodeB =
cHowNet_Api.HowNet_Get_Sememe_Code("ice|冰");

/*To get the distance between the sememes"crop|庄稼"和"ice|冰",
its value: 6*/
BYTE btDistance =
cHowNet_Api.HowNet_Get_Smemme_Distance
(wSememeCodeA, wSememeCodeB);
```

(11) double HowNet_Get_Smemme_Similarity (WORD AwSememeCodeA, WORD AwSememeCodeB)

Function Description: To measure the similarity between the frames of two sememes;

Return Value: If the code of any one of the sememes is erroneous, return -1; if the frame of two sememes can be searched, return their distance; if neither frames exist or one of the two frames does not exist, return 0.

Parameters:

AwSememeCodeA: code of first sememe
AwSememeCodeB: code of second sememe

Remarks: The code of a sememe in the Taxonomy can be obtained by using function HowNet_Get_Sememe_Code().

Sample Code:

*/*To get the similarity between the DEFs of sememes "mean|指代" and "become|成为"*/*

```
#include "HowNet.h"
CHOWNET_API cHowNet_Api;

/*To initialize the data of HowNet system*/
if(!cHowNet_Api.HowNet_Initial())
   return;
/*To get the numbers of the sememes "mean|指代" and "become|成为"*/
WORD wSememeCodeA =
cHowNet_Api.HowNet_Get_Sememe_Code("mean|指代");
WORD wSememeCodeB =
cHowNet_Api.HowNet_Get_Sememe_Code("become|成为");

/*To get the similarity between the DEFs of sememes "mean|指代" and "become|成为", its value: 0.666667.*/
/*The frame of "mean|指代":{be|是:isa={*},relevant={*}}*/
/*The frame of"become|成为":{be|是:isa={*},relevant={*}};{be|是:descriptive={*},relevant={*}}*/
double dSim =
cHowNet_Api.HowNet_Get_Smemme_Similarity
(wSememeCodeA,wSememeCodeB);
```

(12) double HowNet_Get_Concept_Similarity(DWORD AdwUnitIDA, DWORD AdwUnitIDB, float AfA = 1.6, float AfB1 = 0.1, float AfB2 = 0.1, float AfB3 = 0.7, float AfB4 = 0.1)

Function Description: To measure the similarity between two concepts;

Return Value: Similarity value;

Parameters:

AdwUnitIDA	serial number of Record a
AdwUnitIDB	serial number of Record b

AfA	parameter α, $\alpha = 1.6$
AfB1	parameter $\beta1$, $\beta1 = 0.1$
AfB2	parameter $\beta2$, $\beta2 = 0.1$
AfB3	parameter $\beta3$, $\beta3 = 0.7$
AfB4	parameter $\beta4$, $\beta4 = 0.1$

Sample Code:

*/*To compute the similarity between "policeman" and "criminal police"*/*

```
#include "HowNet.h"
CHOWNET_API cHowNet_Api;
```

*/*To initialize the data of HowNet system*/*

```
if(!cHowNet_Api.HowNet_Initial())
   return;
```

*/*To initialize the data of synonymous, antonymous and converse words and expressions; if it fails, it gives error message*/*

```
if(!cHowNet_Api.HowNet_InitialSynAtnCon())
return;
```

*/*To get the serial number of "policeman". To search using HowNet_Search_Keyword with the exact search mode, then to get all the serial numbers using HowNet_Get_SearchResult.*/*

*/*To assign English to the language mode; to assign exact to the search mode*/*

```
S_HOWNET_SEARCHMODE sSearchMode;
sSearchMode.language  = HOWNET_LANGUAGE_ENGLISH;
sSearchMode.mode      = HowNet_SearchMode_Exact;
```

*/*To search "policeman" with the exact search mode*/*

```
cHowNet_Api.HowNet_Search_Keyword
("policeman", sSearchMode);
```

*/*To get all the serial numbers of the record searched/**

```
DWORD* pdwSuccessID1=
cHowNet_Api.HowNet_Get_SearchResult();
```

*/*To get the serial number of "criminal policeman". To search using HowNet_Search_Keyword with the exact search mode, then to get all the serial numbers using HowNet_Get_SearchResult.*/*

*/*To search "criminal policeman" with the exact search mode*/*

```
cHowNet_Api.HowNet_Search_Keyword
("criminal police", sSearchMode);
```

*/*To get all the serial numbers of the record searched*/*

```
DWORD* pdwSuccessID2=
cHowNet_Api.HowNet_Get_SearchResult();
```

*/*To compute the similarity between "policeman" and "criminal police", the result: 0.900000.*/*

```
double dSimilarity =
cHowNet_Api.HowNet_Get_Concept_Similarity
(dwSuccessID2[0], pdwSuccessID2[0]);
```

Chapter 13

NEW RESOURCES ACTIVATING NEW TECHNOLOGY — SOME APPLICATIONS OF HOWNET

Since the first release of HowNet in 1999, it has been widely used in various research areas of NLP, especially in the semantic-related subfield of Chinese NLP. This chapter will not repeat all the successful applications that have already been achieved in the past few years. Instead, it will be devoted to exhibit some novel technologies that HowNet may bring forth and to discuss some potential contributions that HowNet may make to HLT. As the case study we would like to focus on two issues which are believed to help broaden users' horizons.

13.1. Word Sense Disambiguation (WSD)

Generally speaking, lexical ambiguity may be either featured in syntactic origin or semantic origin. This section is confined only to discussion about word sense disambiguation in semantics, especially of the words and expressions of the same part-of-speech. WSD has been a hard nut ever since the earliest days of computer treatment of language in the 1950s. It underwent a long way from one paradigm to another and various approaches, AI-based or corpus-based. It is surprising to find that only little progress seems to have been made in nearly 60 years. Though much recent experimental work cites high-level results, only limited achievements have been gained in large-scale real texts processing such as machine translation and information retrieval.

13.1.1. *Types of semantic ambiguity*

We consider that painstaking observation on sense ambiguity reasonable classification, and construction of various sorts of resources are necessary for advancing the work. Word sense ambiguity in semantics can be classified into the following types:

(1) noticeable context activating: The senses of a polysemous word or expression usually activate contexts with noticeable features owing to their strong distinctness, for instance,

"bank" (2 senses)
a financial institution
riverside

"shoot" (3 senses)
to fire a weapon
to kick, throw, etc., a ball to make a point in a game
to make a photograph or film

(2) unnoticeable context activating: The senses of a polysemous word or expression usually activate contexts with insignificant features owing to their poor distinctness, for instance,

"condition" (2 senses)
a state at a particular time
something stated as desirable for something else

"earth" (2 senses)
the earth's surface
soil in which plants grow

"run" (2 senses)
to move fast by using one's feet
to escape or flee

(3) broad sense-distinction: The senses are strongly distinct or go wide apart so that the disambiguation between them becomes relatively easy. Usually in the contexts in which the target words exist, some very distinct words and expressions may be expected, for instance,

"crane" (2 senses)
a lift
a wading bird

"target" (2 senses)
a reference point to shoot at
the goal intended to be attained

"take off" (2 senses)
depart from the ground
remove clothes

(4) close sense-distinction: The senses are of poor distinctness or the difference between them is rather obscure. Very few clear-cut words and expressions can be found in the context which the target words exist in, for instance,

"state" (2 senses)
a country considered as a political organization
as a province: *California State*

"cotton" (2 senses)
cotton plant
silky fibers from cotton plants

"serious" (4 senses)
thoughtful, solemn
to be considered as sincere
not slight
of an important kind

To sum up, lexical ambiguity is not only very common but also rather complicated. No wonder it has been reported that only little progress has been made. We believe some revolutionary technology and new resources are expected. We consider we first need to build some divergent sorts of special resources to hit the above-listed different types of polysemy. One of the initial objectives of HowNet is to make it special resources for word sense ambiguity.

13.1.2. *Special resources in HowNet for WSD*

HowNet provides three kinds of resources that may meet the needs for tackling different types of word sense ambiguity. They were all touched upon previously. In this section we will focus on how to use them in WSD.

(1) Examples in dictionary records

As mentioned above, each sense of a polysemous word or expression in HowNet should normally be provided with as sufficient examples as possible for the purpose of disambiguation. The examples should be featured by broad sense distinction for computer processing not only for explanation for humans. Let us take two senses of the Chinese word "林" as an example. Its first sense is "woods" or "forest", with its concept definition as "{tree|树:quantity={mass|众}}" which means many trees. Its second sense is a Chinese surname with its concept definition as "{surname|姓}". Their HowNet records read as follows:

NO.=071261
W_C=林
G_C=N [lin2]
E_C=树~，森~，~木，竹~，防风~，防沙~，针叶~，阔叶~，枫叶~，桃~，密~深处，山~，~间小路，~中木屋，~地，在~中走失了，在~中迷失方向，承包了一片~地，这片~子，~带，~产，红~尽染，绿~
W_E=forest
G_E=N
E_E=
DEF={tree|树:quantity={mass|众}}

NO.=071262
W_C=林
G_C=N [lin2]
E_C=姓~，~姓，~先生，~太太，~小姐，~女士，老~，小~，
~大哥，~叔，~公，~爷爷，~伯伯，~伯母，~老爷，~处长，
~家老二，~氏家族，~经理，~主任，~校长，~院长，~总理，
~书记，~*教授*，~老师，~大夫，~护士长，~队，~总，~工
W_E=Lin
G_E=N
E_E=
DEF={surname|姓}

Suppose we have a Chinese text with the word "林" which is to be disambiguated:
"请打电话给*林教授*" (Please call Professor Lin)

Then we may find the exact match between the target phrase with "教授" and an instance (marked in italic) in Record 071262.

However, suppose we have a different Chinese text as follows:
"请打电话给*林船长*" (Please call Captain Lin)

As there are none of exact matches, we have to implement similarity computation.

(2) Implementation of word similarity computing

The implementation of word similarity computing for the above example "请打电话给*林船长*" (Please call Captain Lin)" may be conducted as follows:

(a) To use HowNet's Concept Similarity Measure (CSM) to compute the similarity between "*船长* (Captain)" and each word after "~" respectively in the examples of Record NO.=071262; then we may get the similarity values, some of which are shown in Table 13.1.

Table 13.1. Result of CSM (1).

concept1	concept2	similarity value
船长 (Captain)	先生 (Mr.)	0.375000
船长 (Captain)	太太 (Mrs.)	0.340000
船长 (Captain)	大哥 (Brother)	0.375000
船长 (Captain)	伯伯 (Uncle)	0.355556
船长 (Captain)	经理 (Manager)	0.783333
船长 (Captain)	校长 (School master)	0.611765
船长 (Captain)	处长 (Head of a department)	0.936364
船长 (Captain)	总理 (Premier)	0.620000
船长 (Captain)	教授 (Professor)	0.454545

(b) To use CSM again to compute the similarity between "*船长* (Captain)" and each word after "~" respectively in the examples of Record NO.=071261; then we may get the similarity values, some of which are shown in Table 13.2.

Table 13. Result of CSM (2).

concept1	concept2	similarity value
船长 (Captain)	木 (wood)	0.021053
船长 (Captain)	深处 (depths)	0.018605
船长 (Captain)	间 (opening)	0.018605
船长 (Captain)	中 (inside)	0.018605
船长 (Captain)	地 (land)	0.018605
船长 (Captain)	带 (area)	0.018605
船长 (Captain)	产 (production)	0.000624

(c) By comparing the values in these two tables, we can see clearly the similarity values displayed in Table 13.1 are much higher than those in Table 13.2, thus we may easily conclude in disambiguation of the word sense in "请打电话给*林船长*".

Suppose we have a Chinese text with the word "林" which is to be disambiguated as follows:

"*林中*枫叶红，秋色美如画" (With maple woods red, autumn is as beautiful as a painting), Then we may find the exact match between the target phrase with "中" and 3 instances (marked in italic) in Record 071261.

However, suppose we have a different Chinese text and none of exact matches can be found between the target and the instances in the examples in both the records, we would again use HowNet's Concept Similarity Measure (CSM) to measure the similarity as discussed above and the successful disambiguation is believed to be achieved.

13.2. Question Analysis in Question Answering

Information retrieval (IR) techniques have made much progress and have proven quite successful at locating the documents relevant to a user's query. However currently, the user's query is still rather rigid and leaves no alternatives. Is it possible that the IR gives answers to specific questions instead of whole documents? Thus this potential demand has brought forth the development of question answering (QA) techniques. QA as well as IR has long been facing a technical problem: "Can NLP help the techniques?", and "How much can it contribute if it really can?" The reports and proceedings in the recent TREC conferences seem to give an optimistic answer. This section will discuss how HowNet as a knowledge resource can contribute to QA.

Question analysis is regarded as one of the necessary steps in QA. HowNet will be able to help much in the following respects: (1) separation of a question into the question target and the question focus, (2) question categorization (3) mapping of language expressions, (4) answer prediction.

13.2.1. *Separation of questions*

In terms of question analysis, every question can be separated into two parts: (1) question target, which is the subject that the question is used to point to, as labeled as "Q_target" in question analysis; (2) question focus, which is the focal point that the question is raised to actually inquire about, as labeled as "Q_focus". To take some questions selected from TREC test data as examples:

How deep is Crater Lake?
Q_target: Crater Lake
Q_focus: How deep (depth — attribute question)

What is the diameter of a golf ball?
Q_target: a golf ball
Q_focus: What is the diameter (length — attribute question)

Who invented the road traffic cone?
Q_target: invented the road traffic cone
Q_focus: Who (agent — role question)

When did Hawaii become a state?
Q_target: Hawaii become a state
Q_focus: When (time — role question)

13.2.2. *Question type*

Questions can be categorized into two types according to the focus of questions: (1) attribute question, which is used to inquire about an attribute of something as the first two of the above given examples; (2) role question, which is used to inquire about a semantic role in an event or an event itself as a fact or scenario as the last two of the above given examples.

As previously presented, HowNet specifies 247 attribute sememes in 7 subclasses, thus there are altogether 247 types of attribute questions. HowNet specifies 91 semantic roles, there are 92 types of role questions when event itself is included. We use the tags "<Q_focus> attr=" and "<Q_focus> role=" to indicate the actual value of the two types of questions respectively, for example, the tag "<Q_focus> attr=Color|颜色" means that the question is used to inquire about the color of something; the tag "<Q_focus> role=agent" means that the question is used to inquire about the agent of the event, or who did it. Let us take some more questions selected from TREC QA data as examples.

(1) attribute question

(a) {Appearance|外观}

What color is a poison arrow frog?

<Q_focus> attr=Color|颜色

(b) {Measurement|量度}

How far is it from Denver to Aspen?

<Q_focus> attr=Distance|距离

What is the depth of the Nile river?

<Q_focus> attr=Depth|深度

How tall is the giraffe?

<Q_focus> attr=Stature|高矮

How tall is Kilimanjaro?

<Q_focus> attr=Height|高度

How hot is the core of the earth?

<Q_focus> attr=Temperature|温度

How much did a quart of milk cost in the 1930s?

<Q_focus> attr=Price|价格

What is the degree of tilt of Earth?

<Q_focus> attr=Angle|角度

What is the normal blood sugar range for people?

<Q_focus> attr=Range|幅度

(c) {Property|特性}

What was the name of the first Russian astronaut to do a spacewalk?

<Q_focus> attr=Name|姓名

How old was Elvis Presley when he died?

<Q_focus> attr=Age|年龄

What is Nicholas Cage's profession?
<Q_focus> attr=Occupation|职位

What is the habitat of the chickadee?
<Q_focus> attr=Habit|习惯

(d) {Relationship|关系}
What nationality was Jackson Pollock?
<Q_focus> attr=Nationality|国籍

What kind of animal was Winnie the Pooh?
<Q_focus> attr=Kind|类型

What are birds descendents of?
<Q_focus> attr=Source|来源

(e) {Situation|状况}
What is the medical condition of hypertension?
<Q_focus> attr=Circumstances|境况

(f) {Quantity|数量}
How much folic acid should an expectant mother get daily?
<Q_focus> attr=Amount|多少

What is the exchange rate between England and the U.S.?
<Q_focus> attr=Rate|比率

What are wavelengths measured in?
<Q_focus> attr=Unit|单位

(2) role question
(a) main semantic roles
What did John Hinckley do to impress Jodie Foster?
<Q_focus> role=event

Who fired Maria Ybarra from her position in San Diego council?
<Q_focus> role=agent

Who was President Cleveland's wife?
<Q_focus> role=relevant

What is a golden parachute?
<Q_focus> role=isa

Which team won the Super Bowl in 1968?
<Q_focus> role=experiencer

What does the Peugeot company manufacture?
<Q_focus> role=PatientProduct

Which past and present NFL players have the last name of Johnson?
<Q_focus> role=possessor

Whom did the Chicago Bulls beat in the 1993 championship?
<Q_focus> role=partner

(b) peripheral semantic roles
When did Spain and Korea start ambassadorial relations?
<Q_focus> role=time

What city did Duke Ellington live in?
<Q_focus> role=location

Where does most of the marijuana entering the United States come from?
<Q_focus> role=LocationIni

How long did the Charles Manson murder trial last?
<Q_focus> role=duration

How late is Disneyland open?
<Q_focus> role=TimeFin

How did the disciple Peter die?
<Q_focus> role=manner

Why did David Koresh ask the FBI for a word processor?
<Q_focus> role=cause

13.2.3. *Mapping of language expressions*

If we do a mapping of language expressions to each type of question focus, we will find that each type of question focus contains only limited number of language expressions. It would be easy for a QA system to program with a pattern matching model. Table 13.3 and Table 13.4 show the mapping of language expressions to the two types of Q_focus respectively.

Table 13.3. Mapping of language expressions to <Q_focus>attr.

<Q_focus> attr	Language expressions
Depth|深度	How deep... What is the depth of ...
Color|颜色	What color... What is the color of ...
Temperature|温度	How hot ... How cold ... What is the temperature ... What is the boiling point ...
Price|价格	How much ... What is the price of ...

Table 13.4. Mapping of language expressions to <Q_focus>role.

<Q_focus> role	Language expressions
agent	Who wrote ... Who is the author of ...
relevant	Who is ...
duration	How long ...
location	Where ... In what city ... In what country ...

It should be noticed that when we build the pattern matching model, we should pay enough attention to the variations of the language expressions, for example, for "<Q_focus> role=agent", one of the expressions may be: "Who + {event}" or "Who + be + the + {human} agent= {~}".

For "Who + {event}", we may have the following examples:

"Who invented ...", "Who discovered ...", "Who killed ..."
"Who wrote ...", "Who played ...", "Who murdered ..."

For "Who + be + the + {human} agent= {~}, we may have the following examples:

"Who was the inventor of ...", "Who was the author of ...",
"Who was the manufacturer of ...", "Who was the killer of ...",
"Who was the murder of ..."

13.2.4. *Prediction of answers*

When a question like "What color is the sky" is raised in a QA system, the answer may possibly be: "the sky is blue", "the blue sky", or "the sky usually blue in color", and so on and so forth. Therefore we believe that the focus of the answer is able to be predicted when it is known after the analysis of the questions. We consider the following rules may be established as shown in Table 13.5.

Table 13.5. Prediction of answer to Q_focus attr=.

Q_focus attr=	Focus of answer
Color|颜色	color attribute-values
Price|价格	numeral+ {Unit|单位:host={money|货币}
	numeral+ {money|货币}
Distance|距离	numeral+ {Unit|单位:host={Distance|距离}

As all correspondence between attributes and their relevant attribute-values can be found and retrieved in HowNet, any value becomes predictable when a question is raised to inquire about an attribute. For instance, when a question about "color" of something is asked, a possible answer most likely contains one of color values listed by HowNet and when a question about "distance" is asked, a possible answer most likely contains one of units of distance listed by HowNet.

Look at some of the words and expressions of colors and units of distance that HowNet provides:

"black"

black, burned black, dark, dark and liquid, darkly, glossy black, jet-black, pitch-black, pure black, reddish black, sable...

"blue"

azure, azure blue, blue, bluish green, bright blue, cerulean, hydron blue, indigo, indigo-blue, pure blue, reddish blue, sapphire blue...

"white"

pure white, whitish, off-white, shining white, fair dazzlingly white, fairish, deathly pale, egg white, spotlessly white, milky white, pale, snow-white, hoar...

"unit of distance"

astronomical unit, centimeter, centimetre, cm, decametre, decimeter, foot, ft, handbreadth, handsbreadth, hectometre, inch, kilometer, kilometre, km, light-year, man-kilometer, metre, micron, mile, millimeter, millimetre, mm, nautical mile, yard...

Similarly, when a question like "who wrote Hamlet" is raised in a QA system, the answer may possibly be: a person's name like "Shakespeare". So we believe that the focus of the answer is able to be predicted too when it is known after the analysis of the questions. We consider the following rules may be established as shown in Table 13.6.

Table 13.6. Prediction of answer to Q_focus role=.

Q_focus role=	Focus of answer
agent	"named human"
location	{land|陆地},{place|地方},{waters|水域},{sky|空域}, {InstitutePlace|场所}, {building|建筑物},{house|房屋}
time	{time|时间}

To take "time" as an example, if a question is asked as follows:

"When did Spain and Korea start ambassadorial relations?"

We can predict the answer must fall into a list of hyponyms of "time" or a specific time.

To sum up, HowNet can no doubt contribute much to the development of QA systems with its capability of pre-monitoring of question types and of prediction of focus of answers.

13.3. Domain-specific Seed Word List Updating

Domain information is useful to practical applications of HLT, such as information filtering, text categorization, text clustering, WSD, etc. The determination of domains mainly relies on the contexts or the words and expressions closely relevant to a domain. Therefore domain-specific seed word lists are significant and even indispensable for the domain determination.

13.3.1. *Domain-specific seed word lists in HowNet*

We consider that domain-specific seed words are defined as the words and expressions closely related to a specific domain in meaning. HowNet adopts two ways to provide domain information for its words and expressions. First, similar to ordinary dictionaries, the domain information in HowNet is manually coded. Secondly, HowNet forms its domain-specific seed word lists using its secondary device of computation of meaning CRC. HowNet covers 32 domains, including economy, industry, agriculture, education, sports, finance, physics, chemistry, etc. A seed word is a basic word or expression which is frequently used in a specific domain. Every specific domain includes a cluster of seed words and we name the cluster seed word list.

In discussing domain-specific seed word lists in HowNet, we would like to call our readers' attention to the following points:

(1) By using CRC, HowNet can generally provide at least 32 domain-specific seed word lists. In addition HowNet can provide much more seed word lists than the ready-set domains, because every related concepts field is in fact a seed word list. For example, when you call CRC to extract the related concepts field with the two senses of the word "virus", you will get the following two clusters of words and expressions respectively:

"virus" in virology (totals 165)
antibacterial, bactericidal, bacteria-free, antibacterial, antibiosis, antibiotic, final host, host, intermediate host, Au antigen, Australia antigen, Ebola virus, HIV, HS1, HS2, amoeba, animal virus, ascus, amoxil, bacterial vaccine, vaccine, prevent mould, carry disease germs, antibody, antigen, spore, worm, clean room, autoclave, sterilizer, ...

"virus" harmful to computer programs (totals 6)
kill virus, hacker, Y2K, computer virus, fire wall

(2) A seed word list may include a certain amount of words and expressions which belong to the common domain rather than the specific domain. For example, when you call CRC to extract the seed word list of education domain with "textbook", you will get a seed word list of 654 words and expressions and you will find some of them do not have "domain={education|教育}" coded, such as "study abroad", "train", "edify", "construe", etc.

(3) The list is changeable with new words joining and obsolete ones falling out. For example, the word "Y2K" came to usage in the late 90s, at that time it was a new term for "computer virus" list, but now it has faded and even become obsolete.

13.3.2. *Domain-specific seed word list updating*

As a domain-specific seed word list is changeable with new words constantly joining and obsolete ones sometimes outdated at a high frequency, how to keep pace with the change of the lists has become an important issue.

For updating domain-specific seed word lists, HowNet suggests the following measurements:

(1) To extract texts from, say, web pages and build a domain-specific corpus by taking a certain amount of words and expressions from a domain-specific seed word list and setting them as keywords. For

example, by using the “virus” (in virology) list, we can easily build a corpus about bird flu.

(2) To find any frequently occurring words and expressions which are out of the present domain-specific list. For example, in the newly built bird flu corpus, we will find that “H5N2”, “H5N1”, “inactivated vaccine” are frequently-used terms but they are out of the domain-specific seed word list and even out of HowNet vocabulary.

(3) To add the words “H5N2”, “H5N1”, “inactivated vaccine” in the list after human confirmation.

Chapter 14

SOME VIEWS OF CHINESE THROUGH HOWNET

As HowNet is Chinese-oriented to a certain extent, it encounters a lot of problems concerning the Chinese language. Most of them are closely related to some basic and critical nature of Chinese. We would like to concentrate it in this chapter. The readers who are not interested in the issues about Chinese may skip over this chapter or just take a quick browsing. However, we would like to remind the NLP researchers who are dealing with Chinese to pay special attention to these fundamental issues of Chinese.

14.1. Words or No Words

One assertion about Chinese words may be quite popular, even to most of western researchers in the NLP circle, that is, different from English or other western languages, there is no space between Chinese words in written Chinese and thus segmentation of the context into words is necessary for Chinese processing. However, do words really exist in Chinese? It is still a vexing and controversial question. Some Chinese grammarians argue that in Chinese there are no words at all, but there are only characters instead and some express their strong objection.

HowNet considers that the debate about the existence of words is meaningless. Chinese is so strongly semantic-based that it seems somewhat flexible, at least not as rigid or as hard as English or other western languages. Different from Western languages like English, Chinese has no clear-cut demarcation between so-called multi-character words (if we agree on "word") and multi-character phrases. Non-native-Chinese speakers may find it very strange that even in most popular Chinese dictionaries there are no such entries as "鸡蛋(hen egg — egg)", "牛肉(ox meat — beef)", "下雨(fall rain — rain)". Chinese grammarians argue that if they were regarded as words and were chosen as entries in Chinese dictionaries then how we would deal with the following:

鸭蛋 (duck egg)	驴肉 (ass meat)	下雪 (fall snow)
蛇蛋 (snake egg)	鸡肉 (chicken meat)	下雾 (fall fog)
鸟蛋 (bird egg)	鱼肉 (fish meat)	下雹子 (fall hail)

However, we find that all the above-listed are of very high frequency in a 400-million-character corpus, even much higher than those that are usually registered as entries in ordinary Chinese dictionaries, as shown in Table 14.1.

Table 14.1. Examples of dictionary entry and non-dictionary entry.

non-dictionary entry	dictionary entry
鸡蛋 (hen egg) = 5361	鲜蛋 (fresh egg) =409
牛肉 (ox meat) = 3320	鲜菜 (fresh vegetable) =551
下雨 (fall rain) = 1046	鲜果 (fresh fruit) =377

Some Chinese grammarians and computational linguists have been engaged in long debates about the definition of Chinese words, or even about the real existence of Chinese words. They have been trying to find some would-be golden criterion for distinguishing Chinese words and phrases. What should HowNet follow then in the determination of words and expressions and the selection of entries for the vocabulary in its dictionary? We discussed the principles HowNet follows in selecting words and expressions in Chap. 7. Our over 20 years' experience in NLP has told us any effort in determination of Chinese words and demarcation between a word and a phrase is of insignificance, like trying to lift oneself off the ground by pulling one's hair. Chinese is featured by no clear-cut demarcation between so-called "words" and phrases, between phrases and clauses.

14.2. Part-of-Speech — Semantics-first

In Chinese grammarian community there is a consensus that one of the key characteristics of Chinese, completely different from English, is that there is no strict correspondence between parts-of-speech and syntactic functions. Let's compare the following examples:

Chinese	literal English translation
(a) 我昨天午餐*吃鱼*	(a-1) I *ate* fish for lunch yesterday
(b) 我喜欢*吃鱼*	(b-1) I like *to eat* fish
(c) *吃鱼*对身体有好处	(c-1) *Eating* fish is good to health

In English examples we can see the different forms of the verb "eat":

(a-1) finite form used as the predicate in past tense;

(b-1) infinitive with "to", a non-finite form, used as the object of the verb "like";

(c-1) present participle, a non-finite form, used as the subject of the sentence. But in Chinese examples we see no difference at all with the verbs "吃(eat)". In Chinese different syntactic functions do not require any inflexions of the words and expressions. Let us look at some more examples:

Chinese	literal English translation
(d) 房间里很*静*	(d-1) the room is very *quiet*
(e) 请*静*卧三分钟	(e-1) please lie down 3 minutes *quietly*
(f) 她感到令人窒息的*静*	(f-1) She felt a suffocating *quietness*

In the examples (d), (e), (f), the Chinese word "静", without any inflexions, are used in completely different syntactic functions: as the predicative in (d) , as an adverbial modifying the verb "卧(lie)" in (e), and as the object of the verb "感到(feel)" in (f). If these cases happened to English, an English native speaker would be sensitive enough to be aware of grammatical usage with different parts-of-speech (even though the words happen to be of the same form in different parts-of-speech like "quiet"). Chinese grammar prescribes that a Chinese adjective can be used as an attributive, an adverbial and a subject or an object. It must be kept in mind that in Chinese the part-of-speech of a word or expression is fixed, not variable with the syntactic functions it plays in the sentence. In a Chinese Treebank we found a sample as follows:

```
        (IP (NP-SBJ (NN  经济))
              (VP (ADVP (AD  年平均))
                    (VV  增长)
                    (QP-EXT (CD  百分之十七))))
        (PU  ， )
        (IP (NP-SBJ *pro*)
              (VP (VV  高于)
                    (NP-OBJ (NP (DP (DT  全))
                                (NP (NN  国)))
                    (ADJP (JJ  年平均))
                    (NP (NN  增长)
                          (NN  速度))))))
      (PU  。 )))
```

Here the first "年平均 (annually average)" is tagged as an adverb (AD), while the second "年平均" as a noun modifier (JJ); the first "增长 (grow)" is tagged as a verb (VV), while the second "增长" as a noun (NN). The parts-of-speech of the two words "年平均" and "增长" are interdependent on each other. We wonder if this remains the Chinese language that Chinese people really use. Chinese speakers are not as sensitive in parts-of-speech as English speakers. Many Chinese dictionaries, even very popular ones or those for the learners of Chinese-as-second-language, do not give part-of-speech information for the solid words and expressions. Even in the dictionaries that provide part-of-speech information, words like "增长 (grow)", "发展

(develop)/(recruit)", "结束 (conclude)", "计算(calculate)", "生产 (deliver)/(produce)" etc. are coded with only one part-of-speech: verb. As we know, in English, the words like "grow", "develop", "conclude" and "calculate" usually have their derivative nouns meaning the acts of respective verbs, e.g.

grow	growth
develop	development
conclude	conclusion
calculate	calculation
deliver	delivery

Careful readers would find with interest that in popular Chinese-to-English dictionaries these words may have two or more English equivalents, but they rarely have the derivative nouns as their English equivalents, for example:

增长: increase, rise, grow (no "growth")
发展: ① develop, expand, grow (no "development"/ "expansion");
② recruit, admit (no "recruitment"/ "admittance")
结束: end, finish, conclude, wind up, close (no "conclusion")
计算: count, calculate, compute (no "calculation" / "computation")
生产: ① produce (no "production");
② give birth, deliver (no "delivery")

If the so-called part-of-speech of a Chinese verb would vary with its functions it plays in the context, should most of Chinese verbs be specified as both the parts-of-speech, noun as well as verb in the dictionary? Even should those verbs like "去(leave)", "写(write)" be specified as two parts-of-speech? Let us look at the following Chinese sentences:

"其实早在三个月前总经理已萌生*去*意"

Cf. a raw English translation:

"In fact, a plan of *leaving* came to President's mind three months ago"

"那些写手们必须按时把稿子交到'攒书'公司编辑部"

Cf. a raw English translation:

"Those *writers* have to deliver their manuscripts to the editor's of 'the book assembly company'"

In the examples, the Chinese word "去" modifies the word "意", and the word "写" modifies the word "手", similar to "增长" modifying "速度" in the above sample of the Treebank. So we might have to tag the two words "去" and "写" as "NN". In other words, these two verbs should be tagged as nouns in the text. We are facing the question that how we should code part-of-speech of the words "去" and "写" in Chinese dictionary. In reality we have never found noun part-of-speech for these two verbs in any Chinese dictionaries. On the contrary, we find the words "用" coded as verb part-of-speech in similar cases, e.g. "用法 (method for use)", "用品 (articles for use)".

This case is also true with other parts-of-speech of Chinese and English. For example, let us look at the following Chinese sentence:

"如今她已为人妻，也已为人母，虽少了几分少女的可爱和纯真，却有了少妇的成熟和妩媚"

Cf. a raw English translation:

"She got married and became a mother. Although today she has somewhat lost girl's loveliness and naivety, she grows with maturity and charm of a young married woman"

In Chinese dictionaries, when they are coded with parts-of-speech, the words "可爱", "纯真", "成熟" and "妩媚" are all coded as adjectives only. Would it be appropriate to code all the Chinese adjectives with noun part-of-speech although they have no different inflexions?

We do not believe ordinary Chinese people really have a strict scheme of part-of-speech as westerners do. The Chinese language is much more dependent on semantics. Grammatical inflexions and functions are not so important as those of European languages. To Chinese, so-called adjectives are taken always as an attribute value or a property, no matter what functions they would be in a sentence. In fact, the true meanings of the following words in italic have not changed in the sentences like:

她十分*可爱* (She is very lovely)
我被她的*可爱*所吸引 (I was attracted by her loveliness)

Can an ordinary language user tell the difference in actual meaning between the words “lovely” and “loveliness”? In fact both the words “lovely” and “loveliness” indicate the same attribute.

Besides, Chinese adjectives in Chinese-to-English bilingual dictionaries have no derivative adverbs and nouns as their English equivalents, for example:

平静: tranquil (no “tranquilly” / “tranquility”)
小心: cautious (no “cautiously” / “cautiousness”)
熟练: proficient (no “proficiently” / “proficiency”)

Westerners may ask: “Does Chinese really have derivative adverbs and nouns from those adjectives like ‘tranquil’, ‘careful’, ‘beautiful’, ‘peaceful’, etc?” “If it does, why there are none of them in Chinese monolingual dictionaries, and there are no English equivalents to the corresponding adjectives in Chinese-to-English bilingual dictionaries?” Our answer is: “Morphologically, Chinese does not have those derivative adverbs and nouns”.

In conclusion, the problem of Chinese part-of-speech has been a long-term controversy. The strategy we believe in when doing the research and development of HowNet is: Let Chinese be Chinese. Never try to distort it and squeeze it into a non-Chinese grammar frame, or as a Chinese old saying goes, to cut one’s feet to fit the shoes.

14.3. Aspect of Chinese Verbs

HowNet is, in a sense, a strongly semantics-based system. Why does it have to deal with verbal aspect which is generally regarded as a grammatical category? In the secondary features list of HowNet you can find the sememes denoting Chinese aspect as follows:

{aspect|体}
    ├ {Vdirection|动趋}

```
├ {Vprocess|动程}
│  ├ {Vsuppose|假定}
│  ├ {Vstart|发端}
│  ├ {Vgoingon|进展}
│  ├ {Vcontinue|延续}
│  └ {Vend|完结}
└ {Vresult|动果}
   ├ {Vachieve|达成}
   ├ {Vfail|未达成}
   ├ {Vable|能力}
   ├ {Vincapable|没能力}
   ├ {Vpossible|可能}
   ├ {Vimpossible|没可能}
   └ {Vtry|试试}
```

First, the problem is involved with entry selection in HowNet. Nearly all the Chinese aspect markers are homographs. They can be used both as content words and as function words which are tagged as "STRU" (structure word) for their part-of-speech in HowNet. To take the word "着" as an example. We can see that there are 11 meanings and notice that 8 are content words while 3 of them are function words, two of which are aspect markers. Let's look at the following 11 records of "着".

NO.=144957
W_C=着
G_C=STRU [zhe0]
E_C=冲~，沿~，朝~，顺~，照~，为~，向~，对~
W_E=
G_E=
E_E=
DEF={FuncWord|功能词:adjunct={LeChinese|动助}}

NO.=144958
W_C=着
G_C=STRU [zhao2]
E_C=睡~，够~，没睡~，没够~，找~，听不~，被她猜~了，他能踢~你，子弹从他耳旁飞过没打~他

W_E=
G_E=
E_E=
DEF={FuncWord|功能词:aspect={Vachieve|达成}}

NO.=144959
W_C=着
G_C=STRU [zhe0]
E_C=坐~，站~，躺~，靠~，说~说~哭起来了，读~读~他居然睡着了，他正发~言呢，外面正下~雨，她发~烧还是来了
W_E=
G_E=
E_E=
DEF={FuncWord|功能词:aspect={Vgoingon|进展}}

NO.=144960
W_C=着
G_C=V [zhuo2]
E_C=~装，一律~常礼服，身~黑色西服，五一后可以~夏常服
W_E=wear
G_E=V
E_E=
DEF={PutOn|穿戴:aspect={Vgoingon|进展}}

NO.=144961
W_C=着
G_C=V [zhao2]
E_C=~火，火越~越大，火还是没~起来，火还~着吗，干柴一点就~了
W_E=burn
G_E=V
E_E=
DEF={StateChange|态变:StateFin={fire|火}}

NO.=144962
W_C=着

G_C=V [zhuo2]
E_C=~色，~墨
W_E=apply
G_E=V
E_E=
DEF={apply|涂抹}

NO.=144963
W_C=着
G_C=V [zhuo2]
E_C=将~专人前往，~其手下亲往探视
W_E=send
G_E=V
E_E=
DEF={dispatch|差遣}

NO.=144964
W_C=着
G_C=N [zhao1]
E_C=~数，~法，高~，这~棋真妙，都是他在背后支的~
W_E=trick
G_E=N
E_E=
DEF={plans|规划:{deceive|欺骗:method={~}}}

NO.=144966
W_C=着
G_C=V [zhao2]
E_C=头刚一挨枕头就~了
W_E=fall asleep
G_E=V
E_E=
DEF={sleep|睡:aspect={Vachieve|达成}}

NO.=144967
W_C=着

G_C=V [zhao2]
E_C=~凉，~慌，~魔，~迷
W_E=be effected by
G_E=V
E_E=
DEF={suffer|遭受}

NO.=144969
W_C=着
G_C=V [zhao2]
E_C=脚疼得不敢~地，~水就化，~了雨水会烂的
W_E=come into contact with
G_E=V
E_E=
DEF={touch|触}

If we omitted the aspect markers in HowNet, we would again encounter the dilemma of entry selection of content words and function words in Chinese as discussed in Chap. 7.

Secondly, If we did not handle the aspect, we would find it impossible to fully paraphrase the meanings of many words and expressions and to tell the difference between some of the Chinese words and expressions. For example, all the following words and expressions are usually selected as entries in most Chinese dictionaries: "着", "睡着", "入睡", "成寐", "成眠", "进入睡乡". They are a synonymous set meaning "fall asleep", not merely "sleep". "Sleep" is an action of "resting" while "fall asleep" is a state after taking the action of "sleeping". What is more, "fall asleep"(or "be asleep") is regarded as an expected result, or the goal of "sleep". Let's compare the following:

NO.=102627
W_C=睡
G_C=V [shui4]
E_C=~觉，~眠，~不醒，贪~，~着了，~不着，~大觉，早就~下了，早~早起，~不实，~得香，~得很好，昨晚~好了吗，一天~几个小时，~一会儿，倒头就~，一觉~到大天亮

W_E=sleep
G_E=N
E_E=
DEF={sleep|睡}

NO.=144966
W_C=着
G_C=V [zhao2]
E_C=头刚挨枕头就~了
W_E=fall asleep
G_E=V
E_E=
DEF={sleep|睡:aspect={Vachieve|达成}}

NO.=016552
W_C=成寐
G_C=V [cheng2 mei4]
E_C=
W_E=fall asleep
G_E=V
E_E=
DEF={sleep|睡:aspect={Vachieve|达成}}

To take Chinese expression "觅到", "寻获", "寻见", "找到", "找着" as another example. They are a synonymous set meaning "come upon after searching or find location". "Search" or "look for" is an action of "trying to locate" while "find" is a state and can be regarded as an expected result, or the goal of "search". Let us compare the following:

NO.=124584
W_C=寻
G_C=V [xun2]
E_C=
W_E=look for
G_E=V
E_E=
DEF={LookFor|寻}

NO.=124611
W_C=寻获
G_C=V [xun2 huo4]
E_C=
W_E=find
G_E=V
E_E=
DEF={LookFor|寻:aspect={Vachieve|达成}}

Most of the words and expressions in the examples of the kind are taken as entries in Chinese dictionaries. In other words, they are regarded as "words". However, in reality they represent aspect of Chinese verbs. Special attention should be paid to many words which are polysemous themselves when they are used as aspect makers, for example:

NO.=086098
W_C=起来
G_C=STRU [qi3 lai2]
E_C=公司建~了，组织~了，锁~，藏~，关~，存~
W_E=
G_E=
E_E=
DEF={FuncWord|功能词:aspect={Vresult|动果}}

NO.=086099
W_C=起来
G_C=STRU [qi3 lai2]
E_C=她说着说着哭~了，双方对骂~，他们打~
W_E=begin
G_E=V
E_E=
DEF={FuncWord|功能词:aspect={Vstart|发端}}

NO.=086101
W_C=起来
G_C=STRU [qi3 lai2]

E_C=读~，洗~，写~，做~，吃~，喝~，如果他问~，讲起话来
W_E=
G_E=
E_E=
DEF={FuncWord|功能词:aspect={Vsuppose|假定}}

Table 14.2 shows the meanings conveyed by Chinese aspect and its corresponding "aspect markers" and examples.

Table 14.2. Chinese aspect markers and their meanings.

sememe in HowNet	**meaning**	**marker**	**examples**
{Vsuppose|假定}	presupposing	起来	读~流畅
{Vstart|发端}	inceptive	起来	双方对骂~
		上	在一旁聊~了
{Vgoingon|进展}	progressive	在	~发言呢
		正	~睡觉呢
		正在	~干活
		着	说~说~动手了
{Vcontinue|延续}	protractive	下去	谈~会有结果
{Vend|完结}	terminative	过	吃~饭再走吧
{Vachieve|达成}	perfective	出	做~新成绩
		出来	算~了吗
		到	接~人了吗
		得	饭做~了
		过来	错的地方改~
		过去	被我蒙~了
		好	功课做~了
		见	听~了但看不~
		上	吃~一顿饱饭
		下	谈~那笔生意
		着	见~要见的人,
{Vable|能力}	capable	得到	办~
		得过	信~
		得过来	忙~
		得了	一个人干~
		得起	买~
		得下	装~
		起	输~输不~
		下	可以睡~3 个人
		上来	都答~了
{Vincapable|没能力}	incapable	不得	动也动~

sememe in HowNet	meaning	marker	examples
		不过	说~你
		不过来	一个人忙~
		不了	一个人可干~
		不起	负担~
		不下	吃~
{Vpossible|可能}	possible	得	这菜吃~吃不~
{Vtry|试试}	trying	看	穿穿~

When speaking about Chinese aspect, one point we would like to invite readers' special attention that different from the aspect of English, Chinese aspect is featured by its unrelatedness to tense. It is known that English aspect is usually closely related to tenses, for example, English verbs can be used in progressive aspect with various tenses, such as present progressive, past progressive and future progressive tenses.

Bibliography

Alone, Chinatsu, and Douglas Mckee. 1995. Acquiring predicate-argument mapping information from multilingual texts. In Branimir Boguraev and James Pustejovsky (eds.), Corpus Processing for Lexical Acquisition, pp. 175–190, Cambridge, MA: MIT Press.

Alshawi, Hiyan, and David Carter. 1994. Training and scaling preference functions for disambiguation. Computational Linguistics 20: pp. 635–648.

Appelt, D. E., J. R. Hobbs, J. Bear, D. Israel, and M. Tyson. 1993. Fastus: A finite-state processor for information extraction from real-world text. In Proc. 13th IJCAI, pp. 1172–1178, Chambéry, France.

Basili, Roberto, Gianluca De Rossi, and Maria Teresa Pazienza. 1997. Inducing terminology for lexical acquisition. In EMNLP 2: pp. 125–133.

Benson, Morton. 1989. The structure of the collocational dictionary. International Journal of Lexicography 2: pp. 1–14.

Benson, Morton. Evelyn Benson, and Robert Ilson. 1993. The BBI combinatory dictionary of English. Amsterdam: John Benjamins.

Boguraev, Bran, and Ted Briscoe. 1989. Computational Lexicography for Natural Language Processing. London: Longman.

Boguraev, Branimir, and James Pustejovsky. 1995. Issues in text-based lexicon acquisition. In Branimir Boguraev and James Pustejovsky (eds.), Corpus Processing for Lexical Acquisition, pp. 3–17, Cambridge MA: MIT Press.

Boguraev, Branimir K. 1993. The contribution of computational lexicography. In Madeleine Bates and Ralph M. Weischedel (eds.), Challenges in Natural Language Processing. Cambridge: Cambridge University Press.

Bourigault, Didier. 1993. An endogenous corpus-based method for structural noun phrase disambiguation. In EACL 6: pp. 81–86.

Brill, Eric, and Philip Resnik. 1994. A transformation-based approach to prepositional phrase attachment disambiguation. In COLING 15: pp. 1198–1204.

Bruce, Rebecca, and Janyce Wiebe. 1994. Word-sense disambiguation using decomposable models. In ACL 32: pp.139–145.

Chen, Jen Nan, and Jason S. Chang. 1998. Topical clustering of MRD senses based on information retrieval techniques. Computational Linguistics 24: pp. 61–95.

Chomsky, Noam. 1957. Syntactic Structures. The Hague: Mouton.

Chomsky, Noam. 1965. Aspects of the Theory of Syntax. Cambridge, MA: MIT Press.

Chomsky, Noam. 1986. Knowledge of Language: Its Nature, Origin, and Use. New York: Prager.

Church, Kenneth W., and Robert L. Mercer. 1993. Introduction to the special issue on computational linguistics using large corpora. Computational Linguistics 19: pp. 1–24.

Coates-Stephens, Sam. 1993. The analysis and acquisition of proper names for the understanding of free text. Computers and the Humanities 26: pp. 441–456.

Collins, Michael John, and James Brooks. 1995. Prepositional phrase attachment through a backed-off model. In WVLC 3: pp. 27–38.

Cottrell, Garrison W. 1989. A Connectionist Approach to Word Sense Disambiguation. London: Pitman.

Dagan, Ido, and Alon Itai. 1994. Word sense disambiguation using a second language monolingual corpus. Computational Linguistics 20: pp. 563–596.

Dagan, Ido, Lillian Lee, and Fernando Pereira. 1997b. Similarity-based methods for word sense disambiguation. In ACL 35/EACL 8: pp. 56–63.

Dini, Luca, Vittorio Di Tomaso, and Frédérique Segond. 1998. Error-driven word sense disambiguation. In ACL 36/COLING 17: pp. 320–324.

Dolan, William B. 1994. Word sense ambiguation: Clustering related senses. In COLING 15: pp. 712–716.

Dong, Zhendong, 1988. Knowledge description: what, how, and who? Manuscript & Program of International Symposium on Electronic Dictionary, Nov. 24–25, 1988, Tokyo, p. 18.

Dong, Zhendong, 1988. MT Research in China: In Dan Maxwell, Klaus Schubert,Toon Witkam (eds.), New Directions in Machine Translation, Budapest, Foris Publications, pp. 85–92.

Dorr, Bonnie J., and Mari Broman Olsen. 1997. Deriving verbal and compositional lexical aspect for nlp applications. In ACL 35/EACL 8: pp. 151–158.

Fellbaum, 1998. WordNet: An Electronic Lexical Database. Ed. Cristiane Fellbaum, The MIT Press, Cambridge, London, England, 1998.

Fillmore, Charles J., and B. T. S. Atkins. 1994. Starting where the dictionaries stop: The challenge of corpus lexicography. In B.T.S. Atkins and A. Zampolli (eds.), Computational Approaches to the Lexicon. Oxford: Oxford University Press.

Franz, Alexander. 1997. Independence assumptions considered harmful. In ACL35/EACL 8: pp. 182–189.

Gale, William A., Kenneth W. Church, and David Yarowsky. 1992b. A method for disambiguating word senses in a large corpus. Computers and the Humanities 26: pp. 415–439.

Gale, William A., Kenneth W. Church, and David Yarowsky. 1992c. A method for disambiguating word senses in a large corpus. Technical report, AT&T Bell Laboratories, Murray Hill, NJ.

Gale, William A., Kenneth W. Church, and David Yarowsky. 1992d. Using bilingual materials to develop word sense disambiguation methods. In Proc. 4th Int. Conf. Theoretical and Methodological Issues in Machine Translation (TMI–92).

Grefenstette, Gregory, and Pasi Tapanainen. 1994. What is a word, what is a sentence? Problems of tokenization. In Proc. 3rd Int. Conf. on Computational Lexicography

(COMPLEX '94), Budapest. Available as Rank Xerox Research Centre technical report MLTT–004.

Guthrie, Joe A., Louise Guthrie, Yorick Wilks, and Homa Aidinejad. 1991. Subject-dependent co-occurrence and word sense disambiguation. In ACL 29: pp. 146–152.

Guthrie, Louise, James Pustejovsky, Yorick Wilks, and Brian M. Slator. 1996. The role of lexicons in natural language processing. Communications of the ACM 39: pp. 63–72.

Hirst, Graeme. 1987. Semantic Interpretation and the Resolution of Ambiguity. Cambridge: Cambridge University Press.

Ide, Nancy, and Donald Walker. 1992. Introduction: Common methodologies in humanities computing and computational linguistics. Computers and the Humanities 26: pp. 327–330.

Ide, Nancy, and Jean Véronis. 1998. Introduction to the special issue on word sense disambiguation: The state of the art. Computational Linguistics 24: pp. 1–40.

Jacquemin, Christian. 1994. FASTR: A unification-based front-end to automatic indexing. In Proc. RIAO, pp. 37–47, Rockefeller University, New York.

Jacquemin, Christian, Judith L. Klavans, and Evelyne Tzoukermann. 1997. Expansion of multi-word terms for indexing and retrieval using morphology and syntax. In ACL 35/EACL 8: pp. 24–31.

Jensen, Karen, George E. Heidorn, and Stephen D. Richardson (eds.). 1993. Natural language processing: The PLNLP approach. Boston: Kluwer Academic Publishers.

Justeson, John S., and Slava M. Katz. 1991. Co-occurrences of antonymous adjectives and their contexts. Computational Linguistics 17: pp. 1–19.

Justeson, John S., and Slava M. Katz. 1995b. Technical terminology: some linguistic properties and an algorithm for identification in text. Natural Language Engineering 1: pp. 9–27.

Karov, Yael, and Shimon Edelman. 1998. Similariy-based word sense disambiguation. Computational Linguistics 24: pp. 41–59.

Kelly, Edward, and Phillip Stone. 1975. Computer Recognition of English Word Senses. Amsterdam: North-Holland.

Levin, B. 1993. English Verb Classes and Alternations. Chicago, University of Chicago Press.

Levin, B. 1995. Approaches to lexical semantic representation. Automating the lexicon. D. Walker, A. Zampolli and N. Calzolari. Oxford, Oxford University Press.

Levin, B. and S. Pinker, Eds. 1991. Lexical and conceptual semantics. Oxford, Blackwell.

Levine, John R., Tony Mason, and Doug Brown. 1992. Lex & Yacc, 2nd edition. Sebastopol, CA: O'Reilly & Associates.

Li, Hang, and Naoki Abe. 1995. Generalizing case frames using a thesaurus and the mdl principle. In Proc. Recent Advance in Natural Language Processing, pp. 239–248, Tzigov Chark, Bulgaria.

Li, Hang, and Naoki Abe. 1996. Learning dependencies between case frame slots. In COLING 16: pp. 10–15.

Light, Marc. 1996. Morphological cues for lexical semantics. In ACL 34: pp. 25–31.

Martin, James. 1991. Representing and acquiring metaphor-based polysemy. In Uri Zernik (ed.), Lexical Acquisition: Exploiting On-Line Resources to Build a Lexicon, pp. 389–415. Hillsdale, NJ: Lawrence Erlbaum.

McRoy, Susan W. 1992. Using multiple knowledge sources for word sense disambiguation. Computational Linguistics 18: pp. 1–30.

Mercer, Robert L. 1993. Inflectional morphology needs to be authenticated by hand. In Working Notes of the AAAI Spring Syposium on Building Lexicons for Machine Translation, Stanford, CA.AAAI Press.

Miller, 1990, Miller, George A. Nouns in WordNet: a lexical inheritance system. International Journal of Lexicography 3(4), 1990, Revised August 1993.

Miller *et al.*, 1990, Miller, George A., Richard Beckwith, Christiane Fellbaum, Derek Gross and Katherine J. Miller. Introduction to WordNet: an on-line lexical database. International Journal of Lexicography 3(4), 1990, Revised August 1993.

Miller, G. A. 1986. Dictionaries in the mind. Language and Cognitive Processes 1(3): 171–185.

Miller, G. A., and C. Fellbaum. 1991. Semantic networks of English. In Lexical and Conceptual Semantics. B. Levin and S. Pinker (eds.), Cambridge, MA, Blackwell.

Miller, George A., and Walter G. Charles. 1991. Contextual correlates of semantic similarity. Language and Cognitive Processes 6: pp. 1–28.

Nagao, Makoto, 1997. Machine Translation Through Language Understanding, MT Summit VI Proceedings.

Ng, Hwee Tou, and Hian Beng Lee. 1996. Integrating multiple knowledge sources to disambiguate word sense: An exemplar-based approach. In ACL 34: pp. 40–47.

Nunberg, G. 1996. Transfers of meaning. In Lexical Semantics: The Problem of Polysemy. J. Pustejovsky and B. Boguraev (eds.), Oxford, Oxford University Press, pp. 109–132.

Paik, Woojin, Elizabeth D. Liddy, Edmund Yu, and Mary Mckenna. 1995. Categorizing and standardizing proper nouns for efficient information retrieval. In Branimir Boguraev and James Pustejovsky (eds.), Corpus Processing for Lexical Acquisition, Cambridge MA: MIT Press.

Palmer, David D., and Marti A. Hearst. 1997. Adaptive multilingual sentence boundary disambiguation. Computational Linguistics 23: pp. 241–267.

Palmer, F. R. 1994. Grammatical roles and relations. Cambridge, Cambridge University Press.

Pedersen, Ted, and Rebecca Bruce. 1997. Distinguishing word senses in untagged text. In EMNLP 2: pp. 197–207.

Pereira, Fernando, Naftali Tishby, and Lillian Lee. 1993. Distributional clustering of English words. In ACL 31: pp. 183–190.

Poznański, Victor, and Antonio Sanfilippo. 1995. Detecting dependencies between semantic verb subclasses and subcategorization frames in text corpora. In Branimir Boguraev and James Pustejovsky (eds.), Corpus Processing for Lexical Acquisition, pp. 175–190. Cambridge, MA: MIT Press.

Riloff, Ellen, and Jessica Shepherd. 1997. A corpus-based approach for building semantic lexicons. In EMNLP 2: pp. 117–124.

Roark, Brian, and Eugene Charniak. 1998. Noun-phrase co-occurrence statistics for semi-automatic semantic lexicon construction. In ACL 36/COLING 17: pp. 1110–1116.

Roche, Emmanuel, and Yves Schabes. 1997. Finite-State Language Processing. Boston, MA: MIT Press.

Sapir, Edward. 1921. Language: an introduction to the study of speech. New York: Harcourt Brace.

Schütze, Hinrich. 1998. Automatic word sense discrimination. Computational Linguistics 24: pp. 97–124.

Siskind, Jeffrey Mark. 1996. A computational study of cross-situational techniques for learning word-to-meaning mappings. Cognition 61: pp. 39–91.

Sproat, Richard W., Chilin Shih, William Gale, and Nancy Chang. 1996. A stochastic finite-state word-segmentation algorithm for Chinese. Computational Linguistics 22: pp. 377–404.

Suppes, Patrick, Michael Böttner, and Lin Liang. 1996. Machine learning comprehension grammars for ten languages. Computational Linguistics 22: pp. 329–350.

Tsujii, J., Linguistic Knowledge, World Knowledge and Conceptual Knowledge. In Proceedings of the International Symposium on Electronic Dictionaries, in Tokyo, November 1988.

Velardi, Paola, and Maria Teresa Pazienza. 1989. Computer aided interpretation of lexical co-occurrences. In ACL 27: pp. 185–192.

Viegas, Evelyne, Boyan Onyshkevych, Victor Raskin, and Sergei Nirenburg. 1996. From submit to submitted via submission: On lexical rules in large-scale lexicon acquisition. In ACL 34: pp. 32–39.

Voutilainen, A. 1995. A syntax-based part of speech analyzer. In EACL 7: pp. 157–164.

Webster, Mort, and Mitch Marcus. 1989. Automatic acquisition of the lexical semantics of verbs from sentence frames. In ACL 27: pp. 177–184.

Wilkins, W., (ed.) 1988. Thematic Relations. Syntax and Semantics 21. New York, Academic Press.

Wilks, Y. 1977. Good and bad arguments about semantic primitives. Communication and Cognition 10(3): 181–221.

Wilks, Yorick, and Mark Stevenson. 1998. Word sense disambiguation using optimized combination of knowledge sources. In ACL 36/COLING 17: pp. 1398–1402.

Yarowsky, David. 1992. Word-sense disambiguation using statistical models of Roget's categories trained on large corpora. In COLING 14: pp. 454–460.

Zavrel, Jakub, and Walter Daelemans. 1997. Memory-based learning: Using similarity for smoothing. In ACL 35/EACL 8: pp. 436–443.

Zernik, Uri. 1991a. Introduction. In Lexical Acquisition: Exploiting On-Line Resources to Build a Lexicon, pp. 1–26. Hillsdale, NJ: Lawrence Erlbaum.

Zernik, Uri. 1991b. Train1 vs. train2: Tagging word sense in corpus. In Uri Zernik (ed.), Lexical Acquisition: Exploiting On-Line Resources to Build a Lexicon, pp. 91–112. Hillsdale, NJ: Lawrence Erlbaum.

Zipf, George Kingsley. 1935. The psycho-Biology of Language. Boston, MA: Houghton Mifflin.

Zipf, George Kingsley. 1949. Human Behavior and the Principle of Least Effort. Cambridge, MA: Addison–Wesley.

董振东, 1981. 逻辑语义及其在机译中的应用, 中国的机器翻译, 刘涌泉编, 知识出版社, 北京, 1984, pp. 25–45.

董振东, 董强, 2001. 面向信息处理的词汇语义研究中的若干问题, 语言文字应用, 第 3 期, pp. 27–32.

董振东, 董强, 2001. 知网和汉语研究, 当代语言学, 第三卷, 第 1 期, pp. 33–44.

冯志伟, 2001. 计算语言学基础, 北京, 商务印书馆.

黄昌宁, 李涓子, 2002. 语料库语言学, 北京, 商务印书馆.

刘开瑛, 郭炳炎, 1991. 自然语言处理, 科学出版社.

刘群, 李素建, 2002. 基于《知网》的词汇语义相似度计算，Computational Linguistics and Chinese Language Processing, Vol. 7, No. 2, August 2002, pp. 59–76.

苏培成, 2001. 现代汉字学纲要, 北京, 北京大学出版.

吴立德, 1997. 大规模中文文本处理, 上海, 复旦大学出版社.

姚天顺等, 2002. 自然语言理解 — 一种让机器懂得人类语言的研究, 北京, 清华大学出版社, (第二版).

俞士汶等, 2003. 现代汉语语法信息词典详解 (第二版), 北京, 清华大学出版社.

A Chinese-English Dictionary (Revised Edition), Foreign Language Teaching and Research Press, 1995.

Contemporary Chinese Dictionary (Chinese-English Edition), Foreign Language Teaching and Research Press, 2002.

Contemporary Chinese Standard Dictionary, Foreign Language Teaching and Research Press, Beijing Publishing House, 2004.

LONGMAN English-Chinese Dictionary Of Contemporary English, UK, Longman Group Limited, 1978.

WordNet 2.0 wordnet.princeton.edu/cgi-bin/webwn

Appendix

Part I

As part of Appendix, an accompanying CD-Rom containing the Mini-HowNet system is attached to the book. Mini-HowNet contains the HowNet knowledge database with all the entry records from A to D in Chinese Pinyin, and the HowNet's devices of computation of meaning: Browser, Concept Relevance Calculator, Concept Similarity Measure, and Query Expansion Tool.

Part II

The second part of Appendix contains Axiomatic relation of events and role shifting.

Axiomatic relation of events and role shifting

{RegardAs|当作} (X) <----> {become|成为} (Y) [consequence];
  patient OF {RegardAs|当作}=relevant OF {become|成为};
  ResultIsa OF {RegardAs|当作}=isa OF {become|成为}.

{dismiss|罢免} (X) <----> BeNot|非 (Y) [consequence];
  patient OF {dismiss|罢免}=relevant OF BeNot|非;
  ResultIsa OF {dismiss|罢免}=isa OF BeNot|非.

{lose|失去} <----> {own|有} [precondition];
  possessor OF {lose|失去}=possessor OF {own|有};
  possession OF {lose|失去}=possession OF {own|有}.

{lose|失去} <----> {obtain|得到} [mutual precondition];
  possessor OF {lose|失去}=possessor OF {obtain|得到};
  possession OF {lose|失去}=possession OF {obtain|得到}.

{BelongTo|属于} <----> {own|有} [interchangeable];
possession OF {BelongTo|属于}=possession OF {own|有};
possessor OF {BelongTo|属于}=possessor OF {own|有}.

{owe|欠} [implication] <----> {OwnNot|无};
possessor OF {owe|欠}=possessor OF {OwnNot|无};
possession OF {owe|欠}=possession OF {OwnNot|无}.

{owe|欠} (X) [implication] <----> {own|有} (Y);
target OF {owe|欠}=possessor OF {own|有};
possession OF {owe|欠}=possession OF {own|有}.

{take|取} <----> {obtain|得到} [consequence];
agent OF {take|取}=possessor OF {obtain|得到};
possession OF {take|取}=possession OF {obtain|得到}.

{give|给} <----> {lose|失去} [consequence];
agent OF {give|给}=possessor OF {lose|失去};
possession OF {give|给}=possession OF {lose|失去}.

{give|给} (X) [implication] <----> {receive|收受} (Y);
target OF {give|给}=possessor OF {receive|收受};
possession OF {give|给}=possession OF {receive|收受}.

{exchange|交换} <----> {lose|失去} [consequence];
agent OF {exchange|交换}=possessor OF {lose|失去};
possession OF {exchange|交换}=possession OF {lose|失去}.

{exchange|交换} <----> {obtain|得到} [consequence];
agent OF {exchange|交换}=possessor OF {obtain|得到};
possession OF {exchange|交换}=possession OF {obtain|得到}.

{exchange|交换} (X) [implication] <----> {lose|失去} (Y);
source OF {exchange|交换}=possessor OF {lose|失去};
possession OF {exchange|交换}=possession OF {lose|失去}.

{exchange|交换} (X) [implication] <----> {obtain|得到} (Y);
target OF {exchange|交换}=possessor OF {obtain|得到};
possession OF {exchange|交换}=possession OF {obtain|得到}.

{buy|买} (X) <----> {sell|卖} (Y) [mutual implication];
agent OF {buy|买}=target OF {sell|卖};
source OF {buy|买}=agent OF {sell|卖};
possession OF {buy|买}=possession OF {sell|卖};
cost OF {buy|买}=cost OF {sell|卖}.

{borrow|借入} (X) <----> {lend|借出} (Y) [mutual implication];
agent OF {borrow|借入}=target OF {lend|借出};
source OF {borrow|借入}=agent OF {lend|借出};
possession OF {borrow|借入}=possession OF {lend|借出}.

{TakeBack|取回} (X) <----> {return|还} (Y) [mutual implication];
agent OF {TakeBack|取回}=target OF {return|还};
source OF {TakeBack|取回}=agent OF {return|还};
possession OF {TakeBack|取回}=possession OF {return|还}.

{MarryFrom|娶} (X) <----> {MarryTo|嫁} (Y) [mutual implication];
agent OF {MarryFrom|娶}=target OF {MarryTo|嫁};
source OF {MarryFrom|娶}=agent OF {MarryTo|嫁};
possession OF {MarryFrom|娶}=possession OF {MarryTo|嫁}.

{CompareTo|比拟} (X) <----> {BeSimilar|相像} (Y) [consequence];
patient OF {CompareTo|比拟}=relevant OF {BeSimilar|相像};
contrast OF {CompareTo|比拟}=contrast OF {BeSimilar|相像}.

{MakeEqual|使相等} (X) <----> {equal|相等} (Y) [consequence];
patient OF {MakeEqual|使相等}=relevant OF {equal|相等};
contrast OF {MakeEqual|使相等}=contrast OF {equal|相等}.

{obey|遵循} <----> {fit|适合} [consequence];
patient OF {obey|遵循}=relevant OF {fit|适合};
content OF {obey|遵循}=contrast OF {fit|适合}.

{disobey|违背} <----> {FitNot|不适} [consequence];
agent OF {disobey|违背}=relevant OF {FitNot|不适};
content OF {disobey|违背}=contrast OF {FitNot|不适}.

{include|纳入} (X) <----> {contain|包含} (Y) [consequence];
patient OF {include|纳入}=PartOf OF {contain|包含};
ResultWhole OF {include|纳入}=relevant OF {contain|包含}.

{include|纳入} <----> {contain|包含} [consequence];
agent OF {include|纳入}=PartOf OF {contain|包含};
ResultWhole OF {include|纳入}=relevant OF {contain|包含}.

{include|纳入} (X) <----> {BeMember|隶属} (Y) [consequence];
patient OF {include|纳入}=relevant OF {BeMember|隶属};
ResultWhole OF {include|纳入}=whole OF {BeMember|隶属}.

{include|纳入} <----> {BeMember|隶属} [consequence];
agent OF {include|纳入}=relevant OF {BeMember|隶属};
ResultWhole OF {include|纳入}=whole OF {BeMember|隶属}.

{discharge|开除} (X) <----> {contain|包含} (Y) [consequence];
patient OF {discharge|开除}=^PartOf OF {contain|包含};
SourceWhole OF {discharge|开除}=relevant OF {contain|包含}.

{withdraw|退出} <----> {contain|包含} [consequence];
agent OF {withdraw|退出}=^PartOf OF {contain|包含};
SourceWhole OF {withdraw|退出}=relevant OF {contain|包含}.

{discharge|开除} (X) <----> {BeMember|隶属} (Y) [consequence];
patient OF {discharge|开除}=^relevant OF {BeMember|隶属};
SourceWhole OF {discharge|开除}=whole OF {BeMember|隶属}.

{withdraw|退出} <----> {BeMember|隶属} [consequence];
agent OF {withdraw|退出}=^relevant OF {BeMember|隶属};
SourceWhole OF {withdraw|退出}=whole OF {BeMember|隶属}.

{tie|关联} (X) <----> {relate|有关} (Y) [consequence];
patient OF {tie|关联}=relevant OF {relate|有关};
partner OF {tie|关联}=partner OF {relate|有关}.

{associate|交往} <----> {relate|有关} [consequence];
agent OF {associate|交往}=relevant OF {relate|有关};
partner OF {associate|交往}=partner OF {relate|有关}.

{MarryFrom|娶} <----> {GetMarried|结婚} [mutual implication];
agent OF {MarryFrom|娶}=agent OF {GetMarried|结婚};
possession OF {MarryFrom|娶}=partner OF {GetMarried|结婚}.

{MarryTo|嫁} <----> {GetMarried|结婚} [mutual implication];
possession OF {MarryTo|嫁}=agent OF {GetMarried|结婚};
target OF {MarryTo|嫁}=partner OF {GetMarried|结婚}.

{MarryTo|嫁} (X) <----> {MarryFrom|娶} (Y) [mutual implication];
agent OF {MarryTo|嫁}=possession OF {MarryFrom|娶};
target OF {MarryTo|嫁}=agent OF {MarryFrom|娶}.

{GetMarried|结婚} (X) <----> {GetMarried|结婚} (Y) [mutual implication];
agent OF {GetMarried|结婚}=partner OF {GetMarried|结婚};
partner OF {GetMarried|结婚}=agent OF {GetMarried|结婚}.

{mating|交配} [precondition] <----> {pregnant|怀孕} ;
agent OF {mating|交配}=experiencer OF {pregnant|怀孕};

{separate|分离} (X) <----> {RelateNot|无关} (Y) [consequence];
patient OF {separate|分离}=relevant OF {RelateNot|无关};
partner OF {separate|分离}=partner OF {RelateNot|无关}.

{separate|分离} (X) <---->{RelateNot|无关} (Y) [consequence];
patient OF {separate|分离}=relevant OF {RelateNot|无关};
SourceWhole OF {separate|分离}=partner OF {RelateNot|无关}.

{SelfMove|自移} <----> {arrive|到达} [consequence];
agent OF {SelfMove|自移}=agent OF {arrive|到达};
LocationFin OF {SelfMove|自移}=LocationFin OF {arrive|到达}.

{arrive|到达} <----> {situated|处于} [consequence];
agent OF {arrive|到达}=existent OF {situated|处于};
LocationFin OF {arrive|到达}=location OF {situated|处于}.

{situated|处于} (X) <----> {CauseToMove|他移} (Y) [implication];
existent OF {situated|处于}=patient OF {CauseToMove|他移};
location OF {situated|处于}=LocationIni OF {CauseToMove|他移}.

{CauseToMove|他移} (X) <----> {SelfMove|自移} (Y) [consequence];
patient OF {CauseToMove|他移}=agent OF {SelfMove|自移};
LocationFin OF {CauseToMove|他移}=LocationFin OF {SelfMove|自移}.

{CauseToMove|他移} (X) <----> {arrive|到达} (Y) [consequence];
patient OF {CauseToMove|他移}=agent OF {arrive|到达};
LocationFin OF {CauseToMove|他移}=LocationFin OF {arrive|到达}.

{pull|拉} (X) <----> {come|来} (Y) [consequence];
patient OF {pull|拉}=agent OF {come|来};
direction OF {pull|拉}=direction OF {come|来};
LocationThru OF {pull|拉}=LocationThru OF {come|来};
LocationIni OF {pull|拉}=LocationIni OF {come|来};
LocationFin OF {pull|拉}=LocationFin OF {come|来}.

{push|推} (X) <----> {go|去} (Y) [consequence];
patient OF {push|推}=agent OF {go|去};
direction OF {push|推}=direction OF {go|去};
LocationThru OF {push|推}=LocationThru OF {go|去};
LocationIni OF {push|推}=LocationIni OF {go|去};
LocationFin OF {push|推}=LocationFin OF {go|去}.

{MoveItUp|上移} (X) <----> {GoUp|上去} (Y) [consequence];
patient OF {MoveItUp|上移}=agent OF {GoUp|上去};
direction OF {MoveItUp|上移}=direction OF {GoUp|上去};
LocationThru OF {MoveItUp|上移}=LocationThru OF {GoUp|上去};
LocationIni OF {MoveItUp|上移}=LocationIni OF {GoUp|上去};
LocationFin OF {MoveItUp|上移}=LocationFin OF {GoUp|上去}.

{lift|提升} (X) <----> {GoUp|上去} (Y) [consequence];
patient OF {lift|提升}=agent OF {GoUp|上去};
direction OF {lift|提升}=direction OF {GoUp|上去};
LocationThru OF {lift|提升}=LocationThru OF {GoUp|上去};
LocationIni OF {lift|提升}=LocationIni OF {GoUp|上去};
LocationFin OF {lift|提升}=LocationFin OF {GoUp|上去}.

{hang|悬挂} (X) <----> {GoUp|上去} (Y) [consequence];
patient OF {hang|悬挂}=agent OF {GoUp|上去};
direction OF {hang|悬挂}=direction OF {GoUp|上去};
LocationThru OF {hang|悬挂}=LocationThru OF {GoUp|上去};
LocationIni OF {hang|悬挂}=LocationIni OF {GoUp|上去};
LocationFin OF {hang|悬挂}=LocationFin OF {GoUp|上去}.

{MoveItDown|下移} (X) <----> {GoDown|下去} (Y) [consequence];
patient OF {MoveItDown|下移}=agent OF {GoDown|下去} ;
direction OF {MoveItDown|下移}=direction OF {GoDown|下去};
LocationThru OF {MoveItDown|下移}=LocationThru OF {GoDown|下去};
LocationIni OF {MoveItDown|下移}=LocationIni OF {GoDown|下去};
LocationFin OF {MoveItDown|下移}=LocationFin OF {GoDown|下去}.

{spray|洒下} (X) <----> {GoDown|下去} (Y) [consequence];
patient OF {spray|洒下}=agent OF {GoDown|下去};
direction OF {spray|洒下}=direction OF {GoDown|下去};
LocationThru OF {spray|洒下}=LocationThru OF {GoDown|下去};
LocationIni OF {spray|洒下}=LocationIni OF {GoDown|下去};
LocationFin OF {spray|洒下}=LocationFin OF {GoDown|下去}.

{swallow|咽下} (X) <----> {GoDown|下去} (Y) [consequence];
patient OF {swallow|咽下}=agent OF {GoDown|下去};
direction OF {swallow|咽下}=direction OF {GoDown|下去};
LocationThru OF {swallow|咽下}=LocationThru OF {GoDown|下去};
LocationIni OF {swallow|咽下}=LocationIni OF {GoDown|下去};
LocationFin OF {swallow|咽下}=LocationFin OF {GoDown|下去}.

{drop|投下} (X) <----> {GoDown|下去} (Y) [consequence];
patient OF {drop|投下}=agent OF {GoDown|下去};
direction OF {drop|投下}=direction OF {GoDown|下去};

LocationThru OF {drop|投下}=LocationThru OF {GoDown|下去};
LocationIni OF {drop|投下}=LocationIni OF {GoDown|下去};
LocationFin OF {drop|投下}=LocationFin OF {GoDown|下去}.

{MoveItBack|回移} (X) <----> GoBackward|后退 (Y) [consequence];
patient OF {MoveItBack|回移}=agent OF GoBackward|后退;
direction OF {MoveItBack|回移}=direction OF GoBackward|后退;
LocationThru OF {MoveItBack|回移}=LocationThru OF GoBackward|后退;
LocationIni OF {MoveItBack|回移}=LocationIni OF GoBackward|后退;
LocationFin OF {MoveItBack|回移}=LocationFin OF GoBackward|后退.

{MoveItInto|内移} (X) <----> {GoInto|进入} (Y) [consequence];
patient OF {MoveItInto|内移}=agent OF {GoInto|进入};
direction OF {MoveItInto|内移}=direction OF {GoInto|进入};
LocationThru OF {MoveItInto|内移}=LocationThru OF {GoInto|进入};
LocationIni OF {MoveItInto|内移}=LocationIni OF {GoInto|进入};
LocationFin OF {MoveItInto|内移}=LocationFin OF {GoInto|进入}.

{inhale|吸入} (X) <----> {GoInto|进入} (Y) [consequence];
patient OF {inhale|吸入}=agent OF {GoInto|进入};
direction OF {inhale|吸入}=direction OF {GoInto|进入};
LocationThru OF {inhale|吸入}=LocationThru OF {GoInto|进入};
LocationIni OF {inhale|吸入}=LocationIni OF {GoInto|进入};
LocationFin OF {inhale|吸入}=LocationFin OF {GoInto|进入}.

{insert|插入} (X) <----> {GoInto|进入} (Y) [consequence];
patient OF {insert|插入}=agent OF {GoInto|进入};
direction OF {insert|插入}=direction OF {GoInto|进入};
LocationThru OF {insert|插入}=LocationThru OF {GoInto|进入};
LocationIni OF {insert|插入}=LocationIni OF {GoInto|进入};
LocationFin OF {insert|插入}=LocationFin OF {GoInto|进入}.

{soak|浸入} (X) <----> {GoInto|进入} (Y) [consequence];
patient OF {soak|浸入}=agent OF {GoInto|进入};
direction OF {soak|浸入}=direction OF {GoInto|进入};
LocationThru OF {soak|浸入}=LocationThru OF {GoInto|进入};
LocationIni OF {soak|浸入}=LocationIni OF {GoInto|进入};
LocationFin OF {soak|浸入}=LocationFin OF {GoInto|进入}.

{inlay|嵌入} (X) <----> {GoInto|进入} (Y) [consequence];
patient OF {inlay|嵌入}=agent OF {GoInto|进入};
direction OF {inlay|嵌入}=direction OF {GoInto|进入};
LocationThru OF {inlay|嵌入}=LocationThru OF {GoInto|进入};
LocationIni OF {inlay|嵌入}=LocationIni OF {GoInto|进入};
LocationFin OF {inlay|嵌入}=LocationFin OF {GoInto|进入}.

{fill|填入} (X) <----> {GoInto|进入} (Y) [consequence];
  patient OF {fill|填入}=agent OF {GoInto|进入};
  direction OF {fill|填入}=direction OF {GoInto|进入};
  LocationThru OF {fill|填入}=LocationThru OF {GoInto|进入};
  LocationIni OF {fill|填入}=LocationIni OF {GoInto|进入};
  LocationFin OF {fill|填入}=LocationFin OF {GoInto|进入}.

{bury|埋入} (X) <----> {GoInto|进入} (Y) [consequence];
  patient OF {bury|埋入}=agent OF {GoInto|进入};
  direction OF {bury|埋入}=direction OF {GoInto|进入};
  LocationThru OF {bury|埋入}=LocationThru OF {GoInto|进入};
  LocationIni OF {bury|埋入}=LocationIni OF {GoInto|进入};
  LocationFin OF {bury|埋入}=LocationFin OF {GoInto|进入}.

{MoveItOut|外移} (X) <----> {GoOut|出去} (Y) [consequence];
  patient OF {MoveItOut|外移}=agent OF {GoOut|出去};
  direction OF {MoveItOut|外移}=direction OF {GoOut|出去};
  LocationThru OF {MoveItOut|外移}=LocationThru OF {GoOut|出去};
  LocationIni OF {MoveItOut|外移}=LocationIni OF {GoOut|出去};
  LocationFin OF {MoveItOut|外移}=LocationFin OF {GoOut|出去}.

{MoveItAway|远移} (X) <----> {leave|离开} (Y) [consequence];
  patient OF {MoveItAway|远移}=agent OF {leave|离开};
  direction OF {MoveItAway|远移}=direction OF {leave|离开};
  LocationThru OF {MoveItAway|远移}=LocationThru OF {leave|离开};
  LocationIni OF {MoveItAway|远移}=LocationIni OF {leave|离开};
  LocationFin OF {MoveItAway|远移}=LocationFin OF {leave|离开}.

{assemble|聚集} (X) <----> ComeTogether|集聚 (Y) [consequence];
  patient OF {assemble|聚集}=agent OF ComeTogether|集聚;
  direction OF {assemble|聚集}=direction OF ComeTogether|集聚;
  LocationThru OF {assemble|聚集}=LocationThru OF ComeTogether|集聚;
  LocationIni OF {assemble|聚集}=LocationIni OF ComeTogether|集聚;
  LocationFin OF {assemble|聚集}=LocationFin OF ComeTogether|集聚.

{hold|拿} [precondition] <----> {CauseToMove|他移};
  agent OF {hold|拿}=agent OF {CauseToMove|他移};
  patient OF {hold|拿}=patient OF {CauseToMove|他移}.

{CeaseCauseTOMove|终止他移} (X) <----> {CeaseSelfMove|终止自移} (Y) [consequence];
  patient OF {CeaseCauseTOMove|终止他移}=agent OF {CeaseSelfMove|终止自移}.

{AimAt|定向} <----> {shoot|发射} [purpose];
  agent OF {AimAt|定向=agent OF {shoot|发射};
  direction OF AimAt|定向=direction OF {shoot|发射};

{AimAt|定向} <----> {firing|射击} [purpose];
agent OF {AimAt|定向}=agent OF {firing|射击};
direction OF {AimAt|定向}=direction OF {firing|射击};

{add|增加} (X) <----> {BecomeMore|增多} (Y) [consequence];
patient OF {add|增加}=experiencer OF {BecomeMore|增多};
quantity OF {add|增加}= (StateFin OF {BecomeMore|增多}) - (StateIni OF {BecomeMore|增多});

{subtract|削减} (X) <----> {BecomeLess|减少} (Y) [consequence];
patient OF {subtract|削减}=experiencer OF {BecomeLess|减少};
quantity OF {subtract|削减}= (StateIni OF {BecomeLess|减少}) - (StateFin OF {BecomeLess|减少});

{exhaust|损耗} (X) <----> {BecomeLess|减少} (Y) [consequence];
patient OF {exhaust|损耗}=experiencer OF {BecomeLess|减少};
quantity OF {exhaust|损耗}= (StateIni OF {BecomeLess|减少}) - (StateFin OF {BecomeLess|减少});

{surplus|剩余} <----> {subtract|削减} [cause];
experiencer OF {surplus|剩余}= patient OF {subtract|削减};
StateFin OF {surplus|剩余}= (StateIni OF {surplus|剩余}) - (quantity OF {subtract|削减});

{create|创造} (X) <----> {ComeToWorld|问世} (Y) [consequence];
PatientProduct OF {create|创造}=experiencer OF {ComeToWorld|问世};

{create|创造} (X) <----> {alive|活着} (Y) [consequence];
PatientProduct OF {create|创造}=experiencer OF {alive|活着};

{CauseToAppear|显现} (X) <----> {exposure|露出} (Y) [consequence];
patient OF {CauseToAppear|显现}=experiencer OF {exposure|露出};

{compile|编辑} (X) <----> {ComeToWorld|问世} (Y) [consequence];
PatientContent OF {compile|编辑}=experiencer OF {ComeToWorld|问世};

{reveal|揭露} (X) <----> {appear|出现} (Y) [consequence];
Patient OF {reveal|揭露}=experiencer OF {appear|出现};

{pregnant|怀孕} [precondition] <----> {reproduce|生殖};
experiencer OF {pregnant|怀孕}=agent OF {reproduce|生殖}.

{tired|疲乏} [cause] <----> {rest|休息};
experiencer OF {tired|疲乏}=agent OF {rest|休息}.

{exercise|锻练} [cause] <----> {BeWell|健壮};
agent OF {exercise|锻练}=experiencer OF {BeWell|健壮}.

{sleep|睡} <----> {awake|醒} [consequence];
agent OF {sleep|睡}=experiencer OF {awake|醒}.

{HungryThirsty|饥渴} [cause] <----> {eat|吃};
experiencer OF {HungryThirsty|饥渴}=agent OF {eat|吃}.

{HungryThirsty|饥渴} [cause] <----> {drink|喝};
experiencer OF {HungryThirsty|饥渴}=agent OF {drink|喝}.

{feed|喂} (X) <----> {eat|吃} (Y) [consequence];
target OF {feed|喂}=agent OF {eat|吃};
patient OF {feed|喂}=patient OF {eat|吃}.

{eat|吃} [precondition]<---->{BeFull|吃饱};
agent OF {eat|吃}=experiencer OF {BeFull|吃饱}.

{consume|摄取} [mutual precondition] <----> {excrete|排泄};
agent OF {consume|摄取}=agent OF {excrete|排泄}.

{compete|比赛} <----> {defeat|战胜} [possible consequence];
agent OF {compete|比赛}=agent OF {defeat|战胜};
partner OF {compete|比赛}=experiencer OF {defeated|输掉}.

{fight|争斗} <----> {defeat|战胜} [possible consequence];
agent OF {fight|争斗}=agent OF {defeat|战胜};
partner OF {fight|争斗}=experiencer OF {defeated|输掉}.

{defeat|战胜} <----> {win|获胜} [consequence];
agent OF {defeat|战胜}=experiencer OF {win|获胜};

{win|获胜} (X) <----> {defeated|输掉} (Y) [mutual implication];
experiencer OF {win|获胜}=contrast OF {defeated|输掉};
contrast OF {win|获胜}=experiencer OF {defeated|输掉}.

{attack|攻打} (X) <----> {resist|反抗} (Y) [mutual implication];
agent OF {attack|攻打}=partner OF {resist|反抗};
patient OF {attack|攻打}= agent OF {resist|反抗}.

{fight|争斗} (X) <---->{fight|争斗} (Y) [mutual implication];
agent OF {fight|争斗}=partner OF {fight|争斗};
partner OF {fight|争斗}=agent OF {fight|争斗};
cause OF {fight|争斗}=cause OF {fight|争斗}.

{SufferFrom|罹患} (X) [cause] <---->{doctor|医治} (Y) ;
experiencer OF {SufferFrom|罹患}=patient OF {doctor|医治};
content OF {SufferFrom|罹患}=content OF {doctor|医治}.

{OutOfOrder|坏掉} (X) [cause] <----> {repair|修理} (Y) ;
experiencer OF {OutOfOrder|坏掉}=patient OF {repair|修理};
content OF {OutOfOrder|坏掉}=content OF {repair|修理}.

{err|出错} (X) [cause] <----> {amend|改正} (Y) ;
experiencer OF {err|出错}=patient OF {amend|改正};
scope OF {err|出错}=content OF {amend|改正}.

{doctor|医治} (X) <----> {BeRecovered|复原} (Y) [possible consequence];
patient OF {doctor|医治}=experiencer OF {BeRecovered|复原}.

{repair|修理} (X) <----> {BeRecovered|复原} (Y) [possible consequence];
patient OF {repair|修理}=experiencer OF {BeRecovered|复原}.

{amend|改正} (X) <----> {BeRecovered|复原} (Y) [possible consequence];
patient OF {amend|改正}=experiencer OF {BeRecovered|复原}.

{wounded|受伤} [cause] <----> {bleed|出血};
experiencer OF {wounded|受伤}=experiencer OF {bleed|出血}.

{wounded|受伤} [cause] <----> {disable|残疾};
experiencer OF {wounded|受伤}=experiencer OF {disable|残疾}.

{labour|临产} <----> {reproduce|生殖} [consequence];
experiencer OF {labour|临产}=agent OF {reproduce|生殖}.

{SufferFrom|罹患} <----> {BeRecovered|复原} [possible consequence];
experiencer OF {SufferFrom|罹患}=experiencer OF {BeRecovered|复原}.

{SufferFrom|罹患} <----> {die|死} [possible consequence];
experiencer OF {SufferFrom|罹患}=experiencer OF {die|死}.

{SufferFrom|罹患} <----> {die|死:cause={ill|病态}} [possible consequence];
experiencer OF {SufferFrom|罹患}=experiencer OF {die|死:cause={ill|病态}}.

{kill|杀害} (X) <----> {die|死} (Y) [consequence];
patient OF {kill|杀害}=experiencer OF {die|死}.

{suicide|自杀} <----> {die|死} [consequence];
agent OF {suicide|自杀}=experiencer OF {die|死}.

{remove|消除} (X) <----> {perish|灭亡} (Y) [consequence];
patient OF {remove|消除}=experiencer OF {perish|灭亡}.

{damage|损害} (X) <----> {OutOfOrder|坏掉} (Y) [consequence];
patient OF {damage|损害}=experiencer OF {OutOfOrder|坏掉}.

{joyful|喜悦} <----> {succeed|成功} [cause];
experiencer OF {joyful|喜悦}=experiencer OF {succeed|成功}.

{sad|忧愁} <----> {fail|失败} [cause];
experiencer OF {sad|忧愁}=experiencer OF {fail|失败}.

{succeed|成功} (X) [cause] <----> {praise|夸奖} (Y);
experiencer OF {succeed|成功}=target OF {praise|夸奖};
scope OF {succeed|成功}=content OF {praise|夸奖}.

{satisfied|满意} [cause] <----> {praise|夸奖};
experiencer OF {satisfied|满意}=agent OF {praise|夸奖};
cause OF {satisfied|满意}=content OF {praise|夸奖}.

{reward|奖励} (X) <----> {obtain|得到} (Y) [consequence];
target OF {reward|奖励}=possessor OF {obtain|得到};
possession OF {reward|奖励}=possession OF {obtain|得到}.

{succeed|成功} (X) [cause] <----> {congratulate|祝贺} (Y);
experiencer OF {succeed|成功}=target OF {congratulate|祝贺};
scope OF {succeed|成功}=cause OF {congratulate|祝贺}.

{succeed|成功} (X) [cause] <----> {admire|羡慕} (Y);
experiencer OF {succeed|成功}=target OF {admire|羡慕};
scope OF {succeed|成功}=cause OF {admire|羡慕}.

{succeed|成功} (X) [cause] <----> {jealous|妒忌} (Y);
experiencer OF {succeed|成功}=target OF {jealous|妒忌};
scope OF {succeed|成功}=cause OF {jealous|妒忌}.

{help|帮助} (X) [cause] <----> {grateful|感激} (Y);
agent OF {help|帮助}=target OF {grateful|感激};
patient OF {help|帮助}=experiencer OF {grateful|感激};
scope OF {help|帮助}=cause OF {grateful|感激}.

{fail|失败} (X) [cause] <----> {sorry|惋惜} (Y);
experiencer OF {fail|失败}=target OF {sorry|惋惜};
scope OF {fail|失败}=cause OF {sorry|惋惜}.

{unfortunate|不幸} (X) [cause] <----> {pity|怜悯} (Y);
experiencer OF {unfortunate|不幸}=target OF {pity|怜悯};
scope OF {unfortunate|不幸}=cause OF {pity|怜悯}.

{soothe|安慰} (X) <----> {AtEase|安心} (Y) [consequence];
target OF {soothe|安慰}=experiencer OF {AtEase|安心}.

{excite|感动} (X) <----> {excited|激动} (Y) [consequence];
target OF {excite|感动}=experiencer OF {excited|激动}.

{please|取悦} (X) <----> {joyful|喜悦} (Y) [consequence];
target OF {please|取悦}=experiencer OF {joyful|喜悦}.

{tease|取乐} <----> {joyful|喜悦} [consequence];
agent OF {please|取悦}=experiencer OF {joyful|喜悦}.

{irritate|激怒} (X) <----> {angry|生气} (Y) [consequence];
target OF {irritate|激怒}=experiencer OF {angry|生气}.

{frighten|吓唬} (X) <----> {fear|害怕 (Y) [consequence];
target OF {irritate|激怒}=experiencer OF {fear|害怕}.

{discourage|泼冷水} (X) <----> {disappointed|失望} (Y) [consequence];
target OF {discourage|泼冷水}=experiencer OF {disappointed|失望}.

{offend|得罪} (X) <----> {angry|生气} (Y) [consequence];
target OF {offend|得罪}=experiencer OF {angry|生气}.

{sorrowful|悲哀} <----> {weep|哭泣} [consequence];
experiencer OF {sorrowful|悲哀}=agent OF {weep|哭泣};
cause OF {sorrowful|悲哀}= cause OF {weep|哭泣};

{die|死} (X) [cause] <----> {condole|致哀} (Y) ;
experiencer OF {die|死}=target OF {condole|致哀}.

{joyful|喜悦} <----> {ShowJoy|示喜} [consequence];
experiencer OF {joyful|喜悦}=agent OF {ShowJoy|示喜};
cause OF {joyful|喜悦}=cause OF {ShowJoy|示喜}.

{grateful|感激} <----> {thank|致谢} [consequence];
experiencer OF {grateful|感激}=agent OF {thank|致谢};
target OF {grateful|感激}=target OF {thank|致谢};
cause OF {grateful|感激}=cause OF {thank|致谢}.

{love|爱恋} <----> {ShowLove|示爱} [consequence];
experiencer OF {love|爱恋}=agent OF {ShowLove|示爱};
target OF {love|爱恋}=target OF {ShowLove|示爱};
cause OF {love|爱恋}=cause OF {ShowLove|示爱}.

{regret|抱歉} <----> {apologize|道歉} [consequence];
experiencer OF {regret|抱歉}=agent OF {apologize|道歉};
target OF {regret|抱歉}=target OF {apologize|道歉};
cause OF {regret|抱歉}=cause OF {apologize|道歉}.

{unsatisfied|不满} <----> {ExpressDissatisfaction|示不满} [consequence];
experiencer OF {unsatisfied|不满}=agent OF {ExpressDissatisfaction|示不满};
target OF {unsatisfied|不满}= target OF {ExpressDissatisfaction|示不满};
cause OF {unsatisfied|不满}=content OF {ExpressDissatisfaction|示不满}.

{unsatisfied|不满} <----> {ExpressAgainst|谴责} [consequence];
experiencer OF {unsatisfied|不满}=agent OF {ExpressAgainst|谴责};
target OF {unsatisfied|不满}= target OF {ExpressAgainst|谴责};
cause OF {unsatisfied|不满}=content OF {ExpressAgainst|谴责}.

{despise|轻视} <----> {IllTreat|慢待} [consequence];
experiencer OF {despise|轻视}=agent OF {IllTreat|慢待};
target OF {despise|轻视}= target OF {IllTreat|慢待};
cause OF {despise|轻视}=cause OF {IllTreat|慢待}.

{angry|生气} <----> {ExpressAnger|示怒} [consequence];
experiencer OF {angry|生气}=agent OF {ExpressAnger|示怒};
cause OF {angry|生气}=cause OF {ExpressAnger|示怒}.

{sense|感觉} <----> {perception|感知} [consequence];
agent OF {sense|感觉}=experiencer OF {perception|感知};
content OF {sense|感觉}=content OF {perception|感知}.

{deceive|欺骗} (X) <----> {misunderstand|误信} (Y) [consequence];
target OF deceive|欺骗}=experiencer OF {misunderstand|误信};
content OF deceive|欺骗}=content OF {misunderstand|误信}.

{HideTruth|瞒} (X) <----> {ignorant|不知} (Y) [consequence];
target OF {HideTruth|瞒}=experiencer OF {ignorant|不知};
content OF {HideTruth|瞒}=content OF {ignorant|不知}.

{TakeVehicle|搭乘} <----> {come|来} [consequence];
agent OF {TakeVehicle|搭乘}=agent OF {come|来}.

{TakeVehicle|搭乘} <----> {go|去} [consequence];
agent OF {TakeVehicle|搭乘}=agent OF {go|去}.

{teach|教} (X) <----> {know|知道} (Y) [consequence];
target OF {teach|教}=experiencer OF {know|知道};
content OF {teach|教}=content OF {know|知道}.

{ask|问} (X) <----> {reply|答} (Y) [mutual implication];
agent OF {ask|问}=target OF {reply|答}
target OF {ask|问}=agent OF {reply|答};
content OF {ask|问}=content OF {reply|答}.

{teach|教} (X) <----> {study|学习} (Y) [mutual implication];
agent OF {teach|教}=source OF {study|学习}
target OF {teach|教}=agent OF {study|学习};
content OF {teach|教}=content OF {study|学习}.

{buy|买} [entailment] <----> {choose|选择};
agent OF {buy|买}=agent OF {choose|选择};
possession OF {buy|买}=content OF {choose|选择};
source OF {buy|买}=location OF {choose|选择}.

{buy|买} [entailment] <----> {pay|付};
agent OF {buy|买}=agent OF {pay|付};
cost OF {buy|买}=possession OF {pay|付};
source OF {buy|买}=taget OF {pay|付}.

{doctor|医治} [entailment] <----> {diagnose|诊察};
agent OF {doctor|医治}=agent OF {diagnose|诊察};
patient OF {doctor|医治}=content OF {diagnose|诊察};
content OF {doctor|医治}=content OF {diagnose|诊察}.

{study|学习} [entailment] <----> {read|读};
agent OF {study|学习}=agent OF {read|读};
content OF {study|学习}=content OF {read|读}.

{study|学习} [entailment] <----> {drill|练习};
agent OF {study|学习}=agent OF {drill|练习};
content OF {study|学习}=content OF {drill|练习}.

{eat|吃} [entailment] <----> {masticate|咀嚼};
agent OF {eat|吃}=agent OF {masticate|咀嚼};
patient OF {eat|吃}=patient OF {masticate|咀嚼}.

{eat|吃} [entailment] <----> {swallow|咽下};
agent OF {eat|吃}=agent OF {swallow|咽下};
patient OF {eat|吃}=patient OF {swallow|咽下}.

{drink|喝} [entailment] <----> {swallow|咽下};
agent OF {drink|喝}=agent OF {swallow|咽下};
patient OF {drink|喝}=patient OF {swallow|咽下}.

{respire|呼吸} [entailment] <----> {inhale|吸入};
agent OF {respire|呼吸}=agent OF {inhale|吸入};
patient OF {respire|呼吸}=patient OF {inhale|吸入}.

{respire|呼吸} [entailment] <----> {exhale|呼出};
agent OF {respire|呼吸}=agent OF {exhale|呼出};
patient OF {respire|呼吸}=patient OF {exhale|呼出}.

Index